Family Therapy in Focus

Counselling & Psychotherapy in Focus

Series Editor: Windy Dryden, Goldsmiths College,
University of London

Counselling & Psychotherapy in Focus is a series of books which
examines the criticisms directed at different forms of counselling
and psychotherapy. Each book in the series reviews the critiques of
a particular approach, presents counter-arguments to the criticisms
and examines the influence that the debates have had in shaping
the approach in question. The books in this series are:

Psychoanalysis in Focus
David Livingstone Smith

Family Therapy in Focus
Mark Rivett & Eddy Street

Person-Centred Therapy in Focus
Paul Wilkins

Family Therapy in Focus

Mark Rivett
and
Eddy Street

SAGE Publications
London • Thousand Oaks • New Delhi

First published 2003

SAGE Publications Ltd
6 Bonhill Street
London EC2A 4PU

SAGE Publications Inc.
2455 Teller Road
Thousand Oaks, California 91320

SAGE Publications India Pvt Ltd
B-42, Panchsheel Enclave
Post Box 4109
New Delhi 110 017

British Library Cataloguing in Publication data

A catalogue record for this book is available
from the British Library

ISBN 0 7619 6235 2 (hbk)
ISBN 0 7619 6236 0 (pbk)

Library of Congress Control Number: 2002109390

Typeset by C&M Digitals (P) Ltd., Chennai, India
Printed in Great Britain by TJ International Ltd, Padstow, Cornwall

Dedication

to
Jean & Leonard
Eddie & Laura
who gave us our appreciation of families

and to
Jan, Joseph & Alex
Anna, Tesni, Jenny & Joe
who remind us of and develop that appreciation

The Manuscript

Gregory Bateson Esalen, October 5, 1978

So there it is in words
Precise
And if you read between the lines
You will find nothing there
For that is the discipline I ask
Not more, not less.

Not the world as it is
Nor ought to be –
Only the precision
The skeleton of truth
I do not dabble in emotion
Hint at implications
Evoke the ghosts of old forgotten creeds.

All that is for the preacher
The hypnotist, therapist and missionary
They will come after me
And use the little that I said
To bait more traps
For those who cannot bear
The lonely
Skeleton
of Truth

'The Manuscript', quoted from Gregory Bateson and Mary Catherine Bateson (1988) *Angels fear: toward an epistemology of the sacred*, New York: Bantam Books. The poem is also printed on page 12 of the January 1981 Esalen catalogue. Reprinted by permission of the Institute for Intercultural Studies.

Contents

Foreword

Family therapy, as an alternative and distinctive way of helping clients, is approximately fifty years old. The oldest family therapy journal, *Family Process*, dates from 1962, but family therapy as an underground movement had started a decade earlier. Sue Walrond-Skinner, an important pioneer, who produced the first British Family Therapy text (*Family therapy: the treatment of natural systems*), recounts the story of how, in 1951, John Bell, who worked at the Mental Research Institute, Palo Alto, visited the Tavistock Clinic while he was in England. He got into discussion with John Sutherland about how John Bowlby was exploring, from a theoretical point of view, the significance of seeing whole families rather than individual clients. According to Sue, Bell misunderstood the convening technique being used by Bowlby, who was not actually seeing families conjointly at that time. He went back to America and was prompted to begin experimenting with convening whole families to family group meetings, thinking that Bowlby had already pioneered such work (Walrond-Skinner, 1976).

I rather like this story about the origins of family therapy. No doubt there are other equally intriguing stories involving other pioneers and how they came to start, but the story does prompt some thoughts about the role of serendipity in developing new ideas. I am reminded of the apple falling on Newton's head and of Fleming's petri dish becoming contaminated with *Penicillium* (a penicillin-producing organism). There is also a certain poignancy in the punctuation created by the story. The Tavistock influences the MRI, which influences the wider growth of family therapy in America and beyond. Obviously, that is a different story from one that takes the MRI as the first point of punctuation.

Sue's historical anecdote prompts other thoughts too – for example, why is it that British family therapists have been so heavily influenced by American theorists? If I think of my own career, which roughly spans the last twenty five years of family therapy's history, then I think of successive waves of American influence: Haley and strategic family therapy, Minuchin and structural family therapy, the MRI and brief therapy, de Shazer and solution-focused therapy. I would also include (paradoxically) the Milan school, because I would argue that Palazzoli and her colleagues did not primarily draw on Italian or even European traditions to develop their model. Their inspiration was primarily the work of Bateson and the MRI. In many ways they took American cybernetic ideas more seriously than any other theorists, but (as I have argued elsewhere (Treacher, 1986; 1995)), in doing so, they created an anti-humanist, expert-driven model (Palazzoli, Boscolo, Cecchin & Prata, 1978), which probably has the most dubious ethical stance of all the multitude of family models that are available to us.

Twenty years on, it is remarkable to look back and remember the popularity of the Palazzoli group. I suspect that their key text, *Paradox and counterparadox*, must still hold the record as the most cited book in the family therapy literature. But do beginning family therapists ever think of reading it now? The seminal work of Boscolo and Cecchin (in their post-Milan phase), and the radical impact of post-modern ideas have effectively erased the original Milan model – an apparently dialectical process which almost makes me believe in the truth of Hegelianism. Unfortunately the third element of Hegel's triad – synthesis, said to arise from the collision of the thesis with the antithesis – has not shown any signs of emerging. Contemporary British family therapy just does not fit such a format. For example, the two most fashionable current models – narrative therapy and solution-focused therapy – are strikingly both non-systemic and both equally antagonistic to the original Palazzoli model.

My concerns about the coherence of family therapy and the problems that arise from shifting paradigms are partly the reflection of my role as a family therapy trainer. Since 1991 I have been involved in co-directing the Diploma in Family and Marital Therapy at the University of Exeter. I have been involved with four cohorts of course members during this time, but, if I am honest with myself, I have to admit that the task of teaching the course has become increasingly difficult for me because I no longer have a firm idea of what should be taught. As I have mentioned elsewhere (Treacher, 1998), I feel like a dinosaur who has been rendered extinct by the rapid conceptual changes that have occurred.

When Eddy and Mark asked me to write the foreword to their book, I was at first not convinced that I should do so. The last thing a book needs is a dinosaur to introduce it! But on reading the manuscript some of my doubts about family therapy's present and future evaporated. Their book is part of a series that will look at all the major forms of psychotherapy from a questioning standpoint. I think Mark and Eddy are very brave to take on the daunting task of putting family therapy under a critical microscope. The task is a huge one because of the complexity of the subject matter. Family therapy is a very diverse field and the conceptual changes that have occurred are, as I have already documented, bewildering. Quite rightly (given the size of the task) they have not attempted to write a definitive text but have instead opted for a less exhaustive approach that deals with selected facets of family therapy. The choices they have made are interesting ones and I am prompted to think what I would have included if I had attempted to write a similar book. In contrasting the so-called first-order approach of general systems theory with the second-order post-modern approaches in the opening chapters of the book is very thought provoking. In reading these chapters I find I drift into a kind of mourning response: I think of the lost opportunities and, above all else, the major problem that family therapy has always confronted – the lack of a major, convincing theory which enables us to have a working understanding of how different types of family function. Thinking along these lines reminds me of the work of Arlene Vetere and Tony Gale whose book *Ecological studies of family life* (Vetere & Gale, 1987) was such a brave attempt to launch such a project. Such a project would not, I think, mesh well with the post-modern ideas that dominate family therapy today, but I resolutely insist on continuing my mourning. Family therapy as a solely hermeneutic tradition does not appeal to me because I have always valued empirical research as a knowledge base that can contribute to the therapy I undertake.

In their next two chapters Eddy and Mark change stance and adopt a sociological lens, looking first at critiques of family therapy and then exploring the rather thin literature which has attempted to answer the question: who are the family therapists? In my book with Sigurd Reimers, *Introducing user-friendly family therapy*, I have explored what I see as a major weakness of family therapy – the failure to explore family members' experiences of being in therapy. It occurs to me (as I read Mark and Eddy's chapter) that family therapists are curiously unvoiced as well. Actually this is not at all surprising – the original general systems theory ideas that were so important in creating the field of family therapy were very dehumanising. On the one hand they rendered individual family members invisible, but on the other they enabled therapists to escape scrutiny because therapists remained experts outside the system they were viewing. Murray Bowen is correctly celebrated for breaking out of this tradition by insisting that the therapist is a vibrant and crucial participant in the process of therapy. More recently second-order theories and the narrative school have encouraged family therapists to recover their voices and examine their role in therapy, but I nevertheless find it significant that Mark and Eddy have so few studies to explore. Narcissism is clearly not a problem we suffer from.

Chapter 7 is an intriguing chapter. Eddy's grounding in Rogerian psychotherapy has always played an important role in his approach to therapy but it is surprising how little attention has been paid to Rogers' approach. Some of the early pioneers of family therapy, and especially Haley, had a mind-set that meant that they rejected other psychotherapy traditions. Paying attention to the nature of selfhood opens the door to asking the almost heretical question: why can family therapy not be undertaken with individuals? Bowen and other transgenerational family therapists were, of course, never bothered by this issue, but it is interesting to see how it has now become a mainstream topic. And there is even some evidence that working individually can be efficacious.

The question of efficacy in family therapy (Mark and Eddy's next topic) is a curious one – for many post-modern theorists such a crude positivist question is anathema. However, throughout my professional career I have always been haunted by the guilty knowledge that the model of family therapy I had espoused really did not possess a substantial efficacy literature. I would have felt much happier if I had felt that the method I was using was tried and tested. The ethical question posed by this chapter is quite clear to me – is it justifiable to practise forms of family therapy that have no clear efficacy? (Narrative therapists may not like the word 'efficacy' but efficacy can be translated into narrative terms quite easily; for example, for 'efficacy' read convincing changes in the stories that the participants tell about being involved in therapy.) Diplomatically, Mark and Eddy do not conclude their chapter with this question but their last chapter does take up this theme.

Chapter 9 is a very ambitious chapter: it attempts to identify core features or dimensions that are responsible for achieving therapeutic change. Much of the work reviewed here is new to me but I am a little bit disappointed that Mark and Eddy do not attempt to make more of what they discover. For instance, what are the training implications of their discoveries?

This same chapter argues towards a conclusion of integration. I'm particularly sympathetic to this chapter because as a therapist I am squirrel-like – I like to hoard everything I have learnt from being exposed (willingly) to a very wide range of models. Intuitively I feel it is impossible for any one model to suit all clients (unless the model is itself an integrative one). I have always worked generically (rather than having a specialised client group) so I always felt that it is necessary to continually expand the repertoire of ideas and techniques (to use a word unfashionable in family therapy) that I can offer my clients. Mark and Eddy comment in the chapter on the work that Sigurd Reimers and myself undertook under the rubric of 'user-friendly family therapy'. Obviously I can't be very objective about this part of the book but personally I am glad that this work is getting a second airing. Writing the book with Sigurd solved something of a professional crisis for myself – I was becoming lost as a family therapist and needed to find a firmer and more personally owned basis that I could use as a springboard for developing my work.

Reading Mark and Eddy's book at the point of retiring has (as I have already hinted) not been an easy task. The retired part of me just wants (among other things) to walk in the Cotswold hills which I have so rapidly got to love (after moving from Devon). The non-retired intellectual part of me has enjoyed the challenges of the book – at times I have agreed and at other times I have disagreed with what they have to say. But overall the book has helped me revisit important issues that I feel remain largely unresolved. I am sure other readers will have a similar experience when reading the book – this is a book that is designed to provoke and stimulate. At times it is elusive and at other times very grounded. That is as it should be since it genuinely reflects many of the puzzling and enriching ideas that family therapy has spawned during its roller-coaster history. Whether the unfolding history will ever be less of a roller-coaster I do not know, but I have a clear preference. I would want to see family therapy based on firmer theoretical and empirical foundations than is currently the case. In other words I take an attachment theory approach to theories – I would prefer to have securer theories to be attached to. And, to wave a (solution-focused) magic wand for a moment, I would have preferred family therapy to place the work of John Bowlby and other attachment theorists (including Allan Schore, 1994) at the centre of its stage. Building therapy on shifting sands may be exciting and energising but I would personally settle for a quieter, less challenging and more professionally secure life.

Andy Treacher
Stroud, Gloucestershire
January 2002

References

Palazzoli, M.S., Boscolo, L., Cecchin, G. & Prata, G. (1978). *Paradox and counter-paradox: a new model in the therapy of the family in schizophrenic transaction.* Northvale, NJ: Aronson.

Reimers, S. & Treacher, A. (1995). *Introducing user-friendly family therapy.* London: Routledge.

Schore, A. (1994). *Affect regulation and the origin of the self. The neurobiology of emotional development.* Hillsdale, NJ: Lawrence Erlbaum Associates.

Treacher, A. (1986). Invisible patients, invisible families. *Journal of Family Therapy, 8*, 267–306.

Treacher, A. (1995). Steps towards a user-friendly approach. In S. Reimers & A. Treacher, *Introducing user-friendly family therapy.* London: Routledge.

Treacher, A. (1998). Psychotherapy and research: a cause for concern? *Context, 39*, 13–15.

Vetere, A. & Gale, A. (1987). *Ecological studies of family life.* Chichester: John Wiley.

Walrond-Skinner, S. (1976). *Family therapy. The treatment of natural systems.* London: Routledge & Kegan Paul.

Preface

Just prior to the turn of the last century a number of celebrations and 'reflections' occurred in the world of family therapy. At its twenty-first birthday celebrations in 1996 there was an 'orgy of reminiscences' (Cooklin, 1996) for the Association for Family Therapy and Systemic Practice (AFT). In 1997 the Association published a magazine 'celebrating British family therapy' (Rivett & Smith, 1997). Whilst, the following year, the *Journal of Family Therapy* invited authors who had contributed articles to its very first edition twenty years before, to reflect upon their earlier ideas in the light of contemporary theory and practice (see Speed & Carpenter, 1998). The metaphor that was most frequently used during these celebrations was one of the life cycle. The 1996 conference was sub-titled 'Coming of Age': the talk was of 'maturing', whilst elsewhere references were made to 'first'- and 'second'-generation therapists. When family therapists looked back at the progress of their practice they naturally thought about growth, evolution and maturation. Indeed, one of the most recent historical reviews written from the standpoint of the 'third generation' of the field has argued that the concept of 'abandoning our parents and grandparents' is a possibility (Dallos & Urry, 1999).

Within this context, this book seeks to ask 'how has family therapy got to where it is now?' and also 'what is it that exists now that is called family therapy?' In one sense we simply here reproduce the circular questions that family therapists use. The difference is that the subject in question is not a problematic interaction, a piece of behaviour, or an emotion. The subject is family therapy itself.

In a field in which metaphors abound, for us the metaphor of evolution or maturation does not quite describe the subject of this book. Certainly, here we have once more both interacted with our professional ancestors and considered future developments. But from the perspective of the different voices that have occupied our minds whilst writing, family therapy's development has seemed to us to involve a complex process of disjunctions, dilemmas and cyclical returns rather than maturation. Understandably, we have therefore wondered about other metaphors that could guide us. In line with Bateson's poem, reproduced here, we certainly have felt that we have attempted to 'read between the lines' and identified the 'baited traps' of others. We have certainly wondered whether 'the lonely Skeleton of Truth' would put in an appearance!

In the end we have realised that we can most clearly describe the process of writing this book by remembering a very simple meditation technique: 'Back to one'. In this method when the meditator loses awareness of the present moment he or she simply returns to the beginning – but a new moment for that beginning. This is how it has seemed writing this book: 'Back to one'. Each perspective from which we have assessed family therapy has led us not to increasing complexity, nor to new revelations, but back to the original insights and practices as well as a development and growth of those insights. These remain at the heart of our passion for family therapy. This passion has been re-awoken in the writing of a book, a book that proposes a critical, and sometimes sceptical, summary of the field. We hope that readers will also experience something of this paradoxical event: doubt serves to stimulate new conviction that is often shorn of its intellectual trimmings. To borrow another Eastern metaphor: this book is a *koan* (or an intellectually unanswerable riddle).

Here we need to comment upon our contexts that constitute the particularities of this book. We undertook our professional training at different times and have differing backgrounds. Eddy is a clinical psychologist with an initial training in individual psychotherapy working in the NHS. Mark, initially a social worker, earns his living both as a family therapist and as a systemic therapist within a national children's charity and teaches family therapy at a university. This unique combination of perspectives has certainly contributed to the product of this book. We each took responsibility for different chapters but the way our drafts were passed back and forth makes all elements of the writing a joint process. A very British book has resulted. By this we mean that the practicality and scepticism of the British is apparent in a way that it might not have been if the book had been written somewhere else in the world. Indeed, again context contributes to this point: family therapy in Britain has all too often seemed to be driven by gurus from other nations. At one time they were American; at another time they were Italian. Currently, it appears to be the turn of Australians and New Zealanders!

Our aim has been to offer a presentation of family therapy in its intellectual and psychotherapeutic context; to try to step over the boundaries that have been used to define our field and in so doing to investigate ideas that are in juxtaposition to ours. All along definitions of family therapy emerge. In the process of doing this we have realised that what at first we saw as being a straightforward task is much more complex. The field itself is of considerable breadth and if, as we have done, one attempts to deal with ideas that are in the academic arena that surrounds us then the task is indeed a mammoth one. We have found that issues that we have only been able to deal with in a paragraph would deserve a chapter in themselves and chapters could have been books! We hope, however, that the critique we offer here will serve as a benchmark for those that follow us. Indeed we now view our text as a benchmarking exercise with all the failings and limitations of such a pursuit.

We begin with an historical perspective in our opening chapter (Chapter 1) which considers both the origins of family therapy and its critique of previous therapies. Following our introduction we consider philosophical critiques which we have separated into chapters exploring systems theory (Chapter 2) and post-modern philosophical developments (Chapter 3) – chapters which, due to family therapy's over-focus on philosophy, also bear something of an historical perspective. These theoretical issues are followed by chapters that consider family therapy from that of sociological (Chapter 4) and social justice critiques (Chapter 6). Interweaved is our version of the sociology of family therapists (Chapter 5). The problems of 'self' are discussed in a chapter on the 'individual' (Chapter 7), which includes a section on the personal development of the therapist. Because of the importance of evidence-based practice, we follow the theoretical chapters with two that consider both the traditional 'outcome' research (Chapter 8) and ways in which research is arguing for 'integration' (Chapter 9). Our final chapter (Chapter 10) draws together our understanding of where our review has alighted from its own journey.

We have written this book with a number of audiences in mind. It is first and foremost intended to stimulate reflection and debate amongst family therapists about their own practice and the place of their inherited theory in that practice. But it is also designed to meet the requirements of family therapy trainees who need to develop a reflective and critical view of their professional literature. All too often professions train their students within an hermetically sealed bubble. In order to prevent this we have drawn on varied sources, some totally unrelated to the closed world of family therapy theory, in order to create an appropriate context for a critical examination of family therapy theory and practice. However, we must assert that the interpretations and analyses in these pages are our own.

We hope that authors who we quote will be generous in allowing us to interpret their words. We also hope that readers will understand that we are not here asserting any certainties. We are contributing to a debate; sometimes asking questions that have not been asked before, or perhaps not in quite this way. Whatever the value of post-modernism to the psychotherapeutic theories of family therapy, we do agree that deconstruction can give valuable insights into texts: this 'family therapy' one in particular. Thus like Don Cupitt we would argue that 'truth is the state of the argument' (1991: 20). If this book stimulates that argument and the enquiry that goes with it, then our hopes will be fulfilled.

Eddy Street
Mark Rivett
Cardiff
December 2001

Chapter 1
Beginning at a beginning: family therapy as critique

There is no first cause. There is a circular cause, in which the beginning, which does not exist, meets the end, which is impossible.

Maurice Maeterlinck

To begin at a beginning ...

The treatment of an entire family, interviewed together regularly as a group, is a new procedure in psychiatry. Just when Family Therapy originated is difficult to estimate because the movement has been largely a secret one. Until recently, therapists who treat whole families have not published on their methods, and their papers are still quite rare – although we may soon expect a deluge. The secrecy about Family Therapy has two sources: those using this method have been too uncertain about their techniques and results to commit themselves to print (therapists of individuals have not let this dissuade them), and there has apparently been a fear of charges of heresy because the influence of family members has been considered irrelevant to the nature and cure of psychopathology in a patient. As a result, since the late 1940's one could attend psychiatric meetings and hear nothing about Family Therapy unless, in a quiet hotel room, one happened to confess that he treated whole families. Then another therapist would put down his drink and reveal that he too had attempted this type of therapy. These furtive conversations ultimately led to an underground movement of therapists devoted to this most challenging of all types of psychotherapy and this movement is now appearing on the surface. (Haley, 1962)

So wrote Jay Haley in the first edition of the pre-eminent journal of the field – *Family Process*. In these opening remarks Haley alludes to a number of features of the family therapy endeavour. Firstly, its origins lie in the developments of the practice of psychiatric psychotherapeutic treatment; secondly, it is a practice utilised by clinicians; thirdly, it is presented as being one thing with a unity of purpose; fourthly, in meeting a resistance from professional hegemony and dogma it has a critical almost delinquent stance. It is on this critical stance that we wish to base our analysis of family therapy.

From its outset family therapy or perhaps more accurately family therapists have seen themselves looking on the world of psychotherapy and mental health provision with a healthy and at time disrespectful scepticism. In this book we wish to use similar critical skills to examine the theory and practice of family therapy itself. We shall examine how family therapy has responded to the critiques of itself and how it has used its own critiques of others to develop itself. Such a self-reflexive examination is necessary if family therapy is to maintain its claim to criticality. More crucially, as 'archaeologists' of family therapy itself (Foucault, 1965) we will seek to highlight particular paths of development that family therapists chose to follow and those they chose not to. In such a telling we are hoping that our reflections on the field do not lead to a view there is only one line of practical and theoretical development that was possible and that is possible. We are hoping that our examination leads simply to a process of continual re-examination.

Typically at this juncture authors would define their terms and set a boundary around their field of interest; however, we need to be cautious about this as in adopting our critical stance it could prove counterproductive. If we are to understand how family therapy has dealt with critiques and developed further we should not prescribe a history. If we are to examine how its clinical methods operate in practice and how its practitioners conduct themselves in the world of clients and professions we cannot strictly limit our definitions of those practices. If we are to assume some unity of purpose in the field we cannot examine that integrity by the field's own concepts; we must move outside its conceptual frame in order to offer a varying perspective. Definition and delineation, if they are appropriate, may come later but only when we have completed our investigations. In a task such as this, of a field as wide as family therapy, we cannot hope to cover every aspect; we can only hope to illustrate and elucidate a reflective, and sometimes reflexive, critical method. We are aware that in order to do this we cannot and indeed should not attempt to provide comprehensive descriptive accounts of many of the positions that we will come to examine, in this we must rest on the reader's appreciation of the subject matter. But we hope that our methodology and the conclusions we arrive at through our examination will cast a different illumination on the family therapy field.

So where do we start? In an examination of any field in which philosophical, sociological, psychological, empirical and practical applications are all dimensions that have relevance, it is not possible to identify a beginning that leads on in some 'logical' manner to all the other points. In a field that well understands the concept of circular causality, we can alight at any point on the circle and begin our journey there. The quote from Haley above illustrates how family therapy began to see itself as a separate therapeutic method in its early days and we will take this as our first access point to examine the field. Each of the characteristics we identified in the quote – the development of a psychotherapeutic practice, a clinical method, a unity of purpose and a critical stance – all carry with them implications for how the field has regarded itself particularly in its development and we can develop our critical methodology here. Let us examine each of these in turn.

Developments in psychotherapy

The standard way of presenting family therapy's historical story is to begin in some way with the emergence of the 'new epistemology' of the application of cybernetic theory to human relationships. Cybernetics began in the work of a mathematician, Norbert Wiener who invented the phrase 'cybernetics' to describe the science of feedback mechanisms in machines and later of communication in human systems. The ideas of cybernetics became fashionable within a certain intellectual circle (just as those of post-modernism have today). Such was the impact of these ideas that there was a series of international conferences between leading scientists called the Macy Conferences in which the breadth of representation was profound. Indeed one crucial member (for the story of family therapy) was Gregory Bateson. He, similar to others, held a cybernetic view that the organisation of events, whether neurological, psychological, behavioural or social, could only be understood in terms of pattern, and information, rather than energy or matter. Wiener and Bateson, as well as others, made the jump from the paradigm of things to the paradigm of pattern and connection. Bateson took these ideas into his anthropological work and in the late 1960s went on to study schizophrenia not as an intrapsychic phenomenon but as an interactional one. His work produced some of the essential papers in the field (1972; 1979). Also because of his status, a group of researchers formed around him who later collectively and independently led the family therapy field. Interestingly when family therapists discuss Bateson's foundational theoretical position there is a tendency to refer only to his work *Steps to an ecology of mind,* whereas his position is clearer and fuller in the work *Mind and nature.* This work is a reflection of his scientific view, an argument intended to unmuddle so much of the muddled thought he saw around him. Yet these ideas have a difficult nature – they seem to turn in on themselves, sometimes to infinitely regress becoming examples of the types of arguments he opposes. Although Bateson was never in any active professional sense a part of family therapy itself, his work is credited by some to have established the field:

> One of the groups with the strongest claim to originating family therapy was Gregory Bateson's schizophrenia project in Palo Alto. (Nichols & Schwartz, 1995: 27)
>
> Although the family was only one of many different types of natural systems that interested Bateson, he is credited as providing the intellectual foundation for the field because of his ideas and studies of patterns and communications. (Dallos & Draper, 2000: 19)

Indeed, what we notice immediately from this account is that the focus is not on the nature of psychotherapeutic practice but on the way that social events in general are considered. So this beginning point of family therapy presents a view of a field that is interested in ideas rather than psychotherapeutic practice. So if we are to suggest another possible starting point for our history where can we begin? What if we begin with the psychotherapeutic origin to which Haley alludes?

In the history of psychotherapy it is easy to see that if one takes Freud as the point of birth for psychotherapeutic practice (which one always does) then one of the main paths of development has been from the intrapsychic/individual focus to an interest in the interpsychic/social processes. This is a line of thought that has been continually present in the history of psychotherapy (see Ackerman, 1958; Brown, 1961). The clinical precursor to much of early family therapy practice was Harry Stack Sullivan. It is through his professional link (a supervisor–supervisee relationship) with Don Jackson that his work had its primary influence on family therapy. Sullivan is best known for his social psychologically based critique of Sigmund Freud's psychoanalytic drive theory. He and his colleagues (including Frieda Fromm-Reichmann, Erik Erikson, Karin Horney, Edward Sapir, Claire Thompson and Harold Lasswell) offered an alternative definition of psychiatry as

> the study of processes that involve or go on between people, the field of interpersonal relations, under any and all circumstances in which these relations exist. It seems a personality can never be isolated from the complex of interpersonal relations in which the person lives and has his being. (Sullivan, 1954: 4–5)

Sullivan challenged the central role of infantile sexual drives in psychological development. Rather he emphasised the role of culture and social context in the determinants of human behaviour and action. Sullivan was critiqued by psychoanalysis and was taken to task for showing an over-concentration on external factors. However, Sullivan pointed out that human experience is a dynamically unfolding interaction between interpersonal, environmental influences and internal (i.e. intrapsychic) meaning. Here the 'self' modifies perceptions and behaviour in response to those external experiences. For Sullivan, understanding an individual's interpersonal relationships involved understanding the way a person interprets his or her experience. This in turn is influenced by the ways the person comes to know the world through the formation of a set of internal assumptions, ideas and fantasies about people and the self. These internal assumptions are based on developmental experiences. (There are many links with these formulations to the writings of the British object-relation theorists, Fairburn, Guntrip and Winnicott, and the Self Psychology of Kohut and Eriksson's psychosocial developmental theory.) Sullivan's journal, *Psychiatry*, reflected his deep-felt belief that psychiatry itself should not emphasise psychopathology but instead focus on the study of interpersonal living and its difficulties. Sullivan's 'interpersonal psychotherapy' was a treatment approach, which focused on the understanding of interpersonal relations and the inner representation of these relations. Learning was the key process for psychotherapeutic change. He introduced the method of obtaining 'collateral data' from families and significant others in the treatment of schizophrenic clients in which the therapist discussed relationships with family members. This clearly presages the future development of family therapy. It needs to be recognised that Sullivan represents a flux of ideas that came from a social understanding. At the time that he was writing there were movements against psychoanalytic orthodoxy and hegemony. Many of Sullivan's theoretical ideas appear well represented and well supported in modern social science including the social construction of reality (see Berger & Luckmann, 1966).

Working at the same time as Sullivan, Otto Rank introduced innovations in therapeutic methods that are also more familiar to family therapists than traditional techniques will have been. He focused more on what was happening in the session itself and less on what had happened in client lives. He introduced his own feelings into sessions rather that remaining detached. An interesting aspect of Rank's contribution was that it provided an important foundational element for the work of Carl Rogers who discussed 'relationship therapy' with regard to the therapy of parents with a child with problems in 1939. Barrett-Lennard (1998) has noted that Rogers' exposition of relationship therapy directly foreshadowed most of the therapeutic principles he set forth and elaborated over the following years. This tradition that encapsulated a social understanding of the development of psychological difficulties and their treatment resulted in a profession led by psychology and counselling. This is opposed to the more medically dominated psychiatric origins of family therapy. It is also worth noting here that the clinical originators of family therapy wished to distinguish themselves not only from psychoanalysis but also from the developing Rogerian field (Haley, 1963).

As we have seen, it was via his link with Sullivan that Jackson developed his foundational ideas and thoughts that were his contribution to the Palo Alto group. From these influences Jackson followed on from Sullivan and his Interactional Theory places emphasis on what is transpiring in the present between people as the primary data relevant to understanding human behaviour. Context and relationship are the focus of attention with little or no emphasis placed on the past, genetic or biochemical explanations of behaviour.

So we can see that a small change of focus provides us with a different history. If we offer a view of family therapy history that privileges the Sullivan lineage as a primary origin then our interest becomes more focused on the processes of psychotherapy and our field's development would not necessarily be seen as a delinquent offshoot that suddenly appeared. It may well have been, and indeed in terms of its clinical practice may just represent, a natural development of a way of thinking that had been slowly developing within psychotherapy's intellectual environment.

A clinical method

To some extent our quote of Haley's suggests more interest in a clinical method than a set of intellectual ideas and it is worth considering the core ideas of clinical practice that were present initially. Sullivan was a clinician rather than a theorist and he refused to be impressed with any theory that could not be demonstrated in practical work with clients. This is an attitude that clearly infiltrated the early family therapists:

> Without doubt this disposition to trust one's experience instead of the reigning dogma characterizes the founders of all the movements (involved in the development of family therapy). (Broderick & Schrader, 1981)

Jackson was the first clinician to uncompromisingly maintain a higher-order cybernetic and constructivist position in the actual practice of therapy. The essence of this model is that the client is seen as a 'family-surrounded individual with real problems in the present day' (Jackson, 1965). Brief in orientation, the primary focus of the model, the questions asked, assignments and tasks given, were always on the relationship between members of the family. Conjoint Family Therapy was a term coined by Jackson to characterise therapy in which two or more people who are vitally important to one another were seen simultaneously in psychotherapy. The family therapist treats the *family*, not the individual. There are a number of clear statements about this within past and recent literature. In the first British text Walrond-Skinner (1976) begins with the following definition:

> family therapy can be defined as the psychotherapeutic treatment of a natural social system, the family, using as its basic medium, conjoint interpersonal interviews. (1976: 1)

In 1984 Speed asserted that:

> one belief which is shared by family therapists is that the focus of concern should be mainly on what occurs between people rather than on what occurs inside an individual. (1984: 2)

Burnham continues to echo this definition:

> family therapy ... looks at problems within the system of relationships in which they occur, and aims to promote change by intervening in the broader system rather than in the individual alone. (1986: 1).

Lastly, Nichols and Schwatz (1998) comment that:

> the animating idea of family therapy is that because most human behavior is interactive, problems can often best be addressed by helping people change the way they interact. (1998: 9)

The clinical method was therefore an uncompromising one in which family members were seen together – hence the name. Even though this interactional, contextual and 'group'-based therapeutic work clearly initially defined the field, we should again note the way that ideas about the origins of problems have dominated family therapy thinking, rather than ideas about the clinical method itself. A consequence of this domination is that the field now incorporates approaches that focus on working with individuals (Boscolo & Bertrando, 1996; White & Epston, 1990). It may well be that in family therapy's journey the core clinical 'family' method has been dropped. How, therefore, should we define the field? If we retain the original clinical method as the defining feature we would arrive at a different definition of 'family therapy' than if we focused on its characterisation of human behaviour as outlined by some non-psychotherapists such as Bateson. If we follow an historical line that focuses on theoretical formulations we arrive at a point that does not necessarily emphasise the family, whereas in following another the family group is central. Here, then, we can discern something of a contradiction, a 'fracture point' or even a paradox. It is paradoxical that in order to exist at that point the individual practitioner may need to hold onto at least two different positions at the same time. Our view is that there are numerous contradictions, fracture points and paradoxes in the family therapy field. In our examination we will attempt to emphasise these points when we believe they are present. We will always wonder whether it is possible to face two directions at the same time.

An implied unity

The discussion above clearly indicates that there are differences and divergences within the field and these are well provided by the histories of family therapy (Nichols & Schwartz, 1998; Goldenberg & Goldenberg, 2000). As we have seen already it is possible just by a reorientation to paint a picture of the diversity. Approaching family therapy in this archaeological manner we can see particular paths of development that family therapists chose to follow and some they have not. Clearly there is more than only one line of practical and theoretical development that led to family therapy. Nichols and Schwartz (1995) comment on this:

> We are by now so used to hearing about 'family therapy' that we may be beguiled into thinking of it as a monolithic enterprise ... [but] as family therapists are well aware, ... *there is not one but many family therapies*, each with distinctly different ways of conceptualizing and treating families.... In fact consensus [between family therapists] never existed. Family therapy was developed by a heterogeneous group of investigators working in distinctly different contexts and with different purposes. These pioneers discovered family therapy before they discovered each other. While it is true that there are unifying principles that most family therapists share, variety not unity has always been a major theme of the story of family therapy. (1995: 1)

We would agree with this: just as there are many histories of family therapy there are many family therapies. Indeed it can be stated with some certainty that family therapy as a homogeneous entity never existed and there have always been disparate voices. Concrete differences emerged in the 1960s in which each school offered a critique of others. The *strategic* school emerged directly out of the early Bateson studies into communication. The MRI group at Palo Alto developed theories about communication that led to a series of techniques that sought to disrupt the communication patterns of families. These therapists were challenged by the emergence of Minuchin's (1974) structural family therapy that essentially expands some of Haley's ideas about the structure of families and adapts these to give a coherent strategy for intervention:

> structural family therapy is a therapy of action ... the therapist joins that system and then uses himself to transform it. (1974: 14)

The next major school of family therapy we shall refer to is the *Milan* school, and as the name suggests had its origins in the work of four Italian family therapists who developed what could be called a new school of strategic therapy. Palazzoli, Boscolo, Cecchin and Prata (1978) worked with a number of families who had anorexic and psychotic members. They also drew on Bateson's work more directly and their interventions were designed not to change the structure or communications of the family but the rules that determined family behaviour:

> the power belongs to neither the one nor the other. The power is only in the rules of the game which cannot be changed by the people involved in it. (1978: 6)

To these schools we can also add a variety of psychodynamically based therapies. Rarely did the founders of these schools admit to be in competition with each other. Yet in practice at conferences and in the way training institutes were set up in the USA and UK there was evidence of competition. Indeed the people who followed one school were often very critical of other approaches. These schools dominated practice and research for two decades, with the psychodynamic school playing a lesser role. However, constructivist, feminist, social constructionist and post-modern critiques of realism have become part of the culture of family therapy over the last twenty years and most family therapists seem to have at least partially welcomed these critiques as an antidote to those early family therapy theories. These critiques we shall examine in more detail in the following chapters. As we develop our arguments we will also emphasise the variety in the field rather than focus on a 'unity of purpose'. In addition, we will concentrate upon the contemporary practice of family therapy in an era when psychotherapy practice has increasingly become professionalised. It may well be that a unity of purpose exists in the activity of a professional group rather than in an overarching framework of psychotherapy practice.

A critical stance

As we have indicated, family therapy is linked to a critique of other approaches to psychotherapy. Conceptually it also inherently contains a critique of many of the worst elements of the mental health world. Hence in a recent text on 'Critical Psychology' (Hare-Mustin & Marecek, 1997) family therapy is applauded as an alternative to traditional medical methods of diagnosis and intervention. Certainly in the early period much of the way that family therapy presented itself was in terms of its criticisms of other therapeutic modalities. Thus the assertion that therapies should deal with interaction represented a critique of those individual and behavioural therapies that sought to treat the individual in isolation from their intimate relationships. Certainly many of the early proponents established their opposition to some of the basic tenets of other psychotherapy schools. The attitude of the time is in an interesting way demonstrated in Jackson's foreword to Haley's *Strategies of psychotherapy:*

> Jay Haley is not a psychiatrist, a psychoanalyst or a clinical psychologist. It will be difficult, therefore, for many psychotherapists to overcome their biases against the unlabeled (or the untouchables) and read this work with the special blend of skepticism and curiosity required of him who would learn something new. (Jackson in Haley, 1963: vii)

Haley's polemical posture is also apparent in a later work of his. In *Leaving Home* he was very explicit:

> When [psychodynamic ideas] were brought into the therapy situation, ... the theory [of repression] was a handicap ... the present, which is all that can be changed was not focused on as an area to be changed ... [Furthermore] the orientation is toward the negative side of people so a positive approach to therapy is impossible. (1980: 13)

At times Haley accepted that his picture of psychoanalysis was possibly 'a parody' (1980: 13) but his interest was to establish the absurdity of treating an individual out of the context of his/her relationships, for a problem that had no definable outcomes and in a manner that was based on insight. Similar objections were raised about other therapeutic methods. Commenting on Rogerian approaches and specifically on the emphasis on conveying empathy Haley (1963) labelled it as a ploy:

> The Rogerian system of ploys where the therapist merely repeats back what the patient says. When the patient accuses the therapist of being no use to him, the therapist replies, 'You feel I'm no use to you'. (1963: 198)

However, the more obvious reason for family therapists critiquing the Rogerian approach was around its concepts of 'non-directive' and 'self-actualisation'. Because family therapy posited a social self, therapists doubted Rogers' ideas about the process of self-actualisation distinct from social interactions. Indeed one of the early concepts, namely that of homeostasis, led to the idea that 'it is the people we love that prevent us from changing' which contradicted Rogers' concept of self.

From a perspective of an historical overview Sprenkle, Blow and Dickey (1999) have provided us with their summary of the early years of family therapy:

> In the first three decades of MFT's [marital and family therapy's] existence, distinctiveness was strongly emphasized over commonality. Family therapy began as a maverick discipline. It was oppositional, even defiant to the prevailing psychotherapy *zeitgeist*. In addition, perhaps because they were rebels of a sort, many of the discipline's founders were feisty and dynamic. They drew attention to their uniqueness and created theories matching their personalities. (1999: 329)

An element of family therapy's conception of itself is therefore of a rather delinquent or even revolutionary therapist following thinking and practices not allowed elsewhere. The matter, however, is not just one of intellectual argument. Family therapists also needed to establish a professional group that had to be different from the already established psychoanalytically trained profession. It therefore served a purpose for early family therapists to ignore the continuities between their practice and that of interactionally interested analysts. Nathan Ackerman (1962), one of the founders of the field, clearly spelt out the issues:

> It is of no small interest today, therefore, to observe how members of the psychoanalytic profession respond to the concept of the family as the unit of mental health and the unit of diagnosis and therapy. Here, as elsewhere, in matters pertaining to theory and practice, psychoanalysts are divided. Once again we discover the familiar split in the psychoanalytic family as between the conservatives and the liberals. (1962: 32)

Family therapy's original position in the psychotherapeutic world is therefore as much due to the socio-political undercurrents of psychotherapeutic practice as it is to the form of ideas that it espoused. The critical stance towards other approaches, however, may have created something of a mind-set for family therapists. Hence, not only is the family therapist a delinquent but he (or she) is also an outsider to the psychotherapy world. The advantage of the outsider perspective is that one can view some processes in a more critical, open manner. But we can also anticipate that there are disadvantages of this perspective. For instance, the outsider might have a general lack of interest, awareness and involvement of what is happening on the 'inside'. Some have indeed argued that this has happened and that family therapy has over-emphasised its distinctiveness to the extent that it is in danger of marginalising itself and becoming irrelevant (Shields, Wynne, McDaniel & Gawinski, 1994).

What history?

In beginning our journey we have taken an early formulation of the field and examined it for its current cohesiveness, to demonstrate our method rather than lay down frameworks. In doing so we have briefly touched on some important historical trends that still may find their echoes in modern-day family therapy. Indeed in our circular tour of family therapy we will find that the critiques we consider and family therapy's response to these critiques all in some way have a relationship to these intial four elements. Certainly family therapy originated from a variety of sources. However, the nature of its development is very different to that of other major psychotherapeutic schools which emphasise a much clearer link to particular foundational thinking. Thus psychodynamic practice can refer back to Freud's early theoretical writing; person-centred therapists can build on Rogers' 'necessary and sufficient conditions' for therapeutic change; and those of a behaviourist persuasion can fall back to the basic stimulus–response formulations of learning theory. It is not as easy as this for family therapists, as the foundational conceptual paradigm for the field – systems theory – has had a troubled ride and it is to this that we turn in our next chapter.

Chapter 2
A troubled legacy? Systems theory and family therapy

Do not, I beg you, look for anything behind phenomena. They are themselves their own lesson.

Goethe

For an idea ever to be fashionable is ominous, since it must afterwards be always old fashioned.

George Santayana

Family therapy and its philosophical foundations

Perhaps more than any other therapeutic tradition, family therapy has resorted to philosophical concepts to justify its theories and practice. It is a school of psychotherapy that appears to rapidly adhere to changes and fashions in ideas and philosophy. Indeed of all the schools of psychotherapy it may well be the most susceptible to philosophical and theoretical movements. In commenting on the field, Rayner (1986) noted that:

> Currently there are a great many individuals able to display their erudition by inventing more and more theories. (1986: 123)

Lask (1987) made some equally telling points about philosophy and family therapy. He drew attention to the fact that within the community of family therapists there would appear to be a 'political correctness' of ascribing to the latest theory:

> No sooner had I realized the importance of the work of Von Bertalanffy, when into the spotlight jump Spinoza, Maturana and a host of others who have become superheroes, revered and worshipped throughout the world of family therapy. (Lask, 1987: 208)

One must ask the question why such a situation exists in which new philosophical ideas tend to dominate discussion and therapist identity. Related to this we must ask whether the field has examined its own philosophical underpinnings in a way that has provided for the development of a rational and cohesive foundation on which to base therapeutic practice. Our view is that being impressed with the 'new' has not necessarily assisted the field in its progression. Different and sometimes opposite philosophical ideas have continued to find their way into family therapy with much rapidity and little forethought. Sometimes such ideas are accepted by the mainstream of the commentators. At other times they have been hotly disputed. In this chapter we wish to examine some foundational concepts and in particular we will examine philosophical criticisms of these concepts in order to assess how valuable they can be as a basis for family therapy practice. Our aim in this chapter will be to concentrate on those concepts that have influenced the field through the application of systems theory as this essentially contributed to the launch of what became known as family therapy.

What is systems theory?

In Chapter 1 we pointed to the role of systems theory in establishing a theory base in the historical development of family therapy. An early British family therapist defined general systems theory in these terms:

> In general systems theory, there exists the system, the systems' environment (supra-system) and the systems' components (sub-systems); and the theory is concerned with the description and exploration of the relationship between this hierarchy. (Walrond-Skinner, 1976:12)

Furthermore:

> General systems theory states that a system is a whole and that its objects ... and their attributes ... can only be understood as functions of the total system ... The character of the system transcends the sum of its components and their attributes and belongs to a higher order of abstraction. (1976: 12)

Such summaries of systems theory abound in both early and later texts of family therapy (Burnham, 1986; Goldenberg & Goldenberg, 2000; Minuchin, 1974; Nichols & Schwartz, 1998; Satir, 1978). In a more recent work, Carr (2000a) delineates fifteen propositions that he believes are central to systems theory (which he also links to cybernetics). These propositions reiterate many of the concepts outlined by the founder of systems theory Bertalanffy (1968). These include the following:

- a family is a system with boundaries and is organised into sub-systems;
- each family member's behaviour is determined by a pattern of interactions;

- these patterns are repetitious and conform to rules that evolve over time;
- these patterns ensure that it is impossible to determine linear causality but rather encourage an appreciation of the circularity of interaction;
- some of these patterns prevent change (homeostasis) whilst others promote change (morphogenesis);
- within the system *feedback* determines which of the above mechanisms take place;
- if the system is unable to adapt to change, one element of the system will 'malfunction', i.e. develop a symptom.

Although this description of general systems theory might appear quite stark, there is no doubt that most family therapists base their understanding of their practice on some, if not all, of the propositions outlined above. Indeed, there is a growing group of therapists who have abandoned the term 'family therapist' altogether in order to adopt the term 'systemic therapist'. These therapists regard systems theory (albeit amended as we shall see) as the essential foundation for their work and which underlies their practice not only with families and couples but also with individuals and work groups.

As we indicated in the historical elements of our introduction in Chapter 1, the adoption of these propositions by family therapists was a gradual one and from the outset controversy surrounded their early application. It has been argued by some (Nichols & Schwartz, 1998) that von Bertalanffy would have disagreed with the largely *mechanistic* interpretations of his theory as initially applied to family therapy. Moreover, it must be seen that these propositions represent a merging of systems theory and cybernetics with cybernetics emphasising the mechanisms of feedback much more. It must also be recalled that these theoretical positions tended to be used *post hoc* by family therapist theorists to justify, on some external theoretical grounds, a practice that was already present. Despite this history the use of the term 'systemic' as a defining adjective for family therapists illustrates how central the appeal is to systems theory. For this reason we discuss various aspects of it theoretically and practically.

The adequacy of systems theory as an overarching theory

It is important to begin to consider the theory in terms of what we would wish it to set out to do. In particular we would wish to ask whether it describes human phenomena and action adequately? This is a theoretical evaluation and specifically this questions the usefulness of systems theory as an overarching and organising theory within this area.

There is no doubt that systems theory created a different approach for thinking about particular phenomena, but the relationship between its abstract theoretical constructs and empirical facts remains tenuous, especially in the study of human social phenomena (Vetere & Gale, 1987). Indeed, it might be more appropriate to describe this theory as a conceptual framework which spans a wide range of disciplines and links up with less general models; hence one encounters a wide range of other models (for example, psychodynamic and cognitive-behavioural) easily being incorporated into explanations based on systems theory. Unfortunately, as a theory it lacks adequate methods of analysis that spring from its formulations. Consequently when engaged in scientific inquiry it is difficult to establish and apply systems principles. This is particularly so in the investigation of family interactions where a major problem has been inadequate operationalisation of concepts so that data may be collected in a meaningful way. Researchers into the psychology of families require a theory that comprehensively presents concepts and that generate testable predictions not only in terms of general human action but also with regard to action specific to the therapeutic situation. Vetere and Gale (1987) list the requirements of such a theory. It should:

1 Describe and explain family and couple structure, dynamics, process and change.
2 Describe invariant interpersonal structures and emotional dynamics within families and couples, particularly concerning the transmission of distress to individuals.
3 Account for family relationships as the interface between the individual and culture; that is to say, how does the family mediate between external environmental events and individual development, thus acting as a filter through which the child interprets the world?
4 Describe the process of individuation and differentiation of the family members.
5 Predict 'health' and 'pathology' within the family; that is, provide a source of hypotheses about family function and what causes dysfunction whether felt or perceived externally.
6 Outline therapeutic strategies for dealing with dysfunction.
7 Account for the seemingly antithetical functions of stability and change, particularly when viewed within the family's developmental cycle.

One can add to and amend this list but here our purpose is merely to begin to assess systems theory as a set of ideas that are helpful in the practical arena of therapy. Clearly as a theory/model/paradigm solely within its own terms systems theory has not met these requirements and indeed cannot meet these requirements. It is the case that it is difficult to make links between the abstract formulations of systems theory and the reality of everyday interaction. Systems theory is therefore not adequate as a general theory in the development of therapeutic models and it would appear to require other formulations to assist in the 'mediation' process. Systems theory is simply capable of being a background framework that requires other ideas in order to give it an application to therapy. That systems theory contributed to the development of the field is not problematic, for, as with other branches of therapeutic practice, a variety of disparate ideas have always played a useful role in theory development. What is unusual in the case of family therapy is that a 'background' theory became, and to some extent still is, a defining contribution. We therefore turn to some issues of difficulty with systems theory as a philosophical base on which to rest therapeutic practice.

Philosophical difficulties with general systems theory

Clearly there are a number of difficulties that the adoption of general systems theory as an organising framework has brought to family therapy. We divide these difficulties into two sections: those that pose problems of *coherency* for the theory and those that pose problems in *applying* the theory to family therapy.

Coherency

From a philosophical point of view, general systems theory and cybernetics as applied by family therapists to their therapy pose ideas that contain incoherencies. The first of these is the idea that human systems constitute a different level of action than that of individual people. Philosophically this idea has been called both *reification* and *reductionist*. In *reification* an aspect or product of human activity becomes distanced from that activity and is invested with autonomy – it becomes a 'thing', something that is not a part of that activity. The outcome of this way of thinking is that the 'thing' is awarded an independent existence in which it is capable of power over individual human behaviour. Radical political theorists have frequently observed *reification* at work. For instance, Marx (1975) wrote about 'human nature' being reified – a 'thing' that can be discussed as separate from actual human beings. It is not surprising, therefore, that a number of critics have responded to the reification of the 'family system' in family therapy. These writers comment that by reifying the family system, family therapists inflated 'the family' into something that exists above the lives of the individuals in it. The family being seen as more than the sum of its members. In an early example of this criticism Pearson (1974) stated that:

> there is a tendency in family therapy to place the family's existence as a thing of primary importance over and above personal well-being. (1974: 148)

An example of this inflation can be seen when family therapists write about domestic violence. Here the language is about 'family violence' and 'family safety' as if they are separate entities where 'family safety' is of a more important order than the welfare of individuals. It also functions as a *reductionist* concept because it simplifies human behaviour within families and implies that this behaviour is *determined* by rules that are outside the control of the family members. This is evident in the idea that dysfunctional families need symptoms. Pearson (1974) notes:

> in family therapy the family needs symptoms. And while symptoms thus signal family imbalance, there is a danger of losing our understanding of them as personal expressions of distress. (1974: 148)

To put it another way, systems theory firstly inflates the role of the family and then conflates the needs/meanings/thoughts of individuals into a collective mass that is seemingly not constructed by those individuals.

These criticisms have also had their proponents within the family therapy world. Speed (1987) stated that:

> many family therapists' interactional thinking has [caused] the relegation of the individual ... to the bottom of the league. (1987: 235)

Here we meet the dilemma continually faced by family therapists: that of balancing 'the family' with 'the individual'.

Difficulties in applying systems theory to families

There are a number of ways in which the application of systems theory to human (family) systems raises philosophical issues. The first most obvious problem is that human beings are not machines. This factor became relevant in the revisions of systems theory that family therapists undertook in the 1990s but it remains a significant issue. This will be more fully discussed later.

The second problem was one that was also noted by early left-wing critics. Pearson (1974) and Poster (1978) both also assert that systems theory as it is applied by family therapists *decontextualised* an individual family. As critics from the 'left', they believed that systems theory failed to account for the societal pressures which lead families into having difficulties. Poster centred his comments around Bateson's use of systems theory and cybernetics. He says:

> **Bateson's position has the serious flaw – one which tends to characterize all family therapy – of isolating the understanding of the family from history and society. (1978: 118)**

Pearson (1974) agrees:

> **family therapy often strips away the contextualized meanings which surround family-systems. (1974: 145)**

Moreover: family theorists snatch the family out of the world (1974: 146) and by doing so ignore the 'social institution' of the family which exerts 'external social constraints' upon us.

This trend within the philosophical critique of family therapy has surfaced at a number of points in its history. On one level it has led to the interest in radical political engagement; on another it has contributed to the developments in post-modern practice that will be reviewed later in the book.

The third problem that therapists have had in applying systems theory to families has been the difficulty of explaining change itself – both 'natural' change and the change process encouraged by psychotherapy. In many papers this difficulty became labelled the 'problem of homeostasis'. Dell (1982) identified this difficulty as the most serious problem for systems theory. He traced the history of how the term *homeostasis* had entered family therapy language from its first use by Bateson's group. He noted that although 'causal descriptions of homeostasis as maintaining the status quo or helping to keep the patient sick are epistemologically incorrect' (1982: 21) the concept continued to complicate therapeutic theory. Dell deconstructs the concept of homeostasis and shows that it is contradictory and 'reifying' a 'conceptual metaphor'. This, he argues, causes therapists to expect a family not to change and expect a system to cause symptoms.

The last comment to make from this conceptual/theoretical perspective is that all these difficulties have occurred because systems theory operates at a level above the individual components. It points to a level of importance above the individual and it has as its axiom that 'the whole is greater than the sum of its parts'. Dallos and Draper (2000) verbalise this sentiment when they write:

A system is ... a set of interacting parts which mutually communicate with and influence each other. The parts are connected so that each part influences and is influenced by each other part. In turn these continually interacting parts are connected together such that they display identifiable coherent patterns. These overall patterns are not simply reducible to the sum of the actions of the individual parts – a system is more than simply the sum of its composite parts. (2000: 24)

From this assumption have come all the above difficulties of coherency and application. Presuming that a whole is greater than the parts leads to reifying the whole, to reduce the value of the components, to decontextualise the system that is being considered and to struggle with notions of therapeutic change. Such issues crystallise the difficulties that family therapists have had with the legacy of their tradition and indeed with other therapeutic traditions. Family therapy is just a different type of therapy; it is not a superior one. We now wish to analyse the various attempts that have been made to deal with this legacy of systems theory.

Revising systems theory thinking for family therapy

Given developments in the field we have to query the extent that systems theory should be considered as foundational for family therapy practice. It undoubtedly has had an historical influence but whether that influence continues and in what form is problematic. Comparing family therapy to other psychotherapeutic schools we can see that although theoretical formulations have moved on from their initial presentations some conceptual link is always retained with their origins. For example, although psychoanalytic therapy has moved some way theoretically from the original ideas of Freud, initial notions such as 'unconscious motivation' still find their echo in modern-day practice. If systems theory is to be seen as a foundational framework, what are the concepts from it that find their use in current thinking about therapy practice? To begin to answer these questions we need to consider how family therapists have attempted to identify and address the problems inherent in systems theory for itself. We find that family therapy theorists have responded in one of three ways. The first way has been to increase the complexity of the theory often by emphasising the cybernetic aspects more than those of general systems theory itself. The second way has been to reinterpret systems theory in a way which emphasises its humanistic qualities. These revisionists tend to adopt a 'meaning' frame for systems theory. The third response has been to ultimately reject systems theory outright. We will outline each of these options.

The solution of increasing complexity

In the previous section we mentioned Dell's response to the problem of homeostasis within systems theory. His response typifies those theorists who have revised systems theory with reference to cybernetics in order to create a more coherent theory and to resolve some of the philosophical difficulties it provides.

Dell (1982) argued that many of the problems with the application of systems theory to families occurred because of errors of logical typing. By this he means that a description is assumed to represent something that exists when in fact the description is merely a metaphor. Using his example, he says that a family might be described as homeostatic but no elements in the family can be ascribed a homeostatic function; for example, the description is one of the system, not parts of the system. Therefore it is incorrect to describe a symptom as homeostatic as the latter description can only be applied to the system itself. Equally, Dell argues that a system cannot have a 'purpose' because such a label implies an external interpretation.

> This is what is meant by systems theorists when they insist that the best explanation of a system is the system itself. In short, there is no *why*; there is only is. (1982: 23)

He concludes his discussion of homeostasis by declaring that, in fact, all systems evolve:

> when a system is perturbed, as all systems are, it tends to seek a steady state that is always *slightly* different from the preceding steady state. In short, homeostasis evolves. (1982: 34)

Movement, change and differentness are clearly continuous and naturally occurring processes. That this happens in human relationships must raise questions about how we view 'stability'. The result of these discussions according to Dell is that systems theory is adequate to explain the contradictions that arise when applying systems theory to family therapy.

In many ways, Keeney (1983) carried this perspective even further. In his closely argued *Aesthetics of change* he returned to Batesonian cybernetics in order to re-establish the role of cybernetic understandings in systems theory and family therapy. Keeney explains that he wants to:

> provide an aesthetic understanding of change, a type of respect, wonder and appreciation of natural systems often overlooked by the various fields of psychotherapy. (1983: 8)

In order to do this he reiterates many of the axioms of systems theory: that non-linear epistemologies are the foundation of cybernetic understandings; that patterns rather than 'material' are where therapists need to work; and that systems are always undergoing change. In the course of his discussion he elaborates the value of second-order cybernetics, which insists that the observer affects what is seen and that change occurs through the perception of difference. Like Bateson, Keeney asserts that the use of conscious purpose largely accounts for human difficulties as conscious purpose itself cannot appreciate the ecological whole. Therefore the therapist must integrate with the family system and by doing so change the way the system changes:

> Therapeutic change of a cybernetic system ... involves change of change – change of how a system's habitual process of change leads to stability. (1983: 177)

However, similar to other strategies, Keeney resorts to a mysticism to explain this mechanism. Therapy, he says, is an art that is founded on cybernetic respect.

This approach has been further expanded by Atkinson and Heath (1990) who address one of the new difficulties caused by this 'respectful' cybernetics. They comment that it is unlikely that a therapist will be able to understand a family system fully because to do so involves the use of external consciousness and this consciousness within a system cannot appreciate the totality of that system.

> It is not possible for any human observer to take in to conscious awareness the recursive complexity of the multiple levels of systems involved in any problem situation. (1990: 148)

The result is that:

> Individuals may be inclined to become passive, not daring to intervene for fear of creating more problems. (1990: 148)

Their answer to this conundrum is to suggest that family therapists must seriously attend to their own belief that they should change a system at all. They argue that:

pragmatic action that is implemented by individuals whose personal contentment is not dependent upon the extent to which their actions are successful in producing desired outcomes. (1990: 151)

This view clearly has some validity: therapists should be aware of their own expectations and how the therapy they undertake fulfils their own desires for power and control. However, as an argument that is seeking to resolve some of the inherited problems of systems theory, it seems to be lacking. Neither Dell's, Keeney's nor Atkinson and Heath's revisions of systems theory adequately solve the problem of coherency, reification of the system or the relegation of the individual.

The solution of humanistic interpretations of systems theory

A number of family therapists have moved to reinterpret systems theory from a humanistic perspective in order to counter the problems we have outlined. The first such commentator is Bogdan (1984). His paper, sub-titled 'An alternative to the reification of family systems', recalled many of the criticisms discussed above; he notes that:

The problem of talking about collective entities without talking non-sense has exercised several minds in philosophy. (1984: 376)

Bogdan comments that despite the appeal of systems theory with its emphasis on interaction, most family therapists

in our unprofessional moments ... are apt to revert to the common-sense view that people act to satisfy their desires or to achieve their goals and that they do this according to their ideals about the nature of the situations in which they are actors. (1984: 375)

In other words, although family therapists act as if their systems theory were true in their practice, in their 'private' thoughts they adopt ideas about self-agency, lineal causation etc. As one satirical commentator noted: 'Get linear; get real!' (Routledge, 1996). Bogdan goes on to comment that although family therapists are happy to state that single parts of a family do not make up the whole, they continue to ascribe reality to concepts such as 'structure' that only exist within individual minds. Indeed, he continues to question all the assumptions that a systemic perspective as adopted by most family therapists entails. He concludes:

The strongest argument against the idea of family homeostasis is neither purely logical nor empirical but is based on the principle of parsimony in scientific explanation. To say that family members behave in certain ways because of a prescriptive rule imposed upon them by a kind of collective organism in which they play a role analogous to that of organs, or perhaps cells, is surely not a simple or commonsense explanation by current standards. (1984: 379)

Bogdan's solution to this is not curiously to ditch systems theory altogether, but to amend it with the concept of 'the family as an ecology of ideas':

The concept of ecology gives us a way of talking about complex systems that does not postulate entities over and above the patterns of interrelationship among the individuals making up such systems. (1984: 380)

Bogdan adds to this an approach which values human meanings:

the core assumption of this paper is that people behave according to how they frame, define or punctuate the situations in which they are actors. (1984: 381)

This interpretation is markedly different from the inherited view that systems theory brought into family therapy. Here people are conscious actors who are not organised by the interactions of the systems in which they live but rather are choosing what they do and think. Bogdan then proceeds to link this perspective to family patterns and argues that patterns evolve because the family members construct ideas about each other that construct a further pattern. He writes:

family structure is simply the name of a class of patterns of communicative behaviour between people. (1984: 383)

Bogdan claims that relying on the concept of an 'ecology of ideas' explains most of the success of previously described therapeutic methods and avoids the difficulties of systems theory.

Bogdan's ideas were criticised by Miller (1984) who believed that the concept of an 'ecology of ideas' added little to the versions of systems theory that were useful to family therapists. Miller also maintained that Bogdan assumes that each family member is a 'methodological individualist' who ultimately would fail to appreciate the 'emergent properties of groups'. In the light of the years that have passed since Bogdan's attempt to revise systems theory, we might acknowledge that his revision appeared to have very little influence on the power of the systemic concept at all. However, two other revisionists have made a remarkable difference to this concept and their developments of systems theory are widely quoted today.

Anderson and Goolishian's (1988) paper entitled 'Human systems as linguistic systems' provides the most competent humanistic revision of systems theory. These authors write:

> Human systems are language generating and simultaneously meaning generating systems ... a sociocultural system is the product of social communication rather than communication being the product of organization ... and a human system is a linguistic or communicative system. The therapeutic system is a linguistic system. (1988: 373)

This, then, was a version of systems theory that by emphasising human meanings and communication sought to avoid some of the mechanistic difficulties posed by other interpretations of systems theory. Indeed, Anderson and Goolishian prefigured the later social constructionist philosophy of family therapy by arguing that meanings are constantly changing according to language usage:

> our theories, as well as our practices of therapy are meant as temporary lenses rather than as representations that conform to a social reality. (1988: 373)

They interpret their position in family therapy development as being in collaboration with an 'emphasis on meaning systems' not 'social systems'. Their interpretation of the history of family therapy was that the great advances promised by it in the 1950s and 1960s had not been justified. They believe that this has to some degree been the result of pursuing the 'social systems' avenue:

> This direction appears to be an extension of the underlying and prevailing paradigm of social science. This derives meaning and understanding from observing patterns of social organization such as structure and role. (1988: 375)

They argue that this model underlies all of the hitherto existing versions of family therapy (and systems theory). Thus:

> concepts ... such as dysfunctional family structure, inadequate generational boundaries, symptom functionality, and inadequate organizational hierarchies are all expressions and extensions of this foundational social theory. (1988: 376)

The alternative that they propose is a version of 'social constructionism' in which:

> Humans ... can be defined as language generating, meaning generating systems engaged in an activity that is intersubjective and recursive. (1988: 377)

This idea leads to some non-systems theory conclusions:

within this framework, there are no 'real' external entities ... there is only the process of the constantly evolving reality of language use. Thus, there are no 'facts' to be known, no 'systems' to be understood, and no patterns and regularities to be 'discovered'. (1988: 378)

In this section we do not wish to continue to elaborate the therapeutic purpose of Anderson and Goolishian's ideas (Anderson & Goolishian, 1986; 1988). The issue here is to consider how successful this revision of systems theory was in addressing the difficulties that we have outlined above. Clearly, the concept of human systems being meaning systems was an attempt to avoid the reification of concepts such as family. Indeed, in their earlier paper Anderson and Goolishian (1986) state 'families do not exist outside of an observer's language' (1986: 9). The emphasis upon language ensured that the 'foundational' assumptions of previous family therapy models was questioned and therefore could not be taken as reality. However, Anderson and Goolishian continued to speak with the language of 'systems'. They talk about 'human systems' and 'problem determined systems', and by using such language themselves are in fact positing the existence (even if in language) of something they call 'system'. Therefore, although they claim to be avoiding reification, it could be argued that they have substituted one version of reification for another. Moreover, many systemic therapists would have agreed with the metaphorical language they use to describe systems. It would appear that this may just be a change of metaphor rather than an actual alteration of conceptual structure.

In terms of the claim that systems theory reduced all experiences to the level of a mechanism, the 'language system' concept is an advance. This new metaphor for experience totally avoided the mechanistic, reductionist inheritance of systems theory. However, it is a version that may seem to posit too much influence for individuals in the making of meaning. Anderson and Goolishian were well aware of this criticism of their ideas. In their 1986 paper they responded to the claim that their rejection of the term 'family' leads them to a 'full circle' position (e.g. to assert the ascendancy of the individual). They reply that 'the individuals communicating about the problem have distinguished the problem' (1986: 9) and are therefore defiant in the face of this criticism. This is also part of their response to the idea that systems theory decontextualises families. Again, although their assertion that language makes for the intersubjectivity of self, they do not build a model as did later social constructionists that emphasises the role of wider systems in the manufacture of problems. In philosophical terms Anderson and Goolishian's answer to the problems of systems theory is a return to the philosophical school of 'idealism' in which it is considered that it is 'mind' that determines reality. In terms of the application of systems theory this simply substitutes one difficulty for another.

It needs to be said that Anderson and Goolishian, like many family therapists before and after them, did not claim to be philosophers who had answers. Indeed, they were at pains to point out that their ideas were not meant to be: 'another family therapy theory or model of therapy' (1988: 375). Moreover, like all family therapists their ideas were designed to be clinically helpful rather that world explaining. Nevertheless, these revisions of systems theory have been taken as valid by many practising therapists and therefore need to be analysed in relation to the original theory they were meant to improve on.

The solution of the 'refusniks'

Throughout the history of family therapy, voices have been heard which have rejected systems theory as an adequate theory for family practice. Some of these practitioners have almost seceded from the field altogether. Box, Copley, Magagna and Moustaki (1981), for example, have placed their theoretical formulations solely within a psychoanalytic framework. Others, such as Michael White (1995) have provided radical critiques when they have already been accepted as leaders in the field. Feminists have also critiqued systems theory and its application to family therapy. In Chapter 6 we will be considering the role of feminism in challenging family therapy practice, but here we need to point to the refusniks of systems theory that emerged from the feminist critique. In her book *The family interpreted*, Luepnitz (1988) outlined her reasons why systems theory was no longer a useful way of conceiving family difficulties. She mounted her criticisms on the plank of feminism and asserted that all cybernetic and systems theories entailed an ahistorical and decontextual analysis of gender. These are clearly specific aspects of the difficulties we have already noted within systems theory itself. Leupnitz concluded that 'general systems theory is no longer helpful' (1988: 163) and further that 'there is not, and I doubt that there ever will be, a feminist cybernetics' (1988: 167). Similarly, one of the early luminaries of the family therapy field, Hoffman (1993) described her leaving of the systems metaphor in 1990:

I was beginning to alter my ideas and to feel that it was time to leave 'systems', in particular 'family systems', behind. (1993: 97)

More recently she has written about the need to 'set aside the model in family therapy' (Hoffman, 1998). She elaborates her theory of family therapy practice that does not rely on systems theory but on the reflectiveness of the therapist. 'Models' she writes 'are heuristic fairy tales, holders of complex realities' (1998: 153). Indeed such a 'model … stays within the Western science paradigm' which is part of the 'blame and change game' that is perpetuated by our theories.

Perhaps the most common source of contemporary scepticism of systems theory, however, is from the solution-focused therapists. These therapists question systems theory from the same perspective as many of the criticisms outlined above: that it is demeaning of individual meaning and that it imposes a theoretical structure on client experiences. But they add the extra perspective that systems theory is rooted in the idea of problems – that it works only if one focuses on problems. No problem, no system! An example of the gradual journey from systems theory to non-systems theory is Steve de Shazer, one of the originators of solution-focused therapy.

In his early books de Shazer (1982, 1985) positioned himself very much within the field of systemic theory. He for instance discussed ways in which the therapist could 'cooperate' with the clients' system (1982: 10). He also gave explanations for the ways in which 'paradoxical' interventions worked. However, by the late 1980s and beyond, de Shazer had begun to jettison references to systems theory in favour of 'what works' pragmatism. Indeed he declared in *Putting difference to work* (1991) that previous family therapy models

> thought that symptoms are the result of some underlying problem … incongruent hierarchies, deviant communication, repressed feelings. (1991: 20)

In 1998 he further commented that solution-focused therapy denounced the 'metanarratives' that were

> simultaneously classifications of clients and their problems, theories that explain clients' life circumstances and their problems. (Miller & de Shazer, 1998: 371)

He added one more (new) criticism of systems theory: that by its nature it assumed 'clients' lives are problem-saturated' (1998: 371). This then would appear to be another atheoretical pragmatic approach that dispenses with systems theory.

Given the popularity of solution-focused brief therapy, we can conclude that many currently practising family therapists have adopted a therapeutic model that is at the very least sceptical of systems theory if not directly hostile to it.

Conclusion

Despite this brief review of the theoretical, conceptual and philosophical difficulties of systems theory, it should be repeated that all contemporary textbooks of family therapy continue to ascribe it as the basis for the therapeutic practice of family therapists. At the start of this chapter, we quoted from a range of American and British texts that credit the paradigm shift from individual to systemic perspectives as being the radical impetus that powered the creation of family therapy. Yet our consideration of the axioms of systems theory with the reflections of external and internal critiques of it, suggest that systems theory provided major difficulties to providing a coherent theory and humanistic practice of family therapy. As a theory it has been much quoted without recognition of its fundamental flaws. In particular we are arguing here that the oft-quoted maxim of family therapists that 'the whole is greater than the sum of the parts' is incorrect and in its promulgation has done a disservice to the field. Philosophically, the statement does not compare like with like: parts of a machine are clearly different from the whole of the machine. Thus to assert that the whole is greater than the parts is tautologous and meaningless. It can only have some meaning if it is assumed that the composite parts grant some mystical entity to the whole. Certainly Bateson may have entertained such notions (Bateson & Bateson, 1987), and indeed in his writings a spiritual theme is implied. But here we must recall yet again that Bateson was not a family therapist and was approaching the phenomena of behaviour in its interactive context from a different perspective than the therapeutic one. Few contemporary family therapists would want to be defending the notion that the family system has some mystical qualities that transcend the qualities of its members. What we can say is that the whole of a system is qualitatively *different* to the sum of its parts but such a statement gives no superiority to that whole.

The problems with systems theory have led to a fracture point in the family therapy world. One group of writers and practitioners continue to assert its validity and importance. Some of these even attempt complex theorising to 'square' the theory with a humanistic and respectful practice. Yet another group seem to disregard it totally and rarely rely upon it to explain their practice. What is difficult to understand given these theoretical problems is how systems theory continues to be presented as a current foundational element of family therapy practice. The problem for family therapy is that if we remove this theory what are we left with? It can certainly be said that family therapists have only seen systems theory as a 'map' and not the 'territory'. But if that view is held how can we explain the lengths to which some authors have gone in trying to 'square' systems theory with family therapy practice. Is there an alternative? In this chapter we have alluded to post-modernism within family therapy. In the next chapter, we turn to this to analyse the place of post-modernism as a theory and as a basis for family therapy practice.

Chapter 3
Family therapy's affair
with post-modernism

I suspect there are more things in heaven and earth than are
dreamed of, or can be dreamed of, in any philosophy. That is the
reason why I have no philosophy myself, and must be my excuse
for dreaming.

J.B.S. Haldane

What is post-modernism?

In the last chapter we explored one of the philosophical and
conceptual legacies of family therapy and suggested that, at least in
part, the dissatisfaction with systems theory had led in the last two
decades to family therapists seeking a different philosophical paradigm for their practice. A major source of the critique of systems
theory-based family therapy was post-modernism and it has been to
this paradigm that family therapists have turned in order to provide
a theoretical framework. In the contemporary field of family therapy,
post-modernism is the most frequently quoted philosophical position
and the literature on this theme has burgeoned (Rivett, 1999). In this
chapter we explain the salient features of post-modernism, describe
how these have been interpreted by family therapists and interrogate
the difficulties that relying on post-modernism as a fundamental
model for practice might hold.

There are a number of readers and texts that define what post-
modernism is (Lyon, 1994; Natoli & Hutcheon, 1993; Smart,
1993; Waugh, 1992); here, therefore, we will attempt to summarise
relevant features in order to make subsequent discussion meaningful.
A first distinction that needs to be made is that post-modernism (the
culture of ideas) and post-modernity (the social embodiment of post-
modernism) are defined in relation to that which is called 'modernist'.
Lyon states that:

The postmodern ... refers above all to the exhaustion of modernity.
(1994: 6)

From the outset, therefore, 'post-modern' has to be seen as having
a definition that relies on 'modernity' – it is one side of a difference;
it is a part of a dichotomy. Thus we must begin with a definition of
the 'modern'. Lyon says that this assumes a

**'foundationalism', the view that science is built on a firm base of
observable facts. (1994: 7)**

This perspective of the 'opposite' nature of the post-modern has
large repercussions in particular to theories of reality and to theories
of power in therapy, as we shall see later. What we need to note here
is the importance of epistemology – the theory of knowledge, to the
post-modern endeavour. In epistemological investigations there is a
reflection on the standards to which knowledge should conform. The
attempt is to characterise the kind of knowledge which a given
method of study might yield about a certain sort of subject matter, and
how far that kind of knowledge conforms to what are taken to be
standards of knowledge in a 'genuine' or 'true' sense (Harre, 1972).
Such is the centrality of this type of philosophical activity to the post-
modern that the most frequently quoted post-modern philosopher,
Lyotard (1986) sub-titled one of his books '*A report on knowledge*'.
Epistemological investigation certainly is a process that focuses on
doubt and within this sceptical perspective is doubt about the validity
of what Lyotard called the 'metanarratives'. These metanarratives are
those assumptions that have dominated Western societies since the
birth of the Enlightenment and include a belief that society will
improve, that technology will emancipate people and that Western
democratic institutions will bring peace and prosperity. Lyotard writes:

**I will use the term *modern* to designate any science that legitimates
itself with reference to a metadiscourse of this kind, making an explicit
appeal to some grand narrative, such as the dialectics of Spirit, the
hermeneutics of meaning, the emancipation of the rational or working
subject, or the creation of wealth. (1986: xxiii)**

In opposition to this Lyotard declares:

**simplifying to the extreme, I define the *post-modern* as incredulity
toward metanarratives. (1986: xxiv)**

Of significance is that this incredulity, this doubt, this scepticism,
includes incredulity to the metanarratives of the left-wing/'socialistic'
philosophy from which many post-modern philosophers evolved,
including Lyotard.

A secondary consequence of this philosophical doubt about metanarratives has been a support for 'local rather than universal' (Lyon,

1994: 7) knowledge. This interest has led to a 'multiplicity of voices' being represented in post-modern texts (see Natoli & Hutcheon, 1993) as well as the famous studies by Foucault (1986). Foucault's studies were in his own terms examples of the *archaeology of knowledge,* in which he attempted to discover the origins of certain ideas and practices. In turn he was able to uncover alternative knowledges that did not become dominant. Sarup (1993) describes Foucault's contribution like this:

> whereas traditional history inserts events into grand explanatory systems ... genealogical analysis attempts to establish and preserve the singularity of events, turns away from the spectacular in favour of the discredited, the neglected and a whole range of phenomena which have been denied a history. (1993: 59)

In a range of areas, Foucault put this method to work to uncover the 'singularities' in the history of the social treatment of madness, the moralities of sexuality and the evolution of medical knowledge (Foucault, 1986). Fiona Williams (1992) summarises the effect of this approach when she reviews the effect of post-modernism on social policy:

> Postmodernism turns away from the overarching analyses of power or function to the study of the fragmentary and the ephemeral, to the unpicking of local discourses. (1992: 206)

So post-modernism is not so much concerned with the conflictual processes between sets of ideas – which often focus on the winning of a battle. It is concerned to ensure that all sets of ideas are seen as relevant and in particular those ideas which did not fare well socially as a result of that conflict.

The third element of post-modernism that has relevance for family therapists is the strand that has come to be called *social constructionism.* This perspective in some ways grows naturally out of both of the above features of post-modernism, but curiously was not given the prominence by post-modernist philosophers that it later was given by family therapy practitioners. This strand asserted that social interaction determined language and therefore reality. *Social constructionists* distinguished themselves from *constructivists* by describing reality as not determined by individuals but by social structures. The most prominent social constructionist within the therapy world is Gergen (1991; 1999) who also co-edited one of the most widely quoted social constructionist texts (McNamee & Gergen, 1992). In this latter text, McNamee and Gergen describe social constructionism in this way:

our formulations of what is the case are guided by and limited to the
systems of language in which we live. What can be said about the
world – including self and others – is an outgrowth of shared conven-
tions of discourse ... in effect what we take to be 'the real and the
good' are largely products of textual histories. (1992: 4)

Language therefore becomes not merely the medium of the communication but the determinant of the relationship between the
communicators and the instructors for what should occur in the
future. (Whether it is the instigator of communication is a moot point
that will be discussed later.) Language initiates a process of social
construction that in turn creates narratives.

Paradoxes and contradictions: critiquing post-modernism

It is important in any critique of post-modernism to underline from
the outset that it is not a singular unified philosophical edifice.
Indeed, post-modernism should be more appropriately labelled *post-
modernisms.* Each of the significant proponents of post-modern
philosophy and post-modern society make different proposals as
befits a movement which values multiplicity. This section is not
therefore intended to provide a rigorous critique of each and every
writer of post-modernism. However, we do seek to highlight a number of arguments that have been made which aim at least to verbalise the inherent paradoxes of post-modern thought. We will do
this with regard to the three essential elements of post-modernism
that family therapists have adopted: a questioning about grand-
narratives; a regard for local knowledges and a view that all narratives
are socially constructed.

Grand-narratives

Commentators on post-modernism note that there is an inherent
contradiction in the claim that all grand-narratives are to be questioned, especially if the statement implies that post-modernity is itself
a new grand-narrative. An example is Lyotard's writing itself. In his
The postmodern condition, on the one hand he rejects narratives
of 'progress' and 'emancipation' (1986: 37) but on the other hand
describes a society in which computerisation and the 'performativ-
ity' of education are becoming the norm. One grand-narrative being
superseded by another? So by post-modernists asserting their views
about knowledge, they are potentially constructing a new grand-
narrative themselves which posits the ascendancy of their views. In

doing so they perpetuate the 'modernist' undertaking of finding the better 'truth'. This paradox has led to debates about whether post-modernism is simply another version of modernism and whether it is appropriate to dismiss the grand-narratives of the Enlightenment at all (see Natoli & Hutcheon, 1993). This problem returns to the place of post-modernism as a set of ideas in contradistinction to modernity. Post-modernism refers to ideas that have their impact when in opposition – the other 'thing' still existing. When this 'other thing' – Enlightment, Modernity etc. – is removed and simply relegated to the dustbin of history (à la Trotsky), post-modernism becomes exactly what it replaces – a grand-narrative.

Local knowledge

Following on from the above commentary, some critics have maintained that post-modernism's emphasis upon the rejection of grand- narratives and the enthronement of local knowledges leads to *relativism*. Relativism suggests that as everything is relative to the nature of the situation there therefore can be no absolute. With the lack of the absolute there is a loss of the basis of morality and ethical action. Some such as Jameson and Callinicos (Lyon, 1994) see post-modernity as merely the expression of 'late capitalism' where consumerism replaces production which itself leads to an ephemeral culture represented by post-modern ephemeral thought. These authors quote Foucault's claim that we should 'prefer what is positive and multiple, difference over uniformity, flows over unities, mobile arrangements over systems' (Lyon, 1994: 76) as examples of the loss of a social ethic of liberation and empowerment. Indeed it has been argued that post-modern thought cannot find a way to describe social structure's institutions, practices and traditions as anything but oppressive and consequently as never productive of 'freedom' (see Natoli & Hutcheon, 1993). Here the critique is one that sees post-modernism as being potentially anarchistic in prognosis, morally barren and absent of ideals.

Social construction

The theme of relativism also poses difficulties for social constructionism. Critics argue that such a philosophy is inherently negative: if all human beings are constrained by the social structure of the language they use, the behaviours they are permitted and the inter-actions that are socially determined, then there is no such thing as freedom nor any real alternatives to that which is known. Smart (1993) describes this as post-modernism having 'no scope for a redemptive politics'. We are not here suggesting that any ideas should lead towards a general political perspective of redeeming the value of persons, freedom and justice. But we are suggesting that therapy by its very nature offers the hope of being valued, free and treated fairly. Therapy suggests something 'better' can be attained in the future and hence we need to be mindful of ideas which are based on other premises.

However, another difficulty of this position when it is combined with the rejection of scientific narratives is that it proves difficult to consider the place of scientific findings in everyday activities. Erwin (1997) for instance, cross-examines the post-modern axioms in order to judge both their clinical relevance and their scientific validity. He concludes that post-modern views about reality being relativistic, observation obscuring what is studied and truth being determined by the 'language game' of the researcher, all add up to a rejection of any standard by which to judge that therapy works. He writes:

> If one argues that clarity, precision, rigorous empirical testing, are unnecessary, what is being rejected is not merely the need for more and better science, but also a firm basis *of any kind* for believing psychotherapeutic claims. The inevitable result of that approach will be continued confusion and sterility. (1997: 80)

Social constructionism therefore can be interpreted as assuming that a practice based on an empirical framework is not possible. In the light of these comments we shall now review how family therapists have responded to these post-modern ideas in their practices.

Adopting post-modernism

Family therapy texts that cited post-modernism as their philosophical support first began appearing in the late 1980 and early 1990s. The most influential of these was White and Epston's (1990) *Narrative means to therapeutic ends*. Indeed this book represented one of the major practice strands that carried post-modernism into family therapy practice. This strand became known as *narrative therapy* and has now expanded as a form of therapy beyond the family therapy community (McLeod, 1997). Indeed in our field this divergence of the 'narrative' school would appear to mark the most significant 'parting of the ways' in terms of the theory, practice and professional organisation of therapy. The other significant strand that uses post-modern ideas as a means of explaining its practice is what has become known as *collaborative* practice. The most significant exponent of this model is Hoffman (1993). In this section of the chapter we will outline the particular post-modern justifications for these therapies that are provided by these authors.

Narrative therapy and post-modernism

White and Epston (1990) begin their book with a review of the various analogies that human beings use in order to typologise their knowledge. They make the common post-modern argument that knowledge is based on an analogy and does not itself constitute 'truth'. They proceed to argue that they prefer analogies that emphasise meaning as opposed to structure and in particular they privilege *narratives* or stories that encapsulate the meaning that individuals ascribe to their lives. The further suggestion is that therapy is about helping people vary the narrative descriptions that dominate their lives. Therapy therefore seeks to find 'unique outcomes' (1990: 16) and 'alternative stories' (1990: 17) in the narratives of clients:

> As alternative stories become available other 'sympathetic' and previously neglected aspects of the person's experience can be expressed and circulated. (1990: 17)

Borrowing from Foucault, White and Epston then propose that since many of the narratives that we accept are socially determined, therapy might often be about resisting the kind of socially repressive narratives that stultify individual freedom and self-expression. They talk about encouraging clients to access 'subjugated knowledges' (1990: 25) which in Foucault's terminology means those ideas that have been relegated because they do not accord with socially acceptable 'norms' or are seen as perniciously deviant.

In another description of his therapeutic method, White (1995) adopts another post-modern method: that of deconstruction. He states that he deconstructs narratives in therapy:

> deconstruction of self-narrative and the dominant cultural knowledges that persons live by; the deconstruction of practices of self and of relationship that are dominantly cultural; and the deconstruction of the discursive practices of our culture. (1995: 35)

Another proponent of narrative family therapy, Parry (1991) also adopts deconstructionism as a crucial element of a post-modern therapy. The therapist works by helping the client vary the elements of the story of her life:

> In the telling of the story there is apt to be little realization of the fact
> that her narration is but a selection of certain events out of a virtually
> unlimited number. (1991: 42)

The therapist's role is therefore to highlight different interpretations of the story and help the client construct a story that is her own story. A narrative therapist, he writes:

> seeks to raise into the foreground of the person's attention alternative
> stories, unexpected interpretations of prevailing stories with the per-
> son's own experience of given events, in order to challenge the
> received text, or life-story in its constraining role. (1991: 52)

This view about narratives, meaning and dominant cultural knowledges presupposes a social constructionist outlook. McLeod (1997) writes:

> a social constructionist view of the world places a sense of the person
> as a story-making and story-consuming being right at the heart of its
> conceptual framework. (1997: x)

Some (e.g. Parry, 1991) believe that the narrative development in family therapy represents one of the 'flowerings' of post-modernism. He sees family therapy as the natural therapeutic expression of post-modernism just as psychoanalysis was for modernism.

Collaborative therapy

The name most frequently associated with developing post-modern ideas into a collaborative therapy is that of Lynn Hoffman (1993). In a series of articles over the end of the 1980s and into the 1990s, Hoffman began to trace the evolution of her model from one dominated by a conception of family systems through to one as mentioned at the end of Chapter 2 that eschews models altogether. She began by beginning to adopt a 'constructivist position for family therapy' which emphasised the ideas of 'second-order cybernetics' that themselves questioned the ability of an outsider to describe a system's patterns. In her 1988 paper, Hoffman outlined the propositions of constructivism as: 'There is no belief in an objective reality' and 'There is no such thing as a "God's Eye View"'. These ideas themselves led to constructivist family therapists being more interested in ideas than behaviours and in attempting to reduce the hierarchy between therapist and client. However, by 1990 Hoffman had begun to embrace not constructivism but social constructionism and post-modernism. Perhaps because she based her therapeutic model on the Milan school of family therapy, she interpreted post-modern practices from a curious, collaborative perspective. She emphasised this aspect of her thinking even when she talked about narratives:

I propose using a post-modern interpretive framework as a banner under which our experiments in co-constructing therapeutic texts might take place. In therapy, we listen to a story and then we collaborate with the persons we are seeing to invent other stories or other meanings for the stories we are told. (1993: 101)

In an admission that mirrors Haley's description of the development of family therapy that we quoted at the beginning of Chapter 1, Hoffman describes almost ashamed developments that ran in the face of the accepted wisdom:

As I began to search for this different voice, I became increasingly uncomfortable with ... technocratic coldness. Actually I never entirely bought it. When unobserved, I would show a far more sympathetic side to clients than my training allowed. I would show my feelings, even weep. I called this practice 'corny therapy', and never told my supervisors about it. ... I began to talk to other women and found that they too used to do secretly what I did and also had pet names for this practice. (Hoffman, 1993: 125)

This quote also highlights that Hoffman has throughout been interested in the role of the therapist and has therefore been placing a greater emphasis on the way the therapist relates to the client. For her issues of power and respect have enabled her to consider the value in Carl Rogers' work and have led to her describing her therapy as collaborative and post-modern. The re-evaluation of the Rogerian perspective in the collaborative frame has led Harlene Anderson (2001) to argue that if alive today Carl Rogers would be closely alongside the developments of collaborative therapy.

Despite various interpretations of the phrase 'collaborative therapy' (Friedman, 1993) the most frequently acknowledged collaborative practice that has been adopted by family therapists has been that of the 'reflecting team'. Tom Andersen first published his ideas about this practice in 1987 in a paper which owed much to the Milan method (a systemic perspective) but which added a 'second-order' perspective in which the team sought to ensure that the family heard a variety of ideas rather than only one interpretation or hypothesis. In later descriptions of this practice, however, the post-modern explanations began to expand:

No description is better than the other ones; they are equally valid. The consequence for clinical work is that we must search for and accept all existing descriptions and explanations of a situation and promote further searching for more explanations and more definitions not yet made. (Andersen, 1991: 26)

Thus reflecting teams are an attempt to both open up the 'expert' power base of therapy and also to encourage families to see their difficulties in a new light by making available new perspectives from the team and the subjugated stories of the family. Reflecting team conversations are activities that embody the post-modern ideal of openness and reflectivity.

Perlesz, Young, Paterson and Bridge (1994) in their review of reflecting team methods recognised that it was 'consistent with second order therapies' (1994: 119) but noted that a distinction should be made between the technique and the process. The technique, for instance, might be applied like any other systems theory-based technique, whereas a stance that places the therapists as reflecting upon their ideas and selves in front of the family inevitably involves a view that approximates the collaborative therapy outlined by Hoffman.

Difficulties in applying post-modernism to family therapy! Does it 'fit'?

In this section we will explore the criticisms of family therapists who have questioned the total acceptance of post-modernism for family therapy. These criticisms will be developed by returning to the categories that critics of post-modernism have used: those of the disadvantages of rejecting all grand-narratives; of enshrining local knowledges and of regarding social constructionism as self-evident.

Maintaining the grand-narratives of family therapy

In Chapter 2 we argued that despite the preponderance of post-modern thinking in contemporary family therapy, our reading of the field is that many practitioners and certainly most of the texts used to train, have not been ready to surrender the 'grand-narrative' of systems theory. On the whole this unwillingness to 'leave the home' of systems theory is unvoiced. However, at least two voices have continued to defend some of the grand-narratives of family therapy against the assault of post-modernism. These have been both traditional family therapists as evinced by Minuchin (1998) and a number of feminist practitioners as evinced by Sanders (1998).

Minuchin was one of the founders of the structural school of family therapy, and certainly it would be hard for anyone to name a school that would be least likely to be acceptable to post-modernists than 'structural'. Indeed, Minuchin's (1974) ideas of family structure have received their fair share of criticism from second-order and post-modernist commentators. Other commentators, however, have reinterpreted his practices from a post-modern perspective (Simon, 1995). Minuchin's more recent critiques of post-modernism have been arguing that this perspective lacks many of the 'knowledges' that were prevalent in family theory generally and family therapy in particular that he developed:

> I began to ask myself whether this metatheory concerning the construction of reality had a theory about families at all. How would this theory explain bonding? Or the affiliations between family members that create subgroups, and sometimes scapegoating? How does it explain the way conflict between parents affects their children's views of themselves? How does it frame the complexities of divorce and remarriage, or the way individual family members select certain family functions and certain styles of interpersonal transactions? (1998: 398)

He summarises this question into the issue of 'can a narrative therapist work with the family as a social system?' (1998: 399). He further describes what this perspective loses:

> The systemic idea that family members co-construct meaning, and that one can observe them in the process of constructing individual and family stories, is lost. (1998: 399)

This concerns Minuchin:

> In the last 40 years a body of research about families has grown up in the disciplines of sociology, anthropology, psychology, genetics, and paediatrics, among others. An understanding of family functioning now spans all types of populations in different cultures, classes and contexts. ... Should this ... be bypassed on the basis of an all-encompassing metatheory? (1998: 400)

Minuchin's criticisms can be summarised as being that the post-modern narrative therapy school has shed a number of essential features of an accepted, acceptable and to some extent proven family therapy. The features which family therapy has lost are:

- the observation of dialogues among family members and their effects on interpersonal patterns;
- the spontaneous and induced enactments that transform a session into a live scenario, with transactions among family members that are multiply voiced and multiply acted out;
- the recognition of the therapist's knowledge as a positive force for healing;
- the realisation that a therapist's participation in the family process provides an experiential connectedness with the family and allows for the use of self as witness, collaborator, expander and enricher of experience;

- the acknowledgement that it is impossible for the therapist to function without bringing a personal bias into the situation.

For Minuchin these are losses but he also recognises that there are a number of positives that family therapy can gain from post-modern practice (1998: 403). It is also evident that some of his criticisms are unfair (particularly the issues of 'self' which in some ways dominate post-modern practice). However, Minuchin argument is nothing less than a defence of various modernist, 'foundationalist' principles that he regards as definitional of family therapy practice itself. He clearly sees the existence of such a knowledge base as being of immense value to those who seek to assist families.

Minuchin, who had been so criticised for his patriarchal and structural views in the 1980s, finds himself in a curious ideological twist as a bedfellow of some feminist thinkers in regards to the nature of his critique of post-modern practice. Sanders (1998), for example, argues that:

> post-structuralism is itself imbued with a conservatism which severely undermines its own radical edge. Most importantly from a feminist perspective, this conservatism is one that works against women. (1998: 112)

This criticism derives from an 'unacknowledged masculism' of post-modern thought. Sanders explains her position:

> [post-structuralism] just like the narrative model derived from it, does itself split off a separate world of language, which has the effect of obscuring its own social, material and historical context ... this split severs the 'selves' it claims to be created by 'language' from aspects of the 'self' which are first and foremost non-linguistic in origin. Indeed, according to post-structuralism, and also social constructionism after it, there are no aspects of the self which are not linguistic in origin: 'selves' have their origins solely in the discursive arena. From my feminist perspective this amounts to a reduction of what is 'social' to the world of linguistic interchange, and as such, represents a disavowal of the contribution of the prelinguistic mother–infant relationship to the production of 'selves'. (1998: 112)

Here Sanders is highlighting a need for an elevation of the contribution of the mother–child relationship in the development of the social self. She is calling for this as a foundational element in how selfhood comes about. This is a need for a grand-narrative and indeed the developing interest in the application of Attachment Theory to family therapy (Byng-Hall, 1995a; Akister, 1998) certainly responds to this call.

Sanders relates the attempt to believe that all experience is language based to be a further example of masculine styles of thinking. She accepts that the concept of 'self' inherited from Foucault frees women 'from the constraints accompanying a notion of the "self" as given essence' (1998: 114). But it also denies difference in the experience of gender and power. Indeed, she argues that his ideas about 'self' subsume the feminine under the masculine. Sanders (1998) supports her argument by returning to the theme of emotions. Gergen, Sanders asserts, conceptualises emotion 'as an expression of an historically contingent social role rather than an internal state' (1998: 116). Sanders criticises the social constructionist view of emotion as being something that is a social construction rather than it emerging from an internal frame of reference. This 'non-internal' hypothesis of emotion is one that Sanders draws some significant therapeutic issues from. She suggests that the obsession with language would lead therapists to ignore the non-verbal and the emphasis on language would also encourage therapists to show less interest in emotionality. Sanders is clearly pointing to the difficulties of focusing on language as thought – for thought is only expressed via language. But in doing this it neglects the other mediums of expression of emotions. This she says, especially in the light of research about the therapeutic alliance, will make for poor therapy:

> My contention is that as long as emotionality remains either untheorised, excluded from notions of the 'self' ... or subsumed within the case of 'language' ... it will continue to exist not only as a chance component of therapeutic interaction, but also as one that is difficult to justify. (1998: 118)

In Sanders' view we cannot neglect the place and role of emotions in families and therapy. It may be the case that in her terms emotionality is 'untheorised', though 'undertheorised' is probably a more accurate term. It appears that post-modernism does not direct therapists towards issues connected to emotionality and it would certainly appear that in the theories of family therapy the 'emotional' is the most neglected of elements of human action and experience.

Thus although Sanders is referring to foundations that relate to the development of the 'self' whilst Minuchin refers back to the foundations of 'family science', both these critics of post-modern practice have based their critiques on the loss of particular grand-narratives.

Local knowledge

In some ways Minuchin and Sanders' critiques reflect upon the view that local knowledges are simply not enough. In one form or other this view can be called that of opposition to *relativism*. The argument is that by rejecting grand-narratives of progress, emancipation etc., post-modernism has forced individuals to find their own moral and ethical perspectives, which may have nothing to do with social moralities. Many of the theories of post-modernity indeed suggest that social change leads to the greater atomisation and individuality of 'consumers' who have only the market to bind them together (Smart, 1993).

It is true to say that many therapeutic post-modernists deny that the model that permeates their work contains a problem of relativism. Indeed, Michael White (1995) has built social criticism into his theory and constructed a political therapy (see Chapter 6). Others, however, have noticed a difficulty with the relativist sequelae to post-modernism:

> Amidst the seeming relativism that post-modernism sponsors, the cry from many of us is: are there no more enduring truths? (Stewart & Amundson, 1995: 71)

Stewart and Amundson are particularly concerned with therapeutic ethics. They state that 'while we may abandon the "truth" of theories that underlie ... our profession, we cannot abandon the "final vocabularies of our ethical principles themselves"' (1995: 71). They therefore argue that just as therapists should be sceptical about the 'absolutist' position, they should not adopt the 'relativist' position as truth.

Another much discussed difficulty with the relativism of post-modernism in therapy is that of therapeutic expertise. There has been a long and distinguished debate about therapist expertise in family therapy in which proponents of 'first-order' or modernist therapy have defended their role in helping families change. In contrast, both 'second-order' and post-modernist therapists have argued that because all knowledge is based on a language game that is socially constructed, therapists do not have a special expertise. Anderson & Goolishian (1988), for instance, argued that the only expertise a therapist had was in 'managing a conversation' whilst Andersen (1991) stated that 'the only person therapists can change is themselves'. Golann (1988), however, concluded that the recourse to a complex theory of power was not necessary:

> It was not the belief in an objective reality that was responsible for excesses or misuses of therapist power and influence in family therapy. It was ... instead the belief that family member's misery ... justified the therapist's use of intrusions, misrepresentations and ordeals. (1988: 56)

This whole issue has led to a consideration of the role of 'not knowing' in family therapy (Larner, 2000). Simply put, this position proposes that in order for therapists to be able to accept the stories and narratives of families, they need to develop a frame of mind in which they do not know about likely outcomes or likely scenarios. This is pointing to the need for the therapist to bring particular qualities to the interaction with the client so they may respond to it in an open way. This actually sounds very similar to the concept of 'congruence' identified by Rogers in his set of 'necessary and sufficient conditions for therapeutic change' (Rogers, 1957). It would appear that family therapists have 'discovered' something by a circuitous route that was already well known and understood in psychotherapeutic circles!

Social constructionism

Social constructionism has evoked the same problems for family therapy as it has for philosophy as a whole. Here we will elucidate these problems from two perspectives: those that return to the question of 'reality'; and those who consider this perspective as deleterious to the development of evidence-based practice.

Questioning of reality

Speed (1991) declared that 'Reality exists OK?', in an article which sought to resist the tide of 'constructed realism' which was spreading in the family therapy world. She recognised that a contructivist stance has always had a role in family therapy thinking and it dated from the work of Watzlawick, Weakland and Fisch (1974) in the 1970s. However, Speed believed that a realist stance was more common with other helping professions and possibly within undeclared family therapy practice. She argues that social constructionism contains contradictions such as:

> from where such ideas [meanings] and dominant narratives emanate. Why are some ideas ideologically and culturally more gripping than others? Do they just happen along in an arbitrary way with one set of ideas becoming more dominant than another because of the relative degrees of influence of the people holding them? (Speed, 1991: 401)

Her conclusion is that a more acceptable model for family therapists is to accept that there is a reality but that there are competing descriptions of it. She argues that essentially reality is 'co-constructed' (1991: 405) and that it is this model that more adequately explains the therapeutic experience. Speed concludes:

> whilst accepting the contribution [of the relative nature of some truths] we should be aware that constructivism and social constructionism, in their denial of the influence of structured reality to what we know, have taken family therapists up a blind alley. (1991: 407)

Held (1995; 1996; 2000) has made similar criticisms of the anti-realist stance of post-modern therapies. She has perhaps been the most consistent critic of post-modernist anti-realism in therapy. She points out (Held, 1996) that in particular solution-focused therapists are being contradictory in claiming that there is no reality outside description and then asserting that they have evidence that their solution talk solves problems. She writes that if some views are 'not true but merely useful for purposes of enhancing solution' then these views are being claimed to have made 'a real difference in their client's lives ... in the client's real experience' (1996: 33).

Held refers to the following situation for us to judge the claims of this anti-realist position:

> as a result of successful solution focused therapy a battered wife says she is no longer beaten, but we cannot take her story as giving us any extralinguistic, objective, behaviourally-based truth or reality about her battered status. That is, she may, despite her story, still be battered, and all we and she have is the story, or lingusitic construction of reality. (1996: 33)

Held makes the very valuable point that post-modernist therapists have confused 'constructing' understandings of reality with reality itself. She writes:

> all theories are themselves linguistic constructions. The active constructing of theories is the business of science, all science. But ... that does not make all scientists constructivists. (1996: 33)

This confuses two things: (1) the linguistic status of the theory, with (2) the extralinguistic reality that the theory is attempting to approximate indirectly. Held also notes that this reducing of all stories to 'stories' is ethically demeaning for clients:

> After all, as therapists we have no business turning our backs on the all-too-harsh realities that our clients have not invented but nonetheless must face in their quests for better lives. (1996: 39)

In a later article, Held (2000) has suggested that anti-realism leads to a stance of being anti-theoretical which is defended in the interests of 'individualising therapy'. However, she contends that there is no necessary connection between these two positions. Indeed, anti-realism can only support individualised practice if it imbues the client's perspective with realism. Furthermore, the anti-realist stance prevents family therapists from being involved in research which will help them understand how to match treatment to individuals:

> How else can therapists take their clients seriously?... theory itself cannot answer the question. ... There is only one court to which we can turn for the best possible judgement ... the court of empirical observation. (2000: 47)

Evidence-based practice

Our earlier arguments have hopefully demonstrated that theories about epistemology are not very helpful in constructing a consensual view of therapeutic outcomes. Held (1996) has suggested that a further difficulty of taking forward a post-modern framework for family therapy is that therapists will fail to engage with researchers to determine what is and what is not evidence of treatment success. She is implying that post-modernism returns family therapy to a new dark age in which research evidence is ignored and practice is even further divided from research. This does not fit the historical legacy of family therapy research, nor does it fit the '*zeitgeist*' of the post-modern era where professional practice must be evidenced and audited. However, her criticism is reflected in the journals of the field. There are increasing numbers of papers that describe research from a positivist viewpoint which are scattered with post-modernist descriptions of practice. Her argument may therefore be true: a fracture is continuing to be shown in the family therapy world between those who talk and practice in a post-modern way; and those who practice with an eclecticism that they do not discuss and who keep an eye on the current evidence to support their therapy.

Revisioning post-modernism

At this point it is necessary to look at the ways that family therapists have attempted to amalgamate post-modernism in a way that is perhaps less extreme than that of the 'convinced post-modernists'. The difficulties described in adopting post-modernism as a model for family therapy have been recognised in the field and the 1990s saw a number of authors make attempts to 'square the circle' and reinterpret post-modernism in a more congenial way. There are those authors who seek a level of integration of the modernist and the post-modernist and those who build post-modernism into an historical framework that allows them to retain a distance from post-modernism itself.

The solution of integrating the modern with the post-modern

One commentator who has provided an integrative model for the modern and post-modern is Larner (1994; 1995). He argues that family therapists should deconstruct post-modernism itself in ways that have been outlined above. However, he wants to establish that deconstruction is not bound by the belief that deconstruction is designed to destroy, but rather is designed to playfully celebrate the paradoxes of life:

> The constraint [on understanding deconstruction] is ... the binary thought of our culture ... This compels us to set up a hierarchy, to theorise, to oppose the true, the real and knowable to meaning, language and the narrative. (1994: 12)

On the contrary, Larner proposes that family therapists adopt *both* the modernist *and* the post-modernist. In doing this he maintains their oppositional and hence relational aspect of their joint definition.

> We look for modernism in post-modernism and post-modernism in modernism. In a deconstructive attitude, all metaphors and approaches in family therapy co-exist in an absurd world of contradicting self-reflexivity. (1994: 14)

He adds:

> Here the question 'what is family therapy?' becomes not a forced choice between cybernetics or discursive theory. Rather family therapy encompasses both the modern and post-modern metaphor. It is not one or the other, but the movement between them, the articulation of their juxtaposition or relation to each other. This calls for a celebration of the difference between the two forms of discourse. (1994: 14)

He calls this attitude, *para-modern* because 'family therapy can be described as neither modern nor post-modern but *both* simultaneously' (1994: 11). In his later article, Larner notes that what he has called *para-modern,* is already evident in post-modern writers who emphasise ambiguity – such as Bateson (1979), Anderson and Goolishian (1988), and Cecchin, Lane and Ray (1993). Larner also uses this metaphor of the *para-modern* to contend that the debate about power in therapy is unhelpful. In fact he states that power is both 'socially constructed and refers to what happens in the real world' (1995: 197).

In a British version of this approach, Pocock (1995) also recounts the difficulties of a post-modern epistemology and recommends that family therapists search for 'the better story' (1995: 159). By this he means that family therapists can adopt any specific theory that helps explain the difficulty they are working with and which points to the most appropriate solution. However:

If one gives up a belief in objective truth ... that *the* explanation for a family's difficulty can be found – but also takes the view that not all stories are equally valid, then what makes one family story better than another? (1995: 160)

Pocock answers that research will help but the overriding issue is 'what is congruent with the family?':

Ideas from a particular model are favoured only if they are clinically more useful at that moment in therapy to that therapist with that family. (1995: 161)

Building on this pragmatic view Pocock provides a number of axes by which to make the judgement about which story is the 'better' one at any particular moment. These refer to:

- which is more congruent with family experience;
- which reflects 'scientific' evidence the best;
- which encompasses more of the experience that the family members have had;
- which is more likely to contain the family's pain;
- which will bind the family in sharing;
- which will evoke emotional reactions;
- which will help the family control their pain;
- which will establish family justice;
- which will provide hope.

This response to the modern/post-modern debate seeks a pragmatic way through the discourse. Pocock summarises the value of his approach by declaring:

Families are so complex we can ill afford to dismiss any theoretical ideas available to us. We should hoard as many stories ... as we can, but use them to serve the therapeutic process rather than attempting to control it. All the thinking and communication of the therapist should be subordinate to helping stimulate potentially useful ideas. Whether and how these are taken into the family story will ultimately be unpredictable and mysterious. (1995: 168)

Both Pocock and Larner therefore seek to go beyond the post-modern/modernist debate and to integrate both perspectives in their practice. In this respect it is interesting to note that both these authors in maintaining their positions make use of and attempt to integrate family therapy ideas with an understanding of psychoanalytic concepts. Again we find developments are now occurring within family therapy that place it within some form of general psycho-therapeutic context.

The solution of re-writing history

Others have tried to re-describe the history of family therapy to explain how the contemporary field has gone beyond the debate itself. In their book *An introduction to family therapy,* Dallos and Draper (2000) acknowledge that the perspective of history they are proposing might be seen as 'fictitious' (2000: xii). However, in an earlier article, Dallos and Urry (1999) suggested that family therapy theory has now moved on beyond the simple juxtapositions of theory. They propose that current practice in fact reflects therapeutic activity that encompasses three stages of theory development:

1   A first-order perspective with a focus on patterns and regularities in families' lives and experiences.
2   A second-order view, with a focus on meaning and the unique-ness of what such actions mean to a particular family.
3   A third-order view in some ways turns back the clock to alerting us to see that family life can be predictable and rule-bound, but with the recognition that this is social constructed by the cultural context rather by the family.

What distinguishes Dallos and Urry's and Dallos and Draper's taxonomy, is that it not only integrates the post-modern/modern discussion into the history of family therapy, but it also takes away the problem of the discussion. In some senses it relativises the very ideas themselves. Pocock (1999) makes a similar point. He notes that history is frequently written by ideologues:

> The term 'first order' came into common use ... by those wishing to distance themselves from certain practices ... earlier still, the term 'linear' helped ... to sort out the psychodynamic family therapists ... from the new Batesonian influenced therapists. (1999: 187)

Pocock therefore implies that these forms of 'history telling' are also 'history making' and thus might obscure the difference that exists in these versions of family therapy. The Dallos and Draper solution is also a pragmatic one in that it clearly implies that where we are is where we stand with current practice in which ideas are linked together by their juxtaposition. This juxtaposition may well have arisen through historical accident. This approach does not lack value but it will result in a lack of cohesiveness of theoretical formulation and it leaves us waiting for philosophical (not therapeutic) developments to let us know what the next step will be.

Conclusions

In this chapter we have described post-modernism, how it has been interpreted by family therapists and what attempts have been made to account for the difficulties that it poses for family therapy. Although at times, the language used to describe the value of post-modernism has been effulgent and grandiose, our discussion has shown some of the values of a post-modern perspective. Post-modernism has ensured that family therapy remains sceptical of its assumptions, respectful of the individual solutions of its clients and it has brought the reflexivity of the therapist into central stage. But all of these insights could have been derived from earlier models of family therapy and all could have been gained from attention to ethical practice and humanistic concerns. We might therefore conclude that just as with its relationship with systems theory, family therapy appears to have a preference for seeking out the most arcane and complex ideas from which to justify its practice. Post-modern family therapy practice is certainly one story but it brings as many paradoxes and contradictions as any other story.

Chapter 4
Freedom or control?
The sociological critique of
family therapy

> See how yond justice rails upon yond simple thief. Hark in thine ear: change places; and handy-dandy, which is the justice, which is the thief?
>
> Shakespeare (*King Lear*)

Psychotherapy and society

A sociological perspective on family therapy provides the focus for the next two chapters. Here we will consider sociological critiques of family therapy substantially concentrating upon family therapy theory, but we also seek to describe a *sociology of family therapy*. In the following chapter (Chapter 5) we will carry this critique further by exploring the *sociology of family therapists*. We begin by considering the sociological criticisms of psychotherapy in general leading us to an exploration of the place of psychotherapy and subsequently family therapy in society.

The history of sociological enquiry into the place of psychotherapy in society has included those who broadly welcome therapeutic involvements (Rieff, 1966) and those with a more critical stance (Rose, 1999). Understandably the span of these enquiries is vast and therefore here we concentrate upon only a few specific reflections by sociologists about psychotherapy.

Psychological reductionism

The argument that all psychotherapies are inherently reductionist is a widespread sociological view. Thus popular novelists like Fay Weldon (1997) have written that 'therapism ... rejects socialism, seeing no solution to human woes through social organisation'. Although Weldon's perspective is specifically from a left-wing political position, she merely echoes more academic views. Pilgrim (1992), for instance, comments that:

all versions of psychotherapy are necessarily psychological in their reasoning, they are prone to psychological reductionism. (1992: 225)

This charge is later repeated:

This ... leads me to a core point about my stance towards psychotherapy. The latter is constituted by a variegated set of social practices. Within the latter, the close attention that is paid to personal and interpersonal change processes has produced a recurring occupational hazard for therapists of different persuasions. There has been a tendency to reify the significance of events in particular isolated contexts (say the patient's unconscious, the transference, or shifts in the group dynamics or the family's functioning) and ignore, or even actively reject, the salience of the wider social context of these events. (Pilgrim, 1997: ix)

What Pilgrim and a number of sociologists argue is that psychotherapy in general makes an assumption that the social world is not relevant to the task of helping its clients. This argument echoes the one outlined in our discussion of systems theory and its critics, and it appears in different guises throughout our overall discussion.

Pilgrim (1992) justifies his charge of psychological reductionism by exploring some psychotherapists' ideas about homosexuality and individualism. He also asserts that this psychological reductionism is a function of the 'subjectivist methodologies' that have been adopted by psychotherapies. He argues that there are three forms of scientific endeavour: *Physical science* (physics, chemistry, astronomy and related engineering sciences); *Natural science* (biology, geology, oceanography, meteorology, economics, psychology, anthropology and sociology); and *Semiotic science* (anthropology, linguistics, psychology and sociology). Although psychology occupies two of these categories, Pilgrim argues that psychotherapists are more likely to value the latter form of science. This category 'involves the production and justification of *interpretations*' (1997: 2) and is thus sceptical of objectivity and the search for causes. Thus psychotherapists are unlikely to explore branches of science that provide sociological explanations for personal suffering. Both Pilgrim (1997) and Totton (2000) maintain that this has led to all the psychotherapies (with a few notable exceptions) being inherently socially conservative.

Professional knowledge and power

The view that psychotherapists depend upon a non-objective knowledge base connects to another sociological critique of their practice: that they become unchallengeable experts in the definitions of problems and solutions. Pilgrim describes the process in which a client comes for therapy:

Clients, as it were, walk into a framed context which has been construed in advance by therapists. It is true that some versions of psychotherapy ... emphasise the unique contribution which clients make to the construction of the personal relationship with their therapists. However, such freedom is at the latter's discretion. (1997: 97)

A number of critics of therapy have made a similar point: psychotherapists are able to define their knowledge in a way that cannot be challenged by other scientific perspectives. Masson (1988; 1992), for instance, in his persistent rejections of therapy noted that therapists can 'act with impunity' because of the 'idea, widely accepted in our society, that therapists, by the very fact of bearing this label, have access to some greater wisdom about the human mind' (1992: 8).

This reliance by psychotherapists on their own forms of knowledge has led to a number of writers comparing psychotherapists to religious sects (Pilgrim, 1997) that are unable to adapt to new knowledge and remain politically conservative.

Contexts of therapy

A more specific sociological perspective that is also developed by Pilgrim (1997) is to explore the *context* of therapy. The overriding context of therapy since its modern inception by Freud, Pilgrim argues, is that of a private relationship, mediated by cash. This leads to therapists lacking an understanding of the 'social history' (1997: 101) of their endeavours and to a severe bias in the *type* of therapy recipients. Pilgrim deconstructs a number of classic psychotherapy texts to show that most authors assume that therapists will be working with paying clients in therapy suites which themselves project an air of social solidity. Therapy, he suggests, is the pursuit of the privileged who pay for services from members of their own class, i.e. people who are privileged in the same way.

This last commentary upon psychotherapy will be explored further in the next chapter. However, if we now gather these elements together, it is possible to outline not only a description of the relationship between society and psychotherapy but to begin to construct a *sociology of psychotherapy*.

A sociology of psychotherapy

Sociology as a discipline has traditionally been divided into two schools: that school which therorises and studies the social factors which lead to *social stability*; and that which theorises and studies

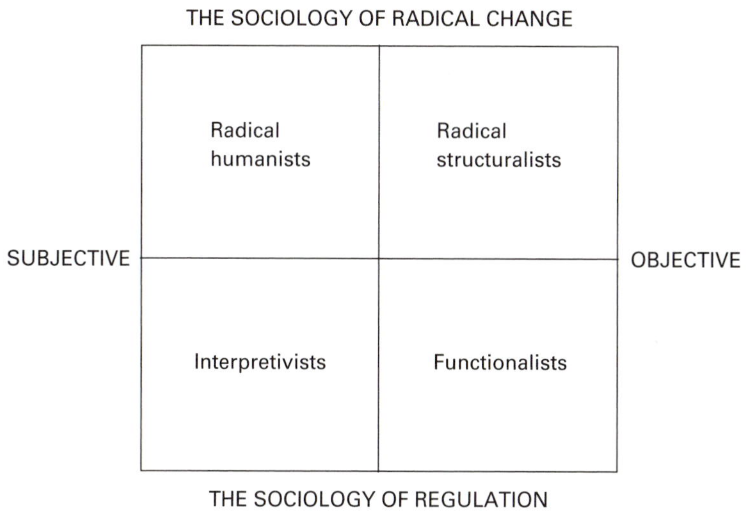

THE SOCIOLOGY OF RADICAL CHANGE

Radical humanists	Radical structuralists
Interpretivists	Functionalists

SUBJECTIVE ⟵   ⟶ OBJECTIVE

THE SOCIOLOGY OF REGULATION

Figure 4.1 *A taxonomy of sociological theories (after Burrell &*
Morgan, 1979)

the social factors that lead to *social conflict* (Macionis & Plummer, 1997). The common examples of these two perspectives have been *functionalism* and *Marxism*. In a *functionalist* analysis, emphasis is placed upon the mechanisms by which society regulates its members in order that social activity is productive. Not surprisingly, *functionalist* sociology was pre-eminent in the 1950s and 1960s at precisely the time that family therapy became popular. Indeed some commentators argue that family studies and family theory as separate areas of interest arose as a means of addressing perceived social problems such as divorce and child neglect (Klein & White, 1996). It was no accident, therefore, that *functionalists* used words like *system* and *roles* to describe their ideas. One of the assumptions of *functionalists* is that society exists to maintain the 'common good' of its members. *Marxists,* on the other hand, have always conceptualised society as a place where conflict is played out and in which forms of regulation were contested. Burrell and Morgan (1979) take this stark categorisation of sociological theory further and suggested four (not two) paradigms for social theory. A version of their categories is reproduced in Figure 4.1.

What is significant about Burrell and Morgan's typology of sociological knowledge is that it includes the categories of 'subjective' and

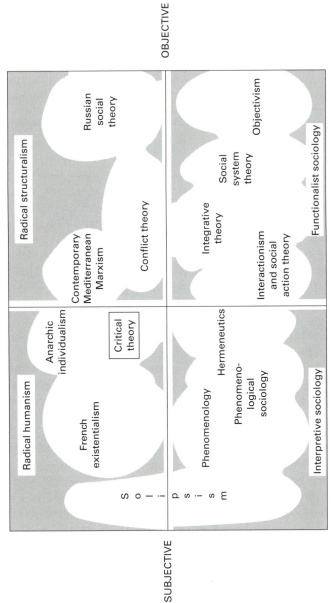

Figure 4.2   *Pilgrim's alterations to Burell and Morgan*

'objective' knowledge. It therefore is more able to encompass the variety of theories that are available by introducing this additional dimension. This model has not been used solely to understand the ideas in an academic way for Howe (1992) has used it to make sense of the theories that underpin social work practice. It has also more recently been used by Pilgrim (1997) to analyse the sociology of psychotherapy by attempting to demonstrate the 'location' of psychotherapy on the model (see Figure 4.2).

Pilgrim asserts that psychotherapy 'fits' in the section of the model devoted to the 'sociology of regulation' and it also shares with phenomenology and hermeneutics a 'subjective' paradigm. He writes:

> psychotherapy is part of a set of social processes which constitute *regulation*. When this term is alternated with that of 'control' it may make little sense, or can cause offence, to psychotherapists, who see their role as facilitating personal freedom. However, the two notions are not incompatible. The outcome of psychotherapy is undoubtedly, in part at least, about improving a person's capacity to cope and function successfully *in their given context*. In this sense, it is about conformity and adaptation and serves to reinforce the status quo. (1997: 22)

From this perspective, therefore, psychotherapy is part of those social structures that reinforce and maintain social cohesion. This raises the important distinction between the theory and ideals of the individual marital and family therapy practitioner and the principles and goals of the agencies in which the practitioner works.

However, it is true that the history of psychotherapy is also littered with radical therapeutic practice and theory. These are described in Totton's (2000) *Psychotherapy and politics* in which he catalogues the work of Reich, Laing and others. One of the distinguishing aspects of these radical theorists is that many of them rejected the three characteristics outlined above: those of psychological reductionism, therapist power and private practice. However, Totton (2000) comments that many of these radical streams within psychotherapy have become subsumed as therapy has become an established profession. Indeed, he quotes contemporary therapists who envisage therapy to be 'a prosthetic substitute for what they portray as women's traditional role of emotional support' (2000: 12). This supports Pilgrim's view that much of psychotherapy functions to maintain social cohesion.

Psychotherapy as oppression

Both Pilgrim's and Totton's analyses of psychotherapy in contemporary society provide a sociology of therapy. They are both characterised by a view that whatever this role, and whatever its ultimate effect, it is largely benign. However, sociologists from other perspectives have produced an analysis of psychotherapy that questions this benevolent view. Most of these sociologists have extended Foucault's studies of the way in which the modern 'self' is formed by society. Foucault's work variously explored the social adoption of ways of understanding deviance, punishment, insanity and sexuality (Rabinow, 1984). What was revolutionary about his approach was that he studied not only how ideas became part of the way social life was defined but also how gradually these social ideas soon defined *what was possible*. Thus in his book *The birth of the clinic*, for instance, Foucault (1976) provided a genealogy for the concept of medical knowledge itself. He traced the social need for medical knowledge to the need to control epidemics in the eighteenth century for economic and military reasons. This in turn led to a construction of the internal world of citizens in which illness and remedies for illness became no longer defined by 'common practice' or 'folk wisdom', but by people with a certain training and knowledge: doctors. This gradually leads to the modern situation in which medical knowledge and medical practitioners are given social status; expertise and medical 'technologies' have become part of our very psyches. Foucault noted that psychotherapy was also an heir to this process and that Freudian concepts were also part of a 'disciplinary power system'.

Other sociologists have, however, carried this analysis further. In his book *Governing the soul*, Rose (1999) provides what he calls 'a genealogy of subjectivity' (1999: vii). He states that:

My claim is that the psy disciplines and psy expertise have had a key role in constructing 'governable subjects' ... in ways that are compatible with the principles of liberalism and democracy. (1999: vii)

Rose's study is an extensive analysis of the way in which our 'selves' have been constructed in the last hundred years. This analysis ranges, for instance, over the way war and work have affected 'subjectivity'. Of relevance to this discussion is his analysis of the role of psychotherapy in this construction. Rose asserts that because Western society is democratic, individuals can no longer be governed by a central powerful state. Therefore:

the government of subjectivity has taken shape through the proliferation of a complex and heterogeneous assemblage of technologies. (1999: 217).

Part of these technologies are the psychotherapies. Rose firstly notes how universal a 'therapeutic' understanding is in contemporary Western society: book shops are full of self-help books, the media are ripe with examples of individuals in pain (whose remedy is to 'talk') and radio even hosts therapeutic 'advice' sessions. Secondly, he notes that there are various explanations for this phenomenon: Marxists have see this growth of therapeutic language as evidence of the atomisation and alienation that occurs in capitalist societies. Other critics have regretted the decline of a community spirit in a culture that emphasises self-fulfilment and individualism. Thirdly, however, Rose argues that the ubiquity of 'psychotherapeutics' has formed part of the 'fabrication of the autonomous self' which then becomes the 'object of expert knowledge' (1999: 221).

Rose explains that as society moved from a rule-bound society in which individuals lived and worked within their 'allotted' place into a society of equal consumers and producers, it was necessary to increase social cohesion by developing an 'internal' discipline. Accordingly, notions of 'normal development', 'individualisation' and 'autonomy' were defined and gained acceptance. He comments that:

> the external constraint of the police was to be translated into an internal constraint upon the conduct of the self. (1999: 227)

In this context, writes Rose, the psychotherapeutic enterprise functions as one other layer in constraining the self. He describes ideas about self-awareness, about autonomy, about personal freedom all of which underlie therapy as ideas that fit a society which wants individuals to 'police' themselves.

> It is here that the techniques of psychotherapeutics come into accordance with new political rationales for the government of con-duct. They are intrinsically bound to this injunction to selfhood and the space of choices that it operates within. They are characteristi-cally sought when individuals feel unable to bear the obligations of selfhood, or when they are anguished by them. And the rationale of psychotherapies ... is to restore to individuals the capacity to func-tion as autonomous beings in the contractual society of the self. (1999: 231)

In this passage, Rose returns to an argument that we have already heard (Pilgrim, 1997) but does so with a different premise: psycho-therapy not only by default encourages conformity; but its whole conceptual base, its whole purpose is irredeemably conformist. Such a proposition therefore makes a mockery of 'radical' therapies

(Totton, 2000) and any such radical therapist would need to respond to this critique in order to justify their practice.

The application of these sociological perspectives to family therapy

Not surprisingly a number of writers have applied these perspectives to the practice of family therapy. Rose (1999) himself, although not conversant with family therapy as such, made some relevant comments. He traced a history in which family relationships became subject to the professional gaze. This history included contributions from the Freudians (Klein & Winnicot), but was also marked by official committees (such as the 1947 Committee on Matrimonial Causes). Such scrutiny eventually led to the emergence of experts who could resolve family difficulties in order to sustain social stability. Rose writes that:

> The modern private family remains intensively governed. ... But government acts not through mechanisms of social control ... but through the promotion of subjectivities, the construction of pleasures and ambitions, and the activation of guilt, anxiety, envy and disappointment. (1999: 213)

This promotes:

> a particular psychological way of viewing our family lives ... urging a constant scrutiny of our inherently difficult interactions with our children and each other ... [which] bonds our personal projects inseparably to expertise. (1999: 213)

It is Howe (1991), however, who has carried this critique directly into the practice of family therapy. Howe (1989) had previously studied consumers' views of family therapy and on the basis of his findings constructed a sociological analysis of family therapy practice. He began by asserting that:

> *family therapy* carries two meanings. ... The first suggests an object of treatment, in this case the family, implying that there is something wrong with the family that needs to be fixed in order to return it to a healthy state. The second ... is to identify a particular method of treatment. (1991: 148)

These meanings translate into various outcomes:

> family therapy offers a disease model of family performance in which families are diagnosed and their way of doing things is seen as pathological. (1991: 148)

Moreover, 'treatment is effected by manipulating the workings of the family itself' (1991: 149). Howe then draws upon ideas that echo those of Rose to argue that family therapy has arisen in order to regulate the private life of the family: 'The private space of the family is politicised' (1991: 153). In particular, the regulation of families can prevent child abuse, delinquency and social breakdown. More crucially, if parents can be encouraged to accept that certain norms of family life are the 'best' ones then the private space itself becomes a replicate of the public space. Within this context family therapists become technicians who not only help families conform to norms but by their very existence bolster up the idea of intervention and normality. In a very radical sense this analysis shows that family therapists cannot be *outside* the social milieu not even within their own thinking processes. This technical use of family therapists occurs at the same time that ideas about normality and individuality suffuse society and implicitly grant family therapists both expertise and legitimacy. Howe also adds that family therapy with its 'disease' roots, its medical language and the objectivist systems theory, is an ideal intervention for welfare bureaucracies. He writes that:

clients ... are made to fit the organisation and its practices. (1991: 159)

These tendencies, Howe says, like critics before him, mean that 'problems are blamed on the family system rather than on the political environment or some inaccessible, untreatable individual pathology'. (1991: 160)

We can now see the extent of a sociological perspective on therapy and on family therapy itself. Some sociologists clearly view these pursuits to be an integral aspect of modern societies in which they serve a function of social conformity. The accusation is that therapy and family therapy in particular reduces individual problems to the level of individual or family 'dysfunction', that they impose their own definitions of difficulties which constitutes a powerful professional position, that they might be the preserve of the privileged and that they are irredeemably connected to social discourses that perpetuate Western capitalist values.

Are these sociological perspectives justified?

Before we move on to explore the reaction of family therapists to these criticisms of their theories and practice, it is appropriate to briefly review a number of concepts that are used by family therapists to see if these perspectives are valid. As always we should make a disclaimer, for as we stated in our opening chapter, 'family therapy' encompasses many varieties and therefore some comments may apply to some forms of practice whilst not to others. That being said we wish to briefly review how family therapists describe a number of their basic concepts in order to assess whether they do indeed apply a psychological reductionism to their work.

The family

We would assume that *family* therapists would have a complex and multi-layered theory of the *family*. We could also assume that within this complex theory, family therapists would consider the sociological aspects of family life and make some response to it. Sadly, on the whole, these assumptions would be wrong. It is true that few would now accept Walrond-Skinner's (1976) opening line of her book:

> Family therapy can be defined as the psychotherapeutic treatment of a *natural* social system. (1977: 1)

In which the use of the word 'natural' is highly problematic. But this distrust of the word would owe more to the feminist and post-modern criticisms of family therapy than to a thoroughgoing sociological analysis of the family. Nor do family therapists routinely refer to the work of family sociologists (Klein & White, 1996). Indeed, it is rare for family therapy texts to address either the social context in which family therapy developed, or the cultural meanings of the term 'family' which of course have changed drastically since the 1960s (Muncie, Wetherall, Langan, Dallos & Cochrane, 1997; Nock, 2000). Moreover, fundamentally, when reading the history of the development of family therapy, the story that emerges is of individual theoreticians and their practice with little reference to the social origins of their ideas (Dallos & Draper, 2000; Nichols & Schwartz, 1998). This is not to say that family therapists have not more recently addressed issues of gender and diversity in their practice (see Chapter 6), but it is to say that an appreciation of family therapy's place in society has not been adopted widely. This is nowhere more explicit than in the frequent starting point for family therapists: the concept of the *family life cycle*. In Carter and McGoldrick's (1989) text with that name, due consideration is made of the varieties of family life and of the impact of poverty and racism upon families. But there is no discussion about *families in relation to society*. Thus, although the authors accept the problematic nature of the idea of 'normal family processes', they do not go further and problematise the 'family' itself.

This brief review points us to the view that family therapists have adopted a psychological reductionism at the expense of a sociological embeddedness in their practice.

Poverty and family therapy: an example of psychological reductionism

But it may well be that this problem dissolves when family therapists turn their attention to an issue that has a clear societal (and hence sociological) frame of reference. Poverty is such an issue. Clearly the poor are identified by particular characteristics that have societal determinants, especially those of economics, whilst poverty as a lived experience undoubtedly has considerable effects on families and their members. Salvador Minuchin famously worked with poor, black families in New York (Minuchin, Montalvo, Guernay, Rosman & Schumer, 1967) and has recently returned to the theme of working with families of the poor (Minuchin, Colapinto & Minuchin, 1998). In this recent book, the authors outline a 'more effective and integrated' way of working with 'multi-crisis' families. This involves a systemic way of working with these families and the agencies that help them. As such it is an excellent restatement of the value of systemic work and clearly has the intention of empowering families who are buffeted by the effects of poverty and state intervention. However, the authors note that:

> we will focus on the details of interaction between professional workers and family members. That interaction is the bottom line of service delivery, more fundamental in efforts to change the system than laws, social policies, or available money. (1998: 30)

Reading these words after reviewing Rose's and Howe's sociological perspectives on therapy, only seems to confirm that family therapy does separate families from society and perhaps it does promote social conformity: poverty is not the target of intervention, rather it is the families' adjustment to it.

Responding to the sociologists

Here we will review the various ways in which family therapists have responded to the critical sociological perspective outlined above.

The 'sympathisers'

A number of family therapists have promoted these critical sociological perspectives within family therapy. Possibly the most outspoken of these has been Epstein (1993). Similar to the sociologists discussed above, Epstein begins by criticising family therapy's psychological reductionism:

> family therapy has become further and further removed from the changing economic and political realities of professional practice as well as the worsening everyday social realities of the many millions of potential clients that the field purports to serve ... theoretical shifts ... remain undecidedly apolitical, decontextualizing therapists and therapy from the larger social and cultural milieus. (1993: 15)

This, he argues, is because fundamentally 'the ideology of therapy entails a generally unquestioned acceptance that the problems brought before the therapist are indeed problems best resolved through therapy'. (1993: 21)

Epstein then examines how this psychological reductionism is played out in systems theory which 'viewed educational, social and occupational failure as indicative of family inadequacy or defect' (1993: 16). As a result of such functionalist theories, 'it was a social imperative for professionals to intervene' (1993: 18) in the lives of the poor and the inadequate. This intervention was legitimated because family therapists had 'extensive training' in 'pathological processes'. But the interventions were 'aimed at changing the socially disturbing behaviours of the individuals and families, not their life circumstances' (1993: 18).

Epstein also addresses the social power of family therapists. Therapy, he argues, is increasingly demanded as a treatment for people who clash with the authorities:

> some clients are forced to go to therapy by their employer, others by an angry spouse or parent. Others are mandated to therapy by the courts, probation officers, child protection services, and other social service agencies. (1993: 20)

In these situations 'the emphasis is still very much upon the expert doing something to and for the clients for their own good' (1993: 20).

All of this misses the point, Epstein maintains. Against a social backdrop of poverty, inequality and social coercion, the issue should be 'whether our society is willing to provide all persons with their basic human needs' (1993: 22), not whether it is willing to subject its citizens to therapy.

Epstein has certainly not been alone in accepting some of the sociological criticisms of family therapy. In Britain, Carpenter (1987) on his return from a visit to India commented that in the face of the poverty and oppression that he witnessed he was tempted to 'think of family therapy as an utterly irrelevant, indeed trivial, pursuit'. (1987: 218)

A number of family therapists in sympathising with the views of this critical sociology have made adjustments to their clinical practice. Here we wish to divide these sympathisers into those who have sought to address three specific perspectives: therapist power, client voices and therapist role in encouraging social resistance.

Therapist power

The ethical issues about therapist power have vexed a number of family therapists ever since Bateson and Haley disagreed about its use (Golann, 1988; Goolishian & Anderson, 1992; Hoffman, 1993; Jones, 1993). Indeed, the philosophical aspects of this have already been noted in Chapter 2. It is important, however, here to return to the debate. The most eloquent supporters of therapists 'shedding power' (Hoffman, 1993) are perhaps Hoffman and Goolishian & Anderson (1992). Hoffman, for instance, has argued that in adopting a reflexive and post-modern approach to therapy she has shifted her practice from attempting to influence her clients. She writes:

you don't strictly speaking, influence *people* – you only influence the *context*. (1993: 29)

Moreover, she commends the reflecting team concept because:

[it] makes the family a party to the thinking of the team. The status structure built into most family therapy models does not apply here, since not only is the family asked to listen in on the deliberations of the experts, but is given the last word. (1993: 52)

Such a revision of the task of family therapy resembles Andersen's own axiom:

The only person I can change ... is myself. (1997: 127)

Goolishian & Anderson (1992) also contend that if the cybernetic model of family therapy is substituted by a social constructionist one then:

therapy is transformed ... into a co-participant conversational action. (1992: 12)

The assumption is that this approach levels the power differentials in therapy. In order to make this view about the 'non-expert' more coherent, Anderson and Goolishian (1992) further developed the concept of 'not-knowing', which as discussed in Chapter 3 emphasises that therapists are 'conversational artists' or 'architects of the dialogical process' rather than experts about family dynamics and development. In fact:

the therapist exercises an expertise in asking questions from a position of 'not-knowing' rather than asking questions that are informed by method. (1992: 28)

They define 'not-knowing':

Not-knowing requires that our understandings, explanations, and interpretations in therapy not be limited to prior experiences or theoretically formed truths, and knowledge. (1992: 28)

There have been a number of responses by other family therapists to this attempt to create a family therapy practice based on equality with clients and on 'not-knowing'. Golann (1988) has argued that whatever the philosophy of open questioning or levelling of power, it does not in itself 'lead to a substantially less intrusive or hierarchical family therapy practice' (1988: 56). Moreover:

the history of psychotherapy research teaches that in order to understand therapy one must look beyond what therapists say they do. (1988: 63)

Larner (2000) notes that:

collaborative therapists must articulate the complexities of knowledge and power involved in a not-knowing stance. This recognises that it is impossible for the therapist not to participate in some hierarchy of knowledge and influence or to take a position that is not culturally, politically or gender informed. (2000: 69)

The general conclusion of these changes to family therapy practice therefore must be that although they do indeed go some way towards answering a sociological critique of family therapy, they do not manage to fully address it. A variety of these approaches has been to involve client voices in both researching and resolving the power differential between therapist and client. It is to this strand that we now turn.

Client voices

Family therapy has a long history of involving its clients in commenting upon its activities (Burck, 1978; Howe, 1989; Kuehl, Newfield & Joanning, 1990; Sells, Smith & Moon, 1996; Strickland-Clark,

Campbell & Dallos, 2000). However, therapists who wish to address the critique that their profession disempowers clients, wish to do more than just listen to them. They want to integrate the views of their consumers into their practice so that their work is less stigmatising and controlling. Conran and Love (1993), for instance, comment that therapists usually only speak to themselves:

> the credibilty of therapist texts is often established by authors proving that they have read and understood other authors. (1993: 2)

This leads to:

> the drowning of client voices in the cacophony of therapists building their credibility with one another, clients are overtly silenced in therapist literature by theoretical disqualification. (1993: 3)

Conran & Love therefore recommend that therapists co-author works with clients in order to emphasise the growing awareness of their egalitarian relationship.

This interest in striving for equality in terms of the story that is told about therapy has led to some notable jointly written articles (Karl, Cynthia, Andrew & Vanessa, 1992). However, it has to be noted that not all such feedback is positive (Howe, 1989) and moreover some research suggests that families want 'both authoritative and collaborative' therapists (Friedlander, 1998). This is clearly not surprising. If the review of sociological ideas about therapy tells us anything, it is that therapy is a social construction within which certain expectations are unavoidable. It is therefore to those family therapists who have not avoided these expectations but resisted them, to whom we now turn.

The solution of the advocates of 'social resistance'

In Chapter 3 we described the development and philosophy of some of the post-modern family therapists. Some of these authors describe their work as if they are seeking to construct a family therapy that takes on criticisms of psychological reductionism and social conformity. Both White and Epston (1990) liberally quote from Foucault and assert that their therapy empowers people who have been oppressed by social norms. This is a curious paradox. Therapists, who according to a Foucaultian analysis are embedded in discourses that encourage conformity, argue that Foucaultian ideas help them transcend their social role.

White (1993), after discussing Foucault's ideas, talks about how he uses them to 'deconstruct the practices of power' (1993: 53):

In therapy, the objectification of these familiar and taken for granted practices of power contributes very significantly to their deconstruction. As the practices of power are unmasked, it becomes possible for persons to take a position on them and to counter the influence of these practices in their lives and relationships. (1993: 53)

His method of achieving this deconstruction is to 'externalise' the practices of power. This method, initially developed for encopretic children (White, 1984), involves inviting the client to consider what personal emotions and thoughts might have their origins in social expectations. These are then 'externalised' as an entity to which the client can relate. White argues that these conversations enable a person to

appreciate the degree to which these practices are constituting of their own lives ... identify those practices ... that might be impoverishing of their lives ... acknowledge the extent to which they have been recruited into the policing of their own lives. (1993: 53)

Since White began to promulgate his ideas, externalisation has been used with a variety of clients. It has been valuable in treating anorexic patients (White, 1995), in helping to empower users of mental health services (White, 1995) as well as a number of socially excluded populations (White, 2000).

However, it remains unclear that this model of family therapy does successfully address the criticisms mounted by a critical sociology. Although it does appear to have responded to some of the comments that Pilgrim (1997) made, it remains doubtful that this form of therapy can avoid apparently helping its clients adjust to the society in which they live. Perhaps they are more empowered by this therapy. But empowerment and personal agency are of course part of the socially oppressive discourse that Rose and Howe described. In short, therapy cannot escape its own social function. If it has a political momentum it has to be within the contours of the society in which it lives.

'So what! It's no bad thing'

The arguments from Pilgrim and Rose have a foundation on a critical position and as such contain views that resonate with the natural radicalism of family therapists. However, the idea that therapy could have a regulatory function in society is not necessarily a negative view. Clearly from some perspectives the need for regulatory mechanisms is a good one with there being a value in supporting social institutions such as 'marriages' and the 'family'. Indeed this is a view that has some common currency in the American professional community and is a view inherent in much of the sociology of the family (Klein & White, 1996). This perspective would argue that we should not neglect the power of social institutions. These institutions, whether they be marriage, parenthood, work or leisure, add a predictability and stability to our social life. These benefits do have some costs in terms of personal freedom and autonomy, but perhaps we should recognise the powerful benefits that flow from regular, organised and patterned relationships. Certainly, the radical critique of such institutions as the family (Barrett & McIntosh, 1982) shows that these institutions need to be changed. But drawing attention to inequality and patriarchy may not constitute the total rejection of these institutions – even if they could be totally rejected! For instance, some research suggests that children do badly from divorce whilst women are more likely to be catapulted into poverty as a result of divorce. Therefore there may be a place for a profession that tries to prevent family breakdown and encourage relationship stability. Thus one side of the coin might be to attempt to liberate partners from the inequitable aspects of traditional marriage. Whilst the other side might be to build on the strengths and resiliencies that families and marriages naturally possess.

This train of thought emphasises the pragmatism of family therapists who might see the feminist, social constructionist and postmodern critiques of therapy as emphasising 'individual rights' to the detriment of 'responsibilities'. This might appear to clash with family therapy's historic commitment to connectedness and interpersonal space. Hence family therapy may have a unique role in intervening when individuals are 'unconnected' or at risk of being 'unconnected' and suffer distress as a result. This might seem to be a compromise with the regulatory role in which family therapists build connectedness in their daily practice by working with relationship strengths. Again we meet something of a paradox: models that emphasise the recognition of client strengths (the non-deficit/competencies models) would seem to be linked with 'regulatory' practices. Thus the sociological criticisms outlined above which propose that 'expert' knowledge is part of a paternalistic and oppressive practice are not the only approaches which constitute a regulatory role.

Whatever the nature of the conundrum this view has underpinned marital services such as Relate and the Catholic Marriage Guidance Service, who seek to support and stabilise adult relationships if not 'marriages'. In the USA there are much larger counterparts of these services (many with similar links to churches) which stress the importance of prevention services with psycho-educational programmes, parent education, marriage education and community-strengthening initiatives in which the skills of family therapists are utilised. Stahmann (2000), for example, writes of the need for marital and family therapists to take up premarital counselling as a professional response. He reports how there are a number of ways in which marital and family therapists can utilise programmes in these areas. A typical case being the extension of the work of D.H. Olson who developed a model for family functioning well known in family therapy circles: the circumplex model. Here a programme called PREPARE is designed to assist premarital couples intending to marry (Olson & Olson, 1999). There is a growing research literature in this field (see Hawley & Olson, 1995). Moreover, the work that began with a consideration of how families can be helped to deal with the 'adversity' of ill health and handicap (Doherty & Baird, 1987; McCubbin, Thompson, Thompson & Frommer, 1998) has been extended by the development of the notion of 'family resilience' (Hawley & DeHaan, 1996; Walsh, 1996). Walsh writes:

> The utility of a resiliency-based framework for family research and intervention is discussed, noting the potential for prevention efforts: providing psychosocial inoculation by strengthening family resilience in high-risk situations. A redirection of inquiry and response is urged from problems and how families fail, to life challenges and how families can succeed in meeting them. In conclusion, it is suggested that, given the increasing family diversity and strains of social and economic upheaval, approaches based on the concept of family resilience are particularly relevant to our times since they prepare families to meet uncertainty and future challenges with the mutual support, flexibility, and innovation that will be needed for evolutionary hardiness in a rapidly changing world. (1996: 261)

Rutter (1999) also argues that a goal for family therapists is to understand and encourage psychosocial resilience and protective mechanisms. To do this they must attend to the interplay between what occurs within families and what occurs in the political, economic, social and racial climates in which individuals perish or thrive. Here then is an approach that is designed to assist 'families to weather and rebound from their life challenges, strengthened as a family unit' (Walsh, 1996: 275). Indeed this 'movement' has led the field in the development of prevention programmes and it is likely that the mental health field with take up this approach more generally as it follows similar developments in the physical health arena.

Conclusion

In exploring a sociological critique of family therapy we have clearly demonstrated that family therapy cannot be 'outside' of the social structures from which it evolved and in which it practises. As Cupitt says: 'The flux is outsideless' (1994: 17). We have also begun to outline another of the paradoxes of family therapy: it retains a critical edge to psychotherapy and yet it manifests in a social setting as a 'typical' psychotherapy. We have also suggested that not only is family therapy inescapably part of social structures, but it may be a valuable part of those structures. The 'radical' and the 'conformist' aspects of family therapy practice may appear irreconcilable. But perhaps a recognition and 'coming to terms' with a regulatory place in society may have personal and professional benefits. In our next chapter it is to these professional benefits that we turn as we begin to explore the pragmatic sociology *of family therapists.*

Chapter 5
Who are the family therapists?

We shape the clay into a pot, but it is emptiness inside that holds whatever we want.

Tao Te Ching

Organising the practice of family therapy

In the last chapter, we explored some of the perspectives of sociologists on the practice of family therapy. After considering the response by therapists to these perspectives, we saw that family therapy in many ways cannot escape some of the roles that society ascribes to the 'helping professions' despite family therapy's critical stance. We wish to take this discussion further by constructing a sociology *of family therapists*. By implication we are drawing a necessary distinction between 'family therapy' as general clinical activity with a boundary that is created of an intellectual/theoretical nature and family therapy as an activity undertaken by specifically defined professionals. The boundaries are different and it could be easy to confuse the two. We do not wish to do this and so in this chapter we focus on family therapy as a professional acitvity.

In the late 1970s and early 1980s the activities of a cult organisation 'the Church of Scientology' had drawn the attention of the government such that official reports recommended that there needed to be some way in which the activities of psychotherapists were regulated. This fitted in well with the professional aims of some psychotherapy organisations and so the United Kingdom Council for Psychotherapy (UKCP) was established. The UKCP has, over the last decade, built up a formidable organisation that has a federal structure (i.e. member modalities adopt standard procedures but 'govern' their own section). Each section then has the power to register its own members as 'psychotherapists' according to general uniform rules. Family therapy is included in the section entitled 'Family, couple, sexual and systemic therapy'. (Other sections are Psychoanalytic and Psychodynamic Psychotherapy, Behavioural Psychotherapy, Humanistic and Integrative Psychotherapy, Hypnotherapy,

Analytical Psychology, Psychoanalytically based Therapy with Children, and Experiential Constructivist Therapies.)

Individual registration with UKCP involves a system of professional monitoring which has codes of ethics, complaints procedures and a method of removing registrants from the list of approved practising psychotherapists. The UKCP publishes its list of registrants regularly (UKCP, 2001). Training within each UKCP section has to reach some level of uniformity and each section has had to design methods of assessing members' 'continuing professional development'. Organisations such as the Association of Family Therapy (AFT) are members of the UKCP, and in conforming to the standards of the organisation and validating those standards on training courses, prepare individuals to apply for registration. However, it should be noted that professional bodies such as the Royal College of Psychiatrists and the British Psychological Society are also represented on the UKCP without them having to prepare their members for registration. They are clearly present to safeguard the interests of their members. But this fact also confirms the view that other professionals are competent to practise as psychotherapists but do not need validation by a body such as UKCP.

This indicates one of the difficulties in formally determining 'who are the family therapists?' Thus although UKCP members registered as family therapists can be identified, there remain a potentially large group of workers who are not individually registered and who may undertake family therapy as a subsidiary activity within their general work. At varying times they could even identify themselves as 'family therapists'. Similarly there are workers who would identify themselves as 'marital therapists' who have little to do with family therapy organisations. The situation is made even more complicated by the existence of other professional regulatory bodies. Although we do not wish to enter into a discussion of the differences between 'counselling' and 'psychotherapy' we should note that family therapy has developed professional links with the 'psychotherapies' not the 'counsellors'. However, the professional organisation of counselling – the British Association of Counselling and Psychotherapy (BACP) – is responsible for the UK Register of Counsellors which contains a division ('Personal, Sexual, Relationship, Family') that undoubtedly has an interest in the clinical practices of family therapy. Clearly some people will identify themselves as counsellors, some as psychotherapists, some as both and some as psychiatrists and psychologists who 'do' family therapy. The matter is clearly confused in the professional sense and this does make it difficult to be clear about whom we mean when we discuss family therapists. Our focus, however, by default of lack of information will be on the largest professional group which sees its activity as psychotherapy and which is likely to be linked through AFT to the UKCP.

Surveys of family therapists

To provide an answer to the question 'who are the family therapists?' we need to turn to a number of recent pieces of research. The first is an American study by Doherty and Simmons (1996) which consisted of a survey of a random sample of members of the American Association for Marital and Family Therapy (AAMFT) in fifteen separate states. Out of the sample, 526 (34.3%) completed an extensive three-stage survey design that included an employment questionnaire, a work analysis description and a consumer satisfaction questionnaire. The authors developed these stages in order to construct a similar employment profile as that already gathered for social work, psychiatry, psychiatric nursing and psychology.

Some significant issues in Doherty and Simmons' study stand out. Firstly, family therapists are clearly older, established professionals with a mean age of fifty-two and mean number of thirteen years practising as family therapists. By implication we might assume that a significant number of these therapists trained as family therapists when they were in their late thirties after working in some other profession. Over 33 per cent of the sample had a Ph.D. and 50 per cent had studied to the level of an M.A. Almost 66 per cent identified themselves as marital and family therapists and 38 per cent had 'dual licensure'. In many states in the United States, professional insurance and legal practice depends upon licensure in a more rigorous way than it does in Britain. Having two licences means that these workers could practise not only as family therapists but as another profession as well. Almost certainly this other licensure preceded that of family therapy. A significant minority of the participants had three licences (12.4%). Another important finding from this survey centres on the 'primary practice setting' of the responders. Nearly 66 per cent of this American sample worked in private practice whilst 13 per cent worked in a 'voluntary agency' setting and only 5.9 per cent worked for 'state' services.

In Britain there have been two surveys that have shed light upon the nature of British family therapists. The first, Street and Rivett (1996), was a survey whose purpose was to explore stress and coping mechanisms within family therapy practice. However, it gathered demographic details of its sample of members of the Association for Family Therapy (AFT), of whom 171 responded (34.5%). Bor, Mallandain and Vetere (1998) published the results of a similar survey of members of the AFT. However, unlike the Street and Rivett survey, the Bor et al. study was designed to replicate the American work reported above and they surveyed the total membership of AFT (1,500) with 495 responses (33%). Table 5.1 presents a comparison of the data from the two British and one US surveys. Both the British surveys have similar figures for age and gender distribution. Street and Rivett found that 26.6 per cent had up to five years' experience in the field whilst 12.0 per cent had over 15 years' experience. Only 14.8 per cent of these workers held a post that designated them as 'family therapists', although 30.5 per cent had job descriptions that included the practice of family therapy. The largest professional background of the sample was social work (45.3%), whereas although this was the largest professional background in the Bor et al. sample the figure of 21.0 per cent was less. Bor and his colleagues also found that 34.0 per cent of the sample had a master's degree (compared with 54.3% of the American sample); 24 per cent describe their practice as that of 'family therapy', whilst 45 per cent use the term 'systemic practitioner'. Bor et al.'s results also show a high number regard 'family therapy' as their primary background with social work being close. Although the British surveys produced different figures for those who work in 'state services' (80% and 64%, respectively) this is the most significant difference between British and American family therapists: the British worker who has allegiance to the title 'family therapist' is a *public agency worker*. We can also see that in the British surveys the proportion of those who work in 'private' practice ways is clearly in the minority (5.3% and 9.0%, respectively).

As we consider these figures, the importance of the family therapist's 'primary' profession clearly retains an importance. This is obviously made so by the British requirement that one cannot begin to train as a family therapist unless one already holds a primary professional qualification. Clearly, as we noted above, some workers in some professional groups may seek to develop their knowledge in family therapy and may wish to adopt the professional title of 'family therapist' even if their job description is of a generic nature. Some workers may wish the opposite: they want to develop their knowledge and skills but choose not to leave their original professional

Table 5.1 *Surveys of family therapists; comparison of data*

Study	Doherty & Simmons	Street & Rivett	Bor et al.
Date	1996	1996	1998
Country	USA	UK	UK
Mean age	52	43	46
Male	45.00%	41.00%	40.00%
Female	55.00%	59.00%	60.00%
Professional background			
Marital and family therapy	60.60%		20.00%
Psychologist	12.00%	9.40%	14.00%
Social worker	7.20%	45.30%	21.00%
Counsellor/ Psychotherapist	6.40%		10.00%
Clergy	4.80%		
Psychiatrist	0.60%	13.50%	14.00%
Nursing	0.60%	10.00%	7.00%
Other medical	0.20%	4.10%	1.00%
Probation		5.30%	0.20%
Practice setting			
Private practice	65.15%	5.30%	9.00%
Voluntary agency	13.00%	11.10%	6.00%
State agency	5.90%	80.10%	
NHS			48.00%
SSD			16.00%
Medical centre	0.80%		
University			3.00%

identity. It is also the case that the structure of professional registration means that any worker who has qualified via a training course might be registered as a family therapist even if they do not hold a family therapy post. As we have suggested, this not only complicates who we can identify as the family therapists but it also misses out many others. These may be workers with no formal family therapy training, who practise family therapy skills, who have no need for any links with family therapy organisations and who do not require their skills to be validated in any institutional way. Clearly the clinical practices of family therapy extend well outside of the organisational ambit of its principal professional organisation.

From the survey information we can make some other assumptions about the social status of family therapists and about the context of their practice. We can also, in passing, partially refute one of Pilgrim's (1997) sociological criticisms of therapy and add a further layer of depth to one of his other criticisms. In their various incarnations, in both America and Britain, we can see that family therapists are well educated, hold a number of professional qualifications, and are generally not at the start of their professional careers. The costs of the extended training undertaken to support these careers have probably involved considerable expense, both personal as well as financial. Moreover, as in many pieces of social research we can make some assumptions on the basis of questions that were *not* asked. None of these surveys asked the participants to record their subjective rating of their social class. Nor did any record the cultural diversity of the sample. These missing details suggest that the researchers did not regard such parameters as significant and indeed they might have assumed the answers to be transparent (May, 1993). That the questions were not asked implies that the answer was assumed: that most family therapists are 'middle class' and white. All of this seems to add up to an obvious proposal: family therapists are indelibly embedded into the societal contexts in which 'helping' occurs. By this we mean that in America, this societal context is structured around private practice, which is itself becoming determined by 'managed care'. In Britain the societal context is one of state-provided services either in the health service or in local government services – services offered by white middle-class professionals, a majority of whom are women.

This returns us to one of Pilgrim's (1997) assertions about the sociology of psychotherapy. In Chapter 4, we commented that he believed that Freud had established the tradition of private practice within psychotherapy. This he argued led to a *skewed* profession, which served the needs of a minority who could afford to pay for therapy. The above surveys imply that at least when it comes to family therapy practice in Britain, this perspective does not hold much credence. We can certainly raise doubts about the representativeness of any of the samples of these studies and note that they were surveys of the membership of an organisation and not a more objective 'workforce' analysis. Nevertheless, the evidence clearly supports the proposal that British family therapists are part of the state welfare system: family therapists are public servants. However, this 'objective' statement does not address a further issue; what do British family therapists aspire to be? We must wonder whether Pilgrim's assertions are more appropriate when applied to the models that occupy the *thoughts* of family therapists – it may well be that the family therapist would hold an 'ideal type' of practice which is independent and free of organisational constraints. Our experience has been that this 'free agent' model informs much of the activity about professional development within the profession. Pilgrim is incorrect when it comes to practical reality but he may well be right about a socially constructed, often unarticulated model of professional aspiration.

Professionalisation and family therapy

A brief history of the profession of family therapy in Britain

In order to begin our consideration of the process of the professionalisation of family therapy in the UK it is helpful to look at the general historical background. In the United States of America, the American Association for Marriage and Family Therapy began in 1942 as a professional organisation for marriage counsellors and only expanded to include family therapists in 1970 (Nichols & Schwartz, 1998). However, in this new guise, it has become the major registering body for family therapy in the USA; indeed by 1998 it represented 23,000 marital and family therapists. In Britain, the Association for Family Therapy (AFT) was founded in 1975 but at that time the idea that it might form the centre of a new 'profession' was far from members' minds. Indeed, it might be said that the formation of the Association was seen by early members to be almost 'anti-establishment' rather than seeking a new establishment (Rivett, 1997). Along with this, the group which met to establish the Association emphasised that their organisation was **for**, not **of**, and it was **for family therapy** not **for family therapists.** At its origin it was what could be termed a 'special-interest group', with a wide definition of that 'interest'.

However, in the time between 1975 and 1992, the discourse began to change. There developed a growing view that family therapy should become a profession and that AFT should have a role in overseeing this growth even though it could not become a 'trade union' of family therapists. The reasons for this change in the professional discourse about family therapy are varied. As always, the context determined most of this change. In the face of a Conservative government that was critical of public services and somewhat attacking of the 'professions' there was a need to clarify and protect certain professional activities and boundaries. In this period one of the products of the cutbacks in public services was that the therapeutic activities of local authority social workers slowly petered out as the needs of the child protection system became all-consuming. In a parallel process, this time also saw the withering away of a large number of multi-agency child guidance services in which family therapy had had a 'protected' niche. As the workers in these settings faced a return to their 'home' agency, they preferred to remain within the world of 'child and family guidance'. The host agency for these teams had to face a loss of experienced staff and in most places this could only be covered by the creation of new family therapy posts (Messent, 2000; Simon, 1991). It is significant that the clear majority of these very experienced workers came from a social work background. It was not unusual for a social worker to be moved out of the child guidance team by her local authority employers only to regain her position as a 'family therapist' employed by the health service.

The shift in discourse about family therapy was also due to some ideological reasons. By 1990, family therapy in Britain had established itself as a distinct treatment method with a number of favourable treatment trials to support it (e.g. Russell, Szmukler, Dare & Eisler, 1987). The contributors to journals and training courses now shared more in common with each other (despite a little factionalism) than they did with colleagues in the professions from which they had come. As with the developments of all professional organisations the desire to regulate the training process was strong. It was also apparent that for some less professionalised and lower remunerated occupations, a post of 'family therapist' brought with it better employment conditions. At the AFT's annual AGM in 1992 all these influences converged in a debate. The outcome of this debate was to grant the executive of the Association the right to proceed with plans to enter the UKCP organisation and to begin the process of registering 'qualified' family therapists. AFT had moved from a special-interest group of professionals to a professional organisation.

The nature of professions

So what does the history above represent? What arguments and factors were influential in constructing a profession of family therapy? Pilgrim and Rogers (1993) argue that the 'professions' have certain sociologically distinguishing factors:

1. Professionals have grown in importance over the last 200 years and have expanded massively in number during this century.
2. Professionals are concerned with providing services to people rather than producing inanimate goods.
3. Though salaried or self-employed, professionals have a higher social status than manual workers.
4. This status tends to increase as a function of length of training required to practice.
5. Generally professionals claim a specialist knowledge about the service they provide and expect to define and control that knowledge.
6. Credentials gain professionals a particular credibility in the eyes of public and government alike. (1993: 81)

Not surprisingly sociologists have varied in their analyses of the professions. As we discussed in the previous chapter, some (functionalists) see professionals as part of the essential fabric of society in that they provide cohesion and regulation. Others (Marxists) argue that the nature of the professional classes is that they control deviancy and resistance to the status quo. The post-structuralists (e.g. Foucault) analyse the language and knowledge structures of professionals to understand how they establish their intellectual hegemony.

In his book *Psychotherapy and society,* Pilgrim (1997) applies this sociological analysis to the profession of psychotherapy. He comments that psychotherapy is a 'stunted profession' partly because it is 'embedded' within 'separate occupational groups' (1997: 115). It has no distinct existence and no unifying training or theoretical position. 'We cannot speak meaningfully at present of a "profession of psychotherapy"' he writes. He adds that 'a drip, drip, drip of criticism' (1997: 124) about psychotherapy has also undermined its legitimacy. There are, he says 'no special experts in human misery' (1997: 135). None of these issues, however, prevented the 1992 AGM of the AFT from pursuing the professional path. The arguments in favour of conforming to UKCP procedures were described in these terms.

Families who use family therapy need to be protected from inadequate therapeutic services ...
    AFT as the national organisation for family therapy should contribute actively in all levels of national context ...
    The setting of high standards for training and practice encourages the development of improved standards ...
    The contemporary context calls for a clear articulation of the therapy on offer and for self regulation by therapists.' (Cred subcommittee of AFT, 1993: 4).

This is the same argument as those in other psychotherapeutic modalities where professionalisation has been pursued (Frankland, 1996). Similarly, as in other modalities, there has been criticism of the process (Bates, 2000; Mowbray, 1995). Treacher, in studying psychiatric hegemony in the NHS, has at various times (Baruch & Treacher, 1978), already opposed this development:

> the process of professionalisation raises important issues about who 'owns' specialised knowledge. Organisations (such as the Association for Family Therapy) which are initially formed to promote the development and communication of knowledge can become barriers to its wide dissemination. (1987: 87)

In 1993, Treacher repeated his worries:

> My biggest fear is that the adoption of these criteria will create another tight, inwardly looking profession that puts its own interests first and its clients' a poor second. If family therapy is to retain any of its radicalism then it needs to avoid being hemmed in by the normal processes of professionalisation ... we should try to avoid the trap which will only benefit therapists who want to set up in private practice and establish upper middle class lifestyles like their American colleagues. (1993:7)

Carpenter (1992) also opposed professionalisation on the grounds that by establishing a specialism, the genericism of the approach would be lost:

> this would lead ... to the marginalisation of family therapy in a way that psychoanalysis is marginal to mainstream health and social services. I can see it being practised by a relatively small group of qualified people who would tend to focus on marriages and families. (1992: 22)

This fear of marginalisation was exactly what Shields et al. (1994) claim had been the result of the professionalisation of family therapy in America. These authors argue that even though family therapy's history had been one of multi-disciplinary variety in 'coming of age' and it had become professsionalised:

> there has been an explosion of family therapy journals, but a decrease in family therapy articles in the journals of other disciplines ... there are few family therapy presentations in the meetings of non-family therapists ... [and] recent proposals for general health and mental health care plans have not yet given much attention to family oriented health care. (1994: 118)

The hypothesis is that as professionalisation has grown so has the isolation of the activity and the professional who practises that activity. Shields et al. believe that the effort to establish family therapy as a 'primary mental health discipline and profession' (1994: 124) has led to the toning down of the earlier radical challenge of family therapy (which in some guises shared ideas with the anti-psychiatry movement (see Sedgwick, 1982). Contemporary practice, Shields et al. contend has led family therapy to be a hand-maiden of psychiatry in the 'diagnosis and treatment of nervous disorders' (1994: 125). This is evident in the struggle to have family systems diagnoses added to the DSM Classification of Mental Disorders (American Psychiatric Association, 1994) whilst other groups are 'fighting against being marginalised by the ... bio-medical establishment' (Shields et al., 1994: 125). They acknowledge that there appear to be advantages to establishing a new profession: autonomy and respect may increase. But they assert that isolation, specialised and thereby limited training also contribute to difficulties in collaborating with other healthcare professions and to the growing gulf between researchers and practitioners. To this we might also add the developments of a tighter specification of what actually constitutes family therapy so that aspects of 'systemic practice', various forms of marital therapy and counselling, and a variety of 'family work' are excluded.

Where does professionalisation leave family therapy in Britain?

Since 1992, when AFT decided to enter UKCP and thereby join the nationwide push to professionalise all the psychotherapies in Britain, family therapy has become an established specialist occupation. AFT now registers training programmes, the graduates of those training programmes, lays down codes of conduct for the practice of family therapy, recommends private practice insurance and has complaints procedures which can lead to the 'striking off' of a registrant. These are only some of the activities that clearly demonstrate that family therapy has been promoted as, seeks to promote itself as and behaves as if it is a fully fledged profession. Webster (2002) has argued that AFT did not intend to create a 'new' profession as its entry criteria for training presumes a previous professional qualification. However, the outcome is clear: a new profession has emerged. The structural and ideological pressures within the community of welfare services have led to family therapy asserting its equality with other professions who practise psychotherapy and are constructing a legitimacy for that practice. This is indeed a remarkable achievement. Most of the older professions have taken much longer to achieve such a status. It is also remarkable because there remain a very small number of specific 'family therapy' posts within welfare services. Estimates as to the exact number vary but it may be no more than a few hundred. If there is any doubt about the direction that family therapy professionally should go, Webster (2002) has again brought the issue into a clear light by stating that:

> **family therapy must decide whether it is a profession and develop a strategy to create a more equitable distribution of posts within the health service or risk losing any access to funding in the battle for funds.** (2002: 146)

She recognises that there is a 'battle' for funds in the NHS and that a strong organised professional group is necessary to fight a corner against other interests. Webster's position is clear: namely, that the needs of family therapy as a profession should dominate, otherwise it will be difficult 'to maintain family therapy in the public sector'.

However, in this development we can discern an interesting changing pattern in the family therapy professional organisation. At first AFT was principally what we have termed a systemic practitioners' organisation (family therapy primary practice/interest – original profession: primary allegiance). Now, however, the organisational and professional needs of the 'professional family therapists' would appear to be becoming primary. Within this process we can note that the original professional background of the family therapists is overwhelmingly social work and nursing. We can anticipate over the forthcoming period that the influences of these particular professional backgrounds will have an impact on how family therapy develops, professionally, organisationally and academically. It is likely that this development will not proceed along the same lines as other psychotherapies, which have principally been established by the psychiatric and psychological professions. We can further anticipate that if there is a neglect of the balancing of the needs of the 'systemic practitioners' against the 'family therapists' that there will emerge a potentially rigid definition of 'family therapy'. This will lead to a separation between standard (what everybody does) and innovative (new, different and perhaps 'risky') practice. There would also be a separation between 'what family therapists do' and a wide range of family and systemic work undertaken by other professionals. We are therefore anticipating that the warnings of Carpenter and Treacher will come to fruition.

Practice, contexts and professionals

Ambivalence and context

As has been suggested in the section above, family therapy in the UK has seen a move from a number of disparate professional contexts to a predomination in the NHS. This is a view borne out by the Bor et al. (1998) survey and we can envisage that this process will continue. In order to provide another perspective upon who family therapists are we will now turn to the context in which they practise. The particular context in question is that of child and adolescent mental health (CAMH).

The fact is that family therapists, in the general sense, have always had somewhat of an ambivalent attachment to the contexts in which they practise. We have noted that one of the criticisms of psychotherapy in general is that it prefers to practise its trade in the privacy of private practice mediated only by cash. Curiously, although we have commented that the evidence is that few UK family therapists practise privately, family therapy intellectually, has its own version of being suspicious of state services. This was most successfully enunciated by Haley in his early paper 'Why a mental health clinic should avoid family therapy' (Haley, 1981a). In this essay, Haley asserted that because family therapy rested upon different views about causation, diagnosis, change and training, it did not fit well with other mental health approaches. Moreover, family therapy was a 'cross-discipline' and therefore it led to a 'shift in the status of the professions' (1981a: 185). In particular, Haley believed that:

> The change brought about by family therapy is most painful to the psychiatrist because he has been highest in status previously and so has the most to lose as the hierarchy changes. (1981a: 186)

Although this paper contained the wit and irony that are a hallmark of Haley, he was pointing out that family therapists ideologically might feel ill at ease in medical settings and might find welfare services a constraint upon their way of working. A number of British authors have commented on this over the years. Carr (1990) noted that family therapists must be careful in how they convince managers to support them. Street and Reimers (1993) described the different agencies in which family therapy was practised and considered which ones gave it a 'better home'. Whilst Rivett, Tomsett, Lumsdon and Holmes (1997) described the sometimes troubled relationship between a family therapy service and its 'host' in-patient unit. Pilgrim (1983) suggested that the 'medical hegemony' which dominates most state-run mental health services is actively inimical to psychotherapy. In the face of these ideas, it would be true to say that the 'curiosity' implicit in most forms of family therapy make it an uncomfortable neighbour to the more 'empirical' and 'scientific bio-medical' approaches to psychological distress that underlie NHS provision. Given this dissonance between family therapy's view of distress and the general ideology of medical settings, it is not surprising that Street and Rivett (1996) found that 'agency expectation' was the factor that was most likely to be experienced as stressful for family therapists.

It is likely that such professional ambivalence will become more evident given the thrust of public policy towards all state-provided services in the last decades (Ranade, 1994; Rogers & Pilgrim, 1996). These policy initiatives have been dominated by a number of themes. One is the increasing emphasis on the local allocation of resources as shown in initiatives such as the purchaser/provider split and community care practice. A recent example of this is the creation of primary care groups whose purpose is to contract for locally needed services. Another theme is the move to make welfare professionals more accountable for their practice. This has been demonstrated in initiatives such as the Patients' Charters, professional audits and the increasing power assigned to managers. Ranade (1994) summarises the latter situation when she says:

> Traditional administration has been supplanted by active management with its focus on results rather than process and year on year improvements in performance. (1994: 97)

Again there are some very recent examples of this pressure to make professionals accountable, such as the introduction of clinical governance and the creation of national bodies that will determine the best methods of intervention for most illnesses (e.g. National Institute for Clinical Excellence). It is against this ideological framework that we can look at family therapy and professional activity in one setting.

CAMHS and family therapy

Given the historical connections between family therapy and the child guidance movement (Carr, 2000a; Child Guidance Special Interest Group, 1975), it is no surprise that most family therapists work in these services. Indeed, in the contemporary context, we can be more specific: the vast majority of family therapists who have designated posts work in child and adolescent mental health services (CAMHS). These services have evolved over the last two decades out of the older child guidance movement. This specialist service has recently become the focus of political interest. For instance, the Health Advisory Service (HAS, 1995) reviewed its structures; the Audit Commission (1994; 1999) researched need and provision; and finally a number of voluntary and state agencies have lobbied for better services (Meltzer, Gatward, Goodman & Ford, 2000; Mental Health Foundation, 2000). Curiously, the result of these pressures has led to very little impetus for the creation of more family therapist posts. The HAS proposals for CAMHS structures recommended that service delivery be focused upon four levels. Tier 1 contained 'primary' services such as social workers, GPs and health visitors. In Tier 2 are to be found professionals with generic child mental health expertise such as community psychiatric nurses (CPNs), child psychiatrists and psychologists. Tier 3 included more specialist services such as day units, substance misuse teams and psychotherapists. Tier 4 includes psychiatric units, forensic services and specialist outpatient teams (for instance, eating disorder teams). This model has been proposed to assist in the strategic planning and commissioning of services and in its acceptance has evolved into an operational blueprint for services. Within this model family therapy is only mentioned at Tier 3 with the assumption being that it can be practised by all professions within CAMHS. AFT (1996) suggested that workers employed as family therapists should be placed in Tier 3, whilst workers using family therapy as part of their general skills would be expected to be employed in Tier 2. The latter, we could assume, would be classed according to our earlier typology as 'systemic practitioners' or 'other professionals practising family therapy'. Interestingly AFT, for all its systemic expertise, has not offered a systemic critique of the tiered model even though some systemic ideas are inherent in its presentation. AFT has focused on posts rather than on a more global ideological view as to how services can be provided and evaluated systemically.

Certainly, given the commissioning of CAMH services it is likely that there is only a need for a very small number of 'family therapists'. Indeed, when the Audit Commission (1999) studied the prevalence of professional groups in CAMHS they found that only 3 per cent were family therapists. This small number belies the amount of family 'work' and 'systemic practice' that is undertaken in CAMHS. The problem for family therapists becomes more serious when we consider that the impetus of social policy in recent years has been to target resources at specific issues and problems rather than at 'global' services (Ranade, 1994; Rogers & Pilgrim, 1996). This has led to a plethora of interventions at Tier 1, rather than at the higher tiers. The Audit Commission for instance noted that:

> The increasing emphasis on prevention and early intervention will make the training and support of Tier 1 workers by specialist CAMHS staff essential. (1999: 38)

Currently we can see these policies being implemented in terms of services to 'looked-after children' (children who are in the care of the local authority) and in terms of early years' services – 'Sure Start', (Ministerial Group on the Family, 1998). In none of these initiatives is a role envisaged for people employed as family therapists, although clearly there are good reasons for systemic practitioners to be involved. Indeed in the USA the profession of family therapy has involved itself in projects such as Head Start (similar to Sure Start) with valuable results (Leitch & Thomas, 1999). It appears, therefore, that current welfare practice as applied to the NHS determines that family therapists will remain a small profession predominantly within CAMHS and the activity of the professional organisation is likely to enhance the working conditions of only a few workers. And yet it is clear that in CAMH services, family therapy methods are a bedrock practice for all professionals.

So who does the work?

Here we need to return to one of the fundamental patterns that have emerged during our exploration of family therapy theory and practice. During the examination of family therapy philosophy we noted how uncertain we are that any specific theory 'grounds' the practice of family therapy. In the last chapter, we noted that family therapists cannot sometimes escape the role of the 'helping' professional in society. So far in this chapter we have cemented this view by pointing out how easily the class of family therapists sits within a picture of welfare 'professionals'. Here another aspect emerges which has a vital implication for our overall consideration of family therapy practice. Insofar as workers without the label 'family therapist' but with family therapy skills operate at any level of service provision they must utilise skills and practices that are *more than* those of 'the' family therapists. Thus a social worker or CPN who works at Tier 2 or 3 might be using family therapy with families, might be adopting systemic skills when working with schools, health visitors and social services departments. But they must also be using other skills – cognitive behavioural skills with adolescents, counselling skills with distressed children and also monitoring the impact of medication on some children with Attention Deficit Hyperactivity Disorder (ADHD) or depression. We must conclude that the vast majority of workers using family therapy skills are not only not in family therapy posts, but are also using other skills equally as much. In the main, family therapy as practised in CAMH services in the UK is more likely to be undertaken by professionals who are not and never will be professional 'family therapists'. To this we can also add that even if someone works in a CAMH service with a professional label of 'family therapist' it is highly likely that that person will be expected to undertake other professional activities that are not a part directly of family therapy training. Not only do 'non-family therapists' practise family therapy but also family therapists do some things that are not 'family therapy'.

Family therapy: an impossible profession?

After the discussion of the last two chapters, we can now begin to summarise some ideas on a sociology of family therapy and of family therapists. We have seen that family therapy at times speaks as if it is outside (even above) society, and yet social myths, expectations and norms suffuse its theory and practice. Despite the apparent radicalism of its ideas, family therapy as a practice contributes to the regulation of society whilst it mitigates the suffering of individuals and families. The places in which family therapy is practised give further evidence that this is the case. Moreover, in the last decade family therapists have further cemented their relationship to a welfare professional system and have become only one of a number of mental health professionals. Their training has a similar structure to these other professions, and the disadvantages highlighted by opponents of professionalisation appear to have been fulfilled with innovation being a possible casualty of the process. However, there are a large group of 'therapists' who are not 'formally' family therapists, who are not part of this established group and for whom a professional organisation is not a representative body. Their activities and needs will be addressed in some way, whether it is through their 'core' established professional organisations, through a change in the focus of the family therapy's professional organisation or through some innovative way. Although family therapy has successfully joined the welfare professionals it also continues to relate to a history that it remembers as radical and due to this history it remains slightly uncomfortable about being closely associated with medical treatments and the like. Whether this radicalism is totally forgotten or recovers to gain an influence over multidisciplinary teams only time will tell. But it still has the potential to retain a critical edge in welfare settings and for some this critical edge is the central aspect of systemic practice. It may well be that although we have suggested that the profession displays some ambivalence, it would be more accurate to see the 'professional' tasks of a family therapist as inherently paradoxical and even more so when placed in a public service context. Before we proceed to examine this paradox in relation to evidence-based practice, we wish to examine one further sociological aspect of family therapy practice: does it contribute to a more just society?

Chapter 6
Social policy, social justice and family therapy

The philosophers have only interpreted the world, the point is to change it.

Karl Marx

Social justice and therapy

In this chapter, we take the sociological perspective on family therapy one stage further: we explore how family therapy contributes to a more just society and we wonder if it works with populations who are socially excluded. We will, during our discussion, take examples of practice that illustrate our exploration (specifically gender equality and cultural diversity) rather than aiming to provide a full comprehensive guide to family therapy and social justice. Before we can begin to unfold this topic, however, we need to consider some of the standard criticisms of therapy from the perspective of social justice.

Chapter 4 provided evidence that many sociological commentators would regard therapists as being unable to theoretically acknowledge either a social justice dimension to their work, or to take on board therapeutic activities that might address social injustice. From Pilgrim's (1997) perspective, however, there is another crucial aspect of this difficulty: therapists have consistently ignored the very populations that are socially excluded. Therapy, he argues, is designed to decrease psychological suffering, therefore it should be concentrated upon those where suffering is at its greatest. If this suffering is to be measured by the incidence of mental distress, then we have ample statistical evidence about which groups these are. He comments:

> Whilst it is a truism that anybody, whatever their social background, can experience varieties of fear, sadness or madness, this does not mean that these occur randomly in society. (Pilgrim, 1997: 41)

Indeed, ever since researchers have studied mental ill health, there has been evidence that certain social variables heavily influence the occurrence of psychological distress. For instance, Brown and Harris (1978) developed an understanding of the *social* origins of depression in women which was related to them having small children and little social support. Cochrane (1983), an early researcher into the prevalence of mental illness within minority ethnic groups, demonstrated that social variables such as class, culture and unemployment as well as gender, differentially affected the mental health of different groups. In terms of class, Pilgrim states:

> The best predictor of general health is social class and, within this trend, mental health follows a class gradient. Class is also relevant in relation to service responses to particular forms of distress. Basically the rich are more likely to receive psychological treatments, and the poor biological treatments. (1997: 41)

Various writers have noted that psychotherapists have rarely recognised the influence of class in the distress of their clients (Parker, Georgaca, Harper, McLaughlin & Stowell-Smith, 1995). Others contend that therapists are more likely to refuse to treat people from lower classes because they are 'unable to benefit' from talking treatments (Pilgrim, 1997).

The influence of gender on psychological distress has also been well researched (Barnes & Maple, 1992; Busfield, 1996; Miles, 1987; Showalter, 1987). Again we know from this research that women seek help for psychological difficulties at a rate of twice that of men; that in certain diagnostic categories women exceed men at a rate of two to one; and that certain psychotropic drugs are more likely to be prescribed for women (Busfield, 1996: Pilgrim & Rogers, 1993). However, referrals to child and adolescent mental health services show a preponderance of boys to girls in the ratio of 3:1 (Health Advisory Service, 1995) which suggests a different gender dynamic in the child population.

The last significant social variable is that of race and ethnicity. Once more there is ample evidence that psychological distress within a person from a minority ethnic culture leads to a different kind of intervention than that in another person. Minority ethnic people are more likely to be diagnosed as having a psychotic illness; they are more likely to be detained under the Mental Health Act 1983 in Wales and England; and they are more likely to enter the psychiatric system via police intervention (Fernando, 1989; 1991; Pilgrim & Rogers, 1993). This representation matches the experience of not only black people but also minority white groups such as Irish people (Pilgrim & Rogers, 1993).

Within sociological circles, there has been a debate about why psychological distress becomes clustered in certain social groups.

Some commentators ascribe this phenomenon to 'social labelling'; for example, groups are given labels because they are socially excluded. Others argue that social exclusion itself leads to higher incidences of illness. We would refer readers to other works to explore this debate more fully (e.g. Pilgrim & Rogers, 1993). Apart from those who question the very basis of objectivist science (radical constructivists), most would agree that distress does in fact increase in these populations. There is then an intimate connection between therapy, social inclusion, social justice and these social variables. We would expect all therapists to be cognisant of these social influences upon the mental health of their clients and perhaps to some degree to address them. A corollary of this knowledge would be an awareness that the gender, class and cultural background of the therapist will have a significant effect on the way the client will be able to relate to the therapeutic encounter. This self-awareness is even more crucial where social constructions are quite likely to be strongly influencing the thoughts and actions of the therapist, especially in cases where sexism and racism might be present. Before we consider these dimensions further, we need to establish whom family therapists work with and what kind of difficulties these people have so that we can assess the impact of social exclusion mechanisms on family therapy practice.

With what problems and with what people do family therapists work?

In order to find some response to this question we can return to the two national studies of family therapy practice – one in America and one in Britain (Bor et al., 1998; Doherty & Simmons, 1996). When marital and family therapists in America were asked to rate their view of their 'treatment competency' (Doherty & Simmons, 1996) 63.4 per cent of therapists believed that they were largely competent to work with minority populations, although most (87.1%) were confident in treating adolescents. These figures also show that 62.8 per cent who felt competent in working with the elderly, 62.4 per cent with children, 53.6 per cent with lesbians and gay men, and 43.8 per cent with the physically impaired. The 'average client profile', however, reveals that many adult clients had attended high school (40.3%) with the largest group having a college education (42.5%). Putting this with the 'type of treatment' provided by these marital and family therapists they recorded that 49.4 per cent of their cases were 'primarily individual' and 23.1 per cent 'primarily couple' (only 12% reported their practice as 'primarily family'). This suggests that American therapists work on the whole with reasonably educated adults in mainly adult combinations.

This was confirmed when the therapists were asked to rate their competency on treating DSM-IV diagnoses. Most felt competent with adjustment disorders (98.8%), anxiety disorders (93.2%) and mood disorders (88.4%). Less than a quarter (23.8%) felt competent in working with schizophrenia and even less with other psychotic disorders (15.9%). This strongly suggests that American family therapists are on the whole not working with 'severe mental illness' and also are probably not working with excluded populations (of note is the fact that class and race were not recorded).

In a number of subtle ways the British survey records a slightly different picture. Bor et al. (1998) found that 16 per cent of family therapists' time was spent with minority ethnic people, 13 per cent with physically disabled service users, 7 per cent with gay men and 4 per cent with lesbians. However, the picture of the problems they worked with has a similarity to that of the American survey. Thus most therapists worked with relationship difficulties (93%), what could be called 'adjustment reactions' and general family disturbances (parent–child problems 86% and marital problems 82%). Fewer worked with the 'severe' mental illnesses such as psychosis/ schizophrenia (38%), obsessive–compulsive disorders (44%) and personality disorders (37%). These surveys therefore give evidence that family therapists may be working to some extent with some socially excluded populations and that British family therapists may be more likely to work with such groups. Thus, not unexpectedly, where the model of practice favours private practice, fewer members of socially excluded groups will be helped. Whereas where state-funded models of practice predominate, more attempts will be made to meet the needs of the socially excluded. In the light of this somewhat uncertain evidence that family therapists engage with the socially excluded, we will now examine how family therapists have altered their practice to address the exclusion of certain populations.

Social inclusion and social justice in mainstream family therapy practice

Here, we will interrogate two areas in which practices of social inclusion and of social justice have entered the mainstream of family therapy practice. These can only be concentrated summations, the purpose of which is to compare practice with the principles of inclusion and justice. The areas that we review are those of gender equity (and the influence of feminism) and of cultural diversity. Feminism, which drastically challenged and altered family therapy practice, promotes justice and equality for women, whilst the requirement to practise with a knowledge of cultural diversity promotes justice and equality for people of all cultures and races. In our discussion we would wish to reiterate the view that these issues have a *self-reflexive* as well as a *social justice* dimension. Pilgrim (1997) criticises the psychotherapies for emphasising only the *self-reflexive* dimension at the expense of the *social justice* dimension. In our discussion we wish to highlight both these aspects, although to some degree the *self-reflexive* component will be more fully explored in Chapter 7.

Family therapy practice and feminism

Before we begin to assess the influence of feminism on family therapy we need to establish the meanings of both *feminism* and *gender-sensitive practice*. Walters (1990) argues that 'any feminist perspective in therapy' needs to have four components:

(1) the conscious inclusion ... of the experience of women growing up, developing, relating to each other, to men, and to social institutions, raising families, working and growing old in a culture largely shaped and defined by male experience.
(2) a critique of therapy practices ... that lend themselves to a devaluing of women,
(3) the integration of feminist theory ... and
(4) the use of female modes and models in the continuing expansion and development of theory and practice. (1990: 13)

Goldenberg and Goldenberg (2000) comment that these components have been translated into a practice which they call gender sensitive (not anti-sexist or pro-feminist which itself has significance). This is a practice that 'attempts to overcome confining sex-role stereotyping in any clinical interventions' (2000: 45). Before we examine the applications of this approach, we will briefly review the interconnection between feminism and family therapy.

A brief history of the relationship between family therapy and feminism

From the vantage point of the beginning of the twenty-first century there are perhaps two predominant impressions that emerge when we examine the relationship between feminism and family therapy. The first is that it is almost inconceivable that family therapy practice in its current form could have existed without the insights of feminism. Linked to this is the disbelief and shame that we experience when we read accounts of early family therapy practice in which well-meaning therapists make interventions with families that only serve to perpetuate gender hierarchies and in which an understanding of the differential experiences of the genders is not respected. The second impression is that it is difficult to clearly specify the origin of feminist critiques of practice and of family therapy in general. They appeared in many places at the same time and it is now quite difficult to trace the development of these critiques. Because of this complex story, we will highlight a few, but obviously not all, of the significant moments in this story.

McGoldrick, Anderson and Walsh (1989) describe their attempts at the 1984 Stonehenge family therapy conference to convene a separate colloquium for women to 'share and build on our mutual efforts to understand the issues of women in families and in family therapy' (1989: 3). This suggestion caused 'surprisingly negative' reactions from both female and male family therapists. It did, however, go ahead and they describe the 'energy, intelligence and power' that were then mobilised in the group of fifty women who took part. This typified the process that in family therapy (as in almost all other fields) lead to feminist insights challenging and then transforming the field. Another example of this process was the forming of the Women's Project in, 1977 by Walters, Carter, Papp and Silverstein. This group of women led the way by running work-shops, writing papers and eventually editing a crucial book (Walters et al., 1989) on gender relationships (see Simon, 1997, for a full description). Other significant early contributions in the story of this relationship were papers by Hare-Mustin (1978), Osborne (1983) and Goldner (1985).

If we were to typify this initial phase of connection between feminism and family therapy, it would be one of challenge. Gradually, feminist practitioners critiqued the theory of family therapy, and then its practice. Thus Walsh & Scheinkman (1989) reviewed all the existing models of family therapy and concluded:

> By and large, the major models of family therapy have not by design promulgated sexist beliefs or practices. However, the architects of our models of family functioning and family intervention have been blind to gender as a fundamental organizing principle in human systems and have not taken into account the differential power and status between men and women in the larger social systems in which families are embedded. (1989: 37)

Luepnitz (1988) went further in analysing the written accounts of the early family therapists in order to highlight how patriarchal and gender stereotypical it had been. Luepnitz places these practitioners 'between two eras of progressive social change'; that is, between the feminist advances of the early twentieth century and the 'second-wave' feminist movement of the 1970s. She comments that:

> It cannot be irrelevant that while early family therapists were writing their first articles and books and seeing their first families, the doctrine of 'separate spheres' for the sexes was a dominant cultural motif. (1988: 27)

During this phase of challenge, a number of family therapists such as Luepnitz reached the conclusion that systems theory itself needed to be rejected because it was too steeped in patriarchal assumptions. Others such as Walrond-Skinner (1987) explored the limitations of applying the methods from feminist therapy to family therapy. However, generally the field began to integrate the insights from feminism in a number of ways. For instance, Jones (1990) comments:

> My grandmother, whenever she heard about a man and woman having marital difficulties, used to say with a twinkle in her eye, 'Well everybody knows these mixed marriages don't work'. Are family therapy and feminism compatible? The answer partly depends on what we mean by family therapy and what we mean by feminism. (1990: 71)

She concludes that she values the double description provided by both feminism and family therapy (e.g. 'compatibility' may not be as important as it is thought to be) and that she is an 'optimist who works like a pessimist' (1990: 79). Walsh and Scheinkman (1989) reach a similar conclusion:

> In contrast to some family therapists who maintain that feminist positions are incompatible with systems theory and practice, we argue that to ignore gender is, in fact, non-systemic. Rather than suggesting that we abandon systems therapies, here we attempt to advance theory and practice by suggesting ways to incorporate an awareness of gender in the various models of family therapy. (1989: 17)

After the insights of this initial phase, therapists began to write about how they integrated feminism into their practice. Schneider (1990), for instance, provided a clinical example of her 'feminist-informed family therapy'. In order to work with a couple whose child had been removed due to physical abuse, Schneider and her team began to explore the gender dynamics of the couple relationship which they believed inhibited the couple from caring for their child appropriately.

One of the gender dynamics was the man's expectation that his partner would accept responsibility for the family's emotional life, and accept the blame if things were not working well. In the therapy Schneider challenged this view by encouraging the man to recognise his own vulnerabilities, and the woman to 'challenge and assert with adult compassion' (1990: 127).

This description typified the growing case examples of how family therapists can use feminist practice in their work with families (Burck & Daniel, 1995; Goodrich, 1991). Indeed the pressure to integrate feminist and family therapy practice led to the establishment of the *Journal of Feminist Family Therapy* in 1988.

The most recent phase in the relationship between family therapy and feminism has been marked by the recognition that not only are there a number of feminisms but also that women's experiences of patriarchal society may be mediated by culture. Almeida (1998) has been the most visible proponent of this perspective:

> The specifics of experience for women along a continuum of race, class and ethnicity have been submerged under one reality by dominant feminist thought: that of gender oppression ... this excludes critical domains of women's experience, as the women in question are not necessarily white, middle-class and heterosexual. (1998: 2)

As in other settings in which the monolith of 'feminism' has been broken down into 'feminisms', this critique of how family therapists have used feminism has led to a wider appreciation of the experience of different women. It has in particular been applied to the area of domestic violence to which we will turn shortly.

How prevalent is a pro-feminist practice in family therapy?

As in previous chapters where we have interrogated theoretical ideas with an assessment of practice, we cannot assume just because feminist practice is taught on training courses and is written about, that family therapists are actively promoting this aspect of social justice when they work with their clients. However, Dankoski, Penn, Carlson and Hecker (1998) provide us with some evidence that this is indeed the case. They sampled 109 marital and family therapists at the AAMFT's conference in, 1995. The respondees were asked to both describe their theoretical orientation (one of which was 'feminist') and to fill in a self-report scale which assessed their awareness of and compliance to a feminist perspective. They found that although very few therapists described themselves as 'feminist' (10% of men and

40% of women), in fact this did not make a significant difference to how they scored on the feminist behaviour checklist. The authors concluded that:

> This study supported the hypothesis that a reluctance to identify one-self as a feminist exists within the field of marriage and family therapy. However, many therapists engage in feminist behaviours in their clinical work. ... The message of feminism, of acknowledging social constraints of gender and the history of gender, is being recognized within the field of marriage and family therapy. (1998: 102)

There is also evidence that therapists are applying feminist ideas to their work with men (Dienhart, 2001; Dienhart & Avis, 1994). Other studies have also suggested that male clients value the challenge and clarity of feminist informed therapy (Werner-Wilson, 1997). Clearly there is a deliberate effort to establish a gender-sensitive approach amongst family therapists. At this point we wish to example the union of family therapy/systemic ideas with a particular project.

Fifth Province re-versings

McCarthy (1998; 2001; Byrne & McCarthy, 1999) and her colleagues have created both a critique of the social construction of female lone parenthood and a therapeutic response to it via feminist practice. This practice begins with acknowledging how women have become 'discursive scapegoats' in contemporary Western societies. McCarthy writes:

> the term/label 'unmarried mother' not only stands proxy for the term 'lone parent' but also for the term 'promiscuity'. It is this latter substitution which switches attention away from the withdrawal of support to mothers and children and justifies the non-support of rising promiscuity in its stead. (2001: 264)

This switch leads to a situation where lone mothers are conceived of as 'unwanted dependant, irresponsible and in need of social correction'. Hence, argues McCarthy, there are social policy initiatives to control access to housing, access to social security and pushes to force women 'back to work' (by providing subsidised childcare).

The practice that emerges from this perspective is one similar to that suggested by White (1993; 1995) in which the therapist encourages the client to resist the social construction of her life. What is perhaps more unique in this approach is that McCarthy and her team work to empower not only individuals, and not only to connect these individuals to an empowering community, but also to empower the community itself. They therefore stimulate supportive networks and community groups to develop their own political voice. Indeed, McCarthy says that she wishes to create a 'politics of listening' in which 'colonizing discourses' (Byrne & McCarthy, 1999: 96) can be uncovered and countered.

Family therapy and domestic violence: a collision with social justice?

So far we have demonstrated that family therapy has adopted a social justice perspective with regard to women's roles in society and in therapy. However, in one area of practice it has not been so smooth an integration. This area is that of domestic violence where feminists have maintained that male control over women is not only symbolised but typified (Pence & Paymar, 1993). Hence, from a number of perspectives feminists have carried out a thoroughgoing criticism of family therapists who engage in couples work where domestic violence has occurred. Indeed, this criticism has at times been acrimonious and forthright (Avis, 1992; Erickson, 1992; Kaufman, 1992). The reasons for this criticism can be summed up in five categories. Firstly, there is ample evidence that family therapists do not ask about or recognise situations where women are being abused despite their own intimate involvement in therapy with these women (Harway, Hansen & Cervantes, 1997). Secondly, family therapists through their preference for interactional and circular theories might assume that the abused woman is in some way responsible for her abuse *and that this might be communicated to her and her abuser* (Anderson & Schlossberg, 1999; Jacobson & Gottman, 1998). This criticism has close parallels with the systemic debate about 'power' (Dell, 1989) in systems and with the reification of the 'family' that was discussed in Chapter 2. It also clearly relates to the first criticism: if a woman feels that the therapist will consider her responsible for the abuse that she experiences, she is unlikely to disclose that abuse in therapy. Thirdly, it has been suggested that couples therapy in itself might be collusive of male abuse of women. Bograd (1984), for instance, asserted that:

> The popular practice of conjoint therapy may be based on certain conventional beliefs or attitudes about women, marriage, and violence. (1984: 563)

She went on to state that couple therapy might implicitly 'perpetuate traditional sex roles' because women are expected to be the 'most responsive' to therapy.

This reinforced

> the traditional notion that women are primarily responsible for the tranquility of the domestic environment. (1984: 565)

Thus by seeing a couple together, the therapist is locating the source of difficulty *implicitly* within the relationship and because of the way society regards women as the 'nurturing gender' (Schneider, 1990) this compounds women's responsibility for the abuse they experience. Fourthly, feminists have argued that couple therapy is not only not safe but also potentially dangerous for the woman. There have been reports that after such therapy, the abusive man is more likely to assault his partner because of what was said in the therapy session and also because of what emotions were exposed (Adams, 1988; Mederos, 1999). Safety might also be compromised because traditionally family therapists work in clinics that have no connection to the Women's Refuge movement, or other protective statutory services (e.g. the police). Therefore they are simply unable to intervene to actively protect a woman if they think she is at risk (Rivett, 2001). Lastly, despite a number of highly publicised couple therapy programmes (Goldner, 1998; 1999; Goldner, Penn, Sheinberg & Walker, 1990), there has been very little research evidence to support couple therapy as a way of reducing violence and abuse (Rivett, 2001).

Responses to the criticisms

Family therapists have responded to these criticisms in a number of ways. Firstly, they have constructed models of therapy that reassert a feminist perspective *alongside* a systemic one. Thus Goldner et al. (1990) write that:

> we were looking for a description [of battering] that was consistent with our beliefs as feminists, and simultaneously consistent with our beliefs as systems thinkers and therapists. We tried to get beyond the reductionist view of men as simply abusing their power, and of women as colluding in their own victimization by not leaving. (1990: 344)

This led to a 'both/and' perspective on battering which included 'four levels of description and explanation: psychodynamic, social learning, sociopolitical and systemic' (1990: 346). In essence this solution to the criticism that family therapists do not support abused women enough, was one that asserted the greater complexity of understanding necessary in such relationships. In a later paper Goldner (1998) proposes another response to this critique: couple therapy is only appropriate in certain cases. Here, she reiterates a view latterly maintained by Bograd and Mederos (1999) that therapists should carefully assess risk before embarking upon couple therapy.

In this way they can screen out the most dangerous situations and recommend other forms of treatment. This will leave a smaller, 'safer' number of relationships in which couple therapy can be undertaken. Anderson and Schlossberg (1999), however, return to what they see as the interactional dynamics of assaults and reassert the value of a systemic perspective. They write that:

> systems theories ... emphasize an inter-personal perspective that focuses upon the social and relational contexts and the unique patterns of interaction that recur within relationships. (1999: 137)

Because research has 'pointed to the importance of the relational context and the patterns of interaction that occur over time in violent relationships' (1999: 138), they believe that systems ideas have simply not been allowed to contribute to an area of study and intervention that are suited to its approach. Indeed, like Brown and O'Leary (1997) these authors comment that since couples are going to continue to ask for couple therapy, family therapists' perspectives should be valued.

Despite this emphasis upon therapy for couples which has been defended by these family therapists, it has to be noted that a number of other family therapists have argued that their systemic skills are better placed in providing *other* forms of treatment. Thus Bograd (1984) herself stated that 'thinking systemically about a couple does not mandate working with the spouses together' (1984: 563). Other family therapists have accepted this early suggestion. Almeida and Bograd (1991) have developed a community response to domestic violence that involves separate treatment for men and women. This response has more recently addressed the differences between cultures and races where domestic violence has been committed (Font, Vecchio & Almeida, 1998). Similar services have been developed by family therapists in Australia (Shaw, Bouris & Pye, 1996).

These responses suggest that family therapists are aware that their preference for couple therapy in situations of domestic violence may not be as appropriate as they had presumed. They also suggest that family therapists are keenly aware of the social justice issues in their work in this field. On the whole, however, the balance would seem to be that they have not yet adequately responded to the feminist critiques of their role in domestic violence.

Gender-sensitive family therapy

We can therefore summarise family therapy's response to this area of social justice. It is evident that family therapy has changed a great deal in relation to gender-sensitive practice. There is evidence that both its theory (excluding the feminist critique of post-modernism that was detailed in Chapter 3) and its practice have made serious efforts to promote gender equality and to challenge gender stereotypes in relationships. This position might not be as clear when we consider domestic violence, but we can still conclude that the majority of family therapists are gender sensitive and many more have a pro-feminist perspective.

Social justice, social exclusion and cultural diversity

Earlier on we highlighted the evidence that culture and ethnicity are crucial factors in determining the incidence and variable social response to mental distress. Just as in gender dynamics, culture and ethnicity are also matters of social justice: racism and institutional racism strongly affect the way individuals are treated in the societies where family therapy is practised (Braham, Rattansi & Skellington, 1992; Skellington & Morris, 1992). In particular the racism that exists within mental health services has been explored and exposed (Fernando, 1989; 1991; Littlewood & Lipsedge, 1982; Rack, 1982). This racism has also been addressed within the theory and practice of family therapy to which we now turn.

Family therapy and cultural diversity

McGoldrick has stated that:

> Like other social institutions, family therapy has been structured in ways that support the dominant value system and keep invisible certain hidden organizing principles of our lives, including culture, class, race, gender and sexual orientation. (1998: 1)

Barratt, Burck, Dwivedi, Stedman & Raval (1999) have explored how this has been played out in family therapy theory. They argue that

> racism is embedded in our society at a number of levels – personal, institutional and cultural – and operates through relationships, and organisational and societal structures of differential and unequal power. (1999: 4)

In particular they regard family therapy theory to have been racist in the way it promoted a Eurocentric vision of family life, of individuation, of emotion, of childhood, of parenting and of the 'self'. A similar argument was made by Fernando (1991):

family therapy ... may be a corrective reaction to the emphasis on the single individual that developed in Western psychiatry ... [this] problem may not be applicable to indigenous systems of healing in other cultures. For it is nothing new for healers in Africa and Asia to involve the family and to take a wide view of problems. (1991: 178)

Just as with feminism, it is possible to analyse the history of the relationship between family therapy and cultural diversity into a number of different phases. Initially, family therapists discussed the applicability of their models of therapy to diverse populations (Bott & Hodes, 1989; Messent, 1992; Wieselberg, 1992). Another strand, however, began to discuss the specific issues that therapists needed to address in working with minority ethnic groups. These were often written by authors from within these cultures and always included an analysis of the impact that racism had upon diverse families (Boyd-Franklin, 1989).

These two phases epitomise, in their different approaches to psychotherapy with diverse populations, a longstanding controversy in the general field of therapy. Briefly, there are two perspectives: one argues that psychotherapy is culturally *generalisable*; the other argues that psychotherapy needs to be designed to be culturally *specific*. The former approach has been labelled the *etic* approach; the latter the *emic* approach.

The *etic* perspective suggests that existing psychological theories and techniques are robust enough to have universal applicability across ethnic or cultural groups. Patterson (1996), for example, believes that a client-centred approach provides all the necessary and sufficient ingredients for effective counselling with any client regardless of ethnicity. A family therapy example of this position is given by Richeport-Haley (1998). She states that Haley's directive approach 'minimizes a focus on ethnicity' because structural changes in families where there are difficulties 'can be similar across ethnic groups' (1998: 78).

Proponents of the *emic* perspective suggest that helping strategies need to be unique to the culture of the client (Sue & Sue, 1990). According to Wohl (1995):

culturally specific approaches are psychotherapy methods designed to be congruent with the cultural characteristics of a particular ethnic clientele, or for problems believed to be especially prominent in a particular ethnic group or ethnic groups in general. (1995: 76)

If we consider one of the techniques developed by some family therapists, we can see that a method developed from one culturally specific group might not be fit for others. Speck and Attneave (1974), for instance, developed a method called 'network therapy' which involved convening the family and wider network together in order to solve a problem within the family. The purpose of these meetings was to stimulate and utilise wider resources that may not be available to individual families themselves. 'Network therapy' was taken up by a number of British therapists in the, 1970s but its application never achieved a mainstream 'popularity'. Given that here were some very useful elements in its practice some therapists have attempted to continue to find a use for this method. In a section of a book chapter entitled 'Networking – the forgotten tradition within family therapy', Treacher (1995) writes:

> Networking is, I believe, the most fundamental answer to the problem of dis-empowerment which is associated with any form of therapy that relies on a professional playing a central role in achieving change. However, since most professional agencies are geared to delivering their service on the basis of individual practitioners working with clients, it requires a radical intervention to establish a networking approach. The type of team involved in networking is radically different, because the team's method of functioning involves breaking out of the confines of the clinical paradigm in order to engage in a whole range of activities which cannot be neatly encompassed in conventional professional–client relationships. (1995: 63)

Here Treacher is clearly lamenting the lack of take-up of network therapy, but this begs the question 'why has its application not been taken up by many?' The answer lies in the history of the approach. Attneave had originally published a paper entitled 'Therapy in a tribal setting and urban network intervention' (Attneave, 1969) in which she had applied systems therapy to Native American clients and it was in this context that network therapy originated. More recently Ivey, Ivey and Simek-Morgan (1993) have described how network therapy can be applied to Native American populations where alcohol misuse is an issue. Here the therapist would arrange for the individual, his or her family and the local community to meet in order to provide a supportive network to help the individual combat the problem. What we therefore have here is the cultural roots of network therapy: it was conceived and continues as an appropriate intervention for a culturally specific population – the Zuni tribe of North America. It is therefore little wonder that it did not receive the take-up lamented by Treacher when it was transported to the traditional English settings of rural Wiltshire, Somerset and Devon. The cultural frameworks of provincial British locations clearly hold different concepts of family and community than do

Native Americans. What is particularly interesting in this light is the recent importation of 'family group conferences' into British child protection systems from Australia (Marsh & Crow, 1997). This may be a form of networking that will find a cultural fit. The networking example above, however, may be an example of the inappropriate generalisation of an *emic* technique. But undoubtedly the pressure and literature presumes that the *emic* approach is the most valid one. Sue, Zane and Young (1994), on the other hand, have argued that despite the existence of a large body of literature on specific techniques there is a relative paucity of clear theoretical models to guide thinking about process and outcome with different ethnic groups. They state:

> most conceptual schemes have focused on specific concrete recommendations for treating ethnic minorities with few ties at current theories of psychotherapy. What is needed are approaches that propose specific hypotheses as to how the psychosocial experiences of ethnic minorities affect certain important processes in psychotherapy. (1994: 809)

In a nutshell, there has been little reference as to why culturally specific interventions are important. Certainly, amongst the literature, which recommends one method of treatment for a certain ethnic population, there are a number of arguments that family therapy remains the treatment of choice. Padilla and De Snyder (1987), among others, suggested that family therapy 'fitted' for Hispanic families who have a strong *familismo* ethic. But this might imply that given the emphasis on individuation and autonomy prevalent in many white, Western families, family therapy might not be the treatment of choice there!

A number of studies have examined ethnic minority participation in therapy and have concluded that there is a preference for similarity between therapist and client (Atkinson & Lowe, 1995). Coleman, Wampold and Casali (1995) believe that this finding might mean that similarity of ethnic background is interpreted by therapist and client alike as evidence that they share a world-view rather than that they are 'alike' in other ways. Nevertheless, such findings cannot be ignored especially given the research significance of the therapeutic alliance (see Chapter 9). Because therapists cannot always represent these similarities (and this applies to age, gender, sexual orientation and disability as well), they must find ways of addressing these differences openly within the therapeutic relationship. This requirement explains why family therapists in particular, and therapists in general, are turning to the concept of *cultural competency*.

Cultural competency

As with the feminist influence upon family therapy, it is difficult to determine when family therapists first began to adopt the concept of cultural competency. But it signifies the most recent phase in the relationship between family therapy and cultural diversity and therefore represents a solution to the *etic* and *emic* debate. O'Hagan (2001) defines cultural competency in this way:

> Cultural competence is the ability to maximise sensitivity and minimise insensitivity in the service of culturally diverse communities. This requires knowledge, values and skills, but most of these are the basic knowledge, values and skills which underpin any competency training in numerous care professions. Their successful application in work with culturally diverse peoples and communities will depend a great deal upon cultural awareness, attitude and approach. The workers need not be (as is often claimed) highly knowledgeable about the cultures of the people they serve, but they must approach culturally different people with openness and respect – a willingness to learn. Self-awareness is the most important component in the knowledge base of culturally competent practice. (2001: 235)

This concept resolves the *emic* and *etic* dichotomy by ensuring that therapists are open to learning about the specific cultural issues of their clients without prejudging them from any 'dominant' cultural perspective. It recognises that there is specific knowledge that therapists need to know, but that they can learn this from their clients themselves. It presumes that the values and skills that underlie therapy are essential in a multicultural context but it also enshrines the principle of 'self-awareness' as a crucial element of culturally diverse practice.

Within family therapy training, Hardy and Laszloffy (1995; 1998; 2000) have made a particular contribution by their description of the 'cultural genogram'. They believe that training programmes have been skewed towards the *emic* approach with 'multicultural content' and 'cultural awareness' rather than encouraging openness and 'cultural sensitivity'. Therefore they propose that trainees complete an analysis of the cultural backgrounds that they bring into their work. They state that the cultural genogram challenges trainees

> to examine how their respective cultural identities influence understanding and acceptance of those who are both culturally similar and dissimilar. (1995: 227)

In the genogram, the person delineates attitudes to diversity, their own cultural diversity and their relationship to their own 'culture' and 'ethnicity' by exploring their families of origin.

Shortly we will return to the impact cultural diversity has had on family therapy practice, and thereby assess family therapy's success in being part of this aspect of social justice. However, just as we used the Fifth Province group as an example of the radical intervention of feminist social justice, here we wish to discuss the New Zealand 'Just Therapy' group as an example of radical culturally diverse practice.

Just Therapy

The Just Therapy group (Tamasese & Waldegrave, 1993; Waldegrave, 1990; Waldegrave & Tamasese, 1993) began adapting family therapy to the cultural conditions in New Zealand in the, 1980s. These conditions included working with Maori, Samoan and white families, each of which had cultural expectations about their heritage as well as expectations about men and women's roles. Waldegrave (1990) states:

> A 'Just Therapy' is one that takes into account the gender, cultural, social and economic context of the persons seeking help. It is our view that therapists have a responsibility to find appropriate ways of addressing these issues and developing approaches that are centrally concerned with the often forgotten issues of fairness and equity. Such therapy reflects the themes of liberation that lead to self-determining outcomes of resolution and hope. (1990: 5)

The implementation of such an approach led to some radical considerations within the group which comprised of men, women, Maori, Samoan and pakeha (white) therapists. In order to ensure that racism, sexism or other injustice was not replicated within their group, they firstly learnt to name the injustices and to avoid being paralysed by it, individualising it or being patronising about it (Tamasese & Waldegrave, 1993). Secondly, they initiated a series of 'cultural sections and gender caucuses' in which injustice could initially be shared with individuals of the same gender/culture. Thirdly, these discussions fed into a new method of accountability in which issues were raised between sections and caucuses. These were raised in a non-individualising way; for example, individuals were not 'blamed' for injustice, but their group was asked to collectively reflect and to take action to prevent the injustice happening again. The Just Therapy group believe that they are able to achieve this accountability because Maori and Samoan culture does not have the hierarchical understanding of relationships that white Western culture has. They write that:

the cultural memories of the subjugated peoples hold vestiges of relationships other than the vertical arrangements of relationships that are characteristic in western nations. (1993: 41)

This radical team approach eventually led to the creation of three separate 'cultural co-ordinators' who jointly manage the agency: thereby the institutional structure symbolises cultural diversity.

Has cultural diversity influenced mainstream family therapy practice?

From the discussion above, it is clear that family therapy has radically altered its theory base and opened up its practice to the scrutiny of cultural diversity. All family therapists now must evidence their cultural competency before being licensed to practice (AFT, 1999). There is also good evidence that the wider focus of 'social justice' is entering the training field (McGoldrick et al., 1999) and there is now a large body of literature to guide therapists (Dwivedi, 1999; Gorell Barnes, 1998; Hill, 1994; McGoldrick, 1998). Almost every edition of the family therapy journals includes articles that concentrate on cultural issues (Allen & Olson, 2001; Shek & Lai, 2001).

Yet some limitations to this picture need to be acknowledged. In previous sections we have noted that we do not have any good evidence that family therapists are working within minority ethnic communities at anything like the numbers that might be expected from the statistics about mental distress quoted earlier. We do not know how many family therapists are themselves from minority ethnic groups. Markowitz (1993) reported that the American Association of Marital and Family Therapists had no people of colour on its executive board. She contrasted this with the equivalent social work association, which had an executive, which by internal rules, had to have at least 10 per cent representation from minority cultures. Moreover, as Chimera, Cooklin and Miller (1999) point out, the institutional racism of the agencies from which most British family therapists work, is unlikely to be avoided by the workers themselves. This might translate into low referral rates from black families which is regarded as 'normal' by a host agency. Moreover, in Britain, there are few radical 'outreach' family therapy services that work within excluded populations unlike the Just Therapy group and others (Pakman, 1995; Piazza & del Valle, 1992).

All these themes open up the debate that to be truly committed to social justice and inclusion, family therapists must adopt a political stance. It is to this theme that we now turn.

Politics and therapy

Implicit in this discussion has been the role of family therapists as agents of social justice: political activists of a kind. How much this aspect of practice is incorporated will vary from practitioner to practitioner. Thus projects such as the Fifth Province group and the Just Therapy group have provided a clear *praxis* (a Marxist term meaning the unity of theory and practice) for their work. Equally, White (1993) interprets the feminist motto that 'the personal is political' as a way of engaging politically with clients whose narratives are subjugated by dominant discourses. One of the differences between these groups is the extent to which they take their form of therapy into the communities that are socially excluded. Most family therapists, however, engage politically from within their own office suites. This in turn means that they are politically influenced by the context of their work. To take an example: a family therapist who is working with an adolescent who is detained within a psychiatric unit might 'externalise' anorexia in order to help the young person gain some control of the socially determined ideas about femininity (and her 'self'). When a similar externalisation is used by a family therapist who works in a community centre on a deprived estate whilst working with a group for lone mothers, the political intent is different. In the one case, the purpose is self-liberation; in the other it might be collective liberation.

The most coherent discussion of the role of politics within family therapy has been that of Goldner (1991). In her discussion of how feminist understandings translate into practice, she writes:

> The error from the left is equally profound. It involves collapsing another distinction, the distinction between words and deeds, between therapy and politics. This is the argument that relies on the aphorism 'therapy is political' as opposed to working with the more precise phrase 'therapy has political aspects'. The problem with the familiar slogan is that it reduces therapeutic conversation to politics, and politics to conversation which trivialises both enterprises. (1991: 58)

She concludes that the best definition of therapy places it firmly in the conversational arena. Therefore:

> psychotherapy is nothing more and nothing less than talk ... it is best to conceive of family therapy as a rhetorical strategy that helps elucidate the dilemmas of love and power between men and women living under a patriarchal society. (1991: 59)

This does not preclude focusing on the challenge within the therapy setting, but it does determine the extent to which family therapists can work towards social justice. If we take the Fifth Province and Just Therapy perspectives, however, there is another vision of therapy. One that is much closer to the radical psychotherapists of other traditions (Totton, 2000). This perspective would argue that therapists cannot confine their social justice activities to their consulting rooms. Interestingly there have been recent signs that family therapists are re-describing the political nature of their work. In a number of ways they have been 'reaching out' to influence the way socially excluded families are treated (Boyd-Franklin & Bry, 2000; Leitch & Thomas, 1999). They also have been reviewing the meaning of political engagement (Samuels, 1999) and of 'community practice' (Doherty & Beaton, 2000). Indeed, Doherty and Beaton (2000) specifically argue that family therapists can orientate themselves into five different levels of 'community involvement'. These range from simply developing community resources for client families, through to using their skills in 'community leadership'. The authors envisage the latter as centring upon specific social problems (child abuse, drug misuse etc.) in which family therapists could be catalysts for social change.

Social policy, social justice and family therapy: a summary

This chapter has charted the role of family therapy within the social policy arena of social justice and social exclusion. We have seen that there are important reasons why family therapy should address these concerns and we have also seen that there is evidence that in at least two areas family therapy practice makes some impact upon them. However, we have also noted the ambivalence that the contexts of work and the nature of psychotherapy bring to a wider social engagement in these matters. In part this relates to the overall themes of the last three chapters: family therapy has a regulatory function and therefore may be classed as 'evolutionary' rather than 'revolutionary' in the way it relates to social policy. At the end of the day, most family therapists have clinical not political skills which might explain why in Britain family therapy has not had any noticeable part in government initiatives designed to end social exclusion. Once more we return to one of our themes: family therapists relieve individual and family suffering and in their work they cannot always attend to the social origins of this suffering. Sometimes, helping families 'cope' with living in an unjust society is the best they can do. This chapter has also introduced the political dimension to family therapy practice: only each individual therapist can reach their own view about how much they wish to work with social justice in their daily work. This social justice takes us back to the 'self' of the therapist. Not surprisingly, it is therefore the 'self', and family therapy's uncertainty about this, that we turn to in the next chapter.

Chapter 7
Where is the individual?

To study the self is to forget the self.
To forget the self is to be enlightened by all things.

Dogen

Introduction

In this chapter we wish to develop the psychological dimension of our analysis of family therapy. This is not, however, as transparent a task as it might at first appear, primarily because many of the psychological criticisms of family therapy could be classed as part of the 'critical psychology' perspective whose general comments about the value and difficulties of psychotherapy have already been subsumed in the feminist, social constructionist and post-modern analyses. Moreover, critical approaches to psychological treatment have applauded the social contextual assumptions of family therapy rather than criticised it (Hare-Mustin & Marecek, 1997).

Nevertheless there is an area of theory and practice in which a psychological perspective can contribute towards a review of this contextual therapy. That is the role of the 'self' and of the 'individual'. The individual and the 'self' in its development and manifestation have after all been the focus of experimentation, theorising and practice since psychology's origins. Indeed, only a cursory look at family therapy texts reveals that there are *assumptions* about individuals that are rarely explored in depth. An example is the inclusion in Dallos and Draper's (2000) book of a chapter entitled 'Ideas that keep knocking at the door' which refers to 'emotions' and 'attachment', both of which are largely presumed to be features of individuals. In this chapter we will therefore expand on the struggle that family therapy has had in relation to its view of individuals and selves in its practice. We will develop themes around this issue that have proved pertinent. As in other chapters, we are aware that we can consider some aspects of this issue but cannot provide a definitive overview. We will begin by discussing the 'problem' that historical theory and practice bequeathed to practitioners when it came to self and individual. We will then explore the *paradox* that has continued to underlie the practice of family therapy in relation to self.

Individuals and systems

In Chapter 2 we noted that one of the philosophical difficulties with systems theory was that it tended to reify the family at the expense of the individual. Undoubtedly, the interactional elements of family therapy ensured that early practitioners theorised about interaction and frequently *ignored* the 'self'. Haley, for instance, asserted that therapy sessions should concentrate upon behaviours and interactions rather than on how individuals *felt* about problems (Haley, 1976). Equally the Milan school sought to construct a therapy that explored meanings and family rules rather than individual experiences (Palazzoli et al., 1978). When family therapists considered how the individual fitted into their therapy, they constantly returned to the differences of their ideas from those of individual therapists. So Willi (1987) asked:

> How do systems therapists' ideas of an individual differ from those of individually oriented therapists? Systems therapists are less interested in stable personality structures than in the contextual variability of a person's behaviour. (1987: 429)

This attitude to the individual led Haley to justify his view that 'interviewing one person is to begin with a handicap' (1978: 10).

There were a number of deeper arguments for this view of the individual. Bateson (1972), for instance, argued that a systemic perspective and a perspective that accepted the existence of a 'self' were mutually incompatible. He notes that even though human beings are part of groups and cultures that are systemic, the nature of individual consciousness of *necessity* blinds the individual to this systemic nature. Others such as Watzlawick et al. (1974) add that one aspect of this systemic 'double bind' is that an individual might think his or her behaviour is an expression of self but *it is also* a communication to others. Ultimately this systemic tussle with the individual points out that *consciousness of self* often delimits *consciousness of relationship*. Because of this various systemic writers have tried to use methods that introduce consciousness of relationship into family therapy theory (Atkinson & Heath, 1990; Keeney, 1983). But other family therapists have been inclined to criticise the idea that systems theory relegated the individual in this way. Nichols (1987) commented that:

Most discussions of change in family therapy are muddled by confusion over who changes. Therapists don't change, systems don't change: people change. To be more exact, therapists initiate change, systems undergo change, but individual persons must make changes ... change ultimately works through individuals within the system. (1987: 38)

Speed (1987) also noted that:

an aspect of many family therapists' interactional thinking has been the relegation of the individual and individual therapy to the bottom of the league. (1987: 235)

Indeed she disagrees with the proposal that 'the context of interaction ... entirely determines the individual's behaviour, rather than anything internal to the individual' (1987: 235). This, she states, is 'the empty box theory of personality' which is clearly wrong because we all have 'a sense of self, emotions, memories, personal history, feelings' (1987: 235).

As family therapy has continued to evolve these critical voices have increased. They have argued that family therapists have rarely considered the self of the client within a family setting, and also have frequently forgotten about the self of the therapist as well. Hildebrand (1998), for instance, has crystallised the view that the family therapist's interactional perspective has ignored the self of the therapist in her book *Building bridges*. She writes:

In the early stages of its development one way of distinguishing family therapy theory and practice from other psychotherapies was by the lack of focus on the person of the systemic therapist. ... I would now suggest that the time has come to reappraise the role of the self and its significance in clinical practice. (1998: 1)

What is clear from this short discussion is that integrating self and system is a complex theoretical and pragmatic task, one to which family therapy comes with a history of prejudices and uncertainties. Before we explore these in more depth we wish to consider how other therapeutic approaches analyse the 'self'.

Self and the psychotherapies

Clearly most if not all psychotherapies assume that their purpose is to bring about some change in the client's 'self' (Erwin, 1997). The definitions of this self are, however, various and the changes intended to this self are equally various. Here we can therefore only discuss the major conceptions of self which have had an influence upon family therapy's development (Baldwin, 1987, provides a fuller description). Parfit (1987) provides a useful orientation to this topic. He divides theories of self into two types: ego and bundle theories. He asserts that ego (his use of the term bears no relation to Freud's use of the term but rather is a more 'common sense' use) theorists believe in a persistent self who is the subject of experiences. The existence of this ego self explains the sense of unity and continuity of experience. Bundle theorists (named after Hume's 'bundle of sensations'), on the other hand, deny there is such a thing as self. They state that the apparent unity is just a collection of ever changing experiences tied together by such relationships as a physical body and memory. Such theories have a link with 'Eastern' views of the self (Brazier, 1995; Rosenbaum, 1998). Interestingly, ego theories seem to represent our everyday lives and thus we all naturally tend to hold onto them. So when we ask ourselves 'who am I?', we would tend to reply with a statement about our qualities, experiences and even essences. Rosenbaum and Dyckman (1995) sum up the dilemma very well:

> There is a pervasive tendency to assume that we each have some core identity that underlies our existence and defines each of us. However, as soon as one assumes that a substantive identity exists, which has an intrinsic essence separate from its interactions with the world, then a gap arises between 'I' and 'it,' 'me' and 'you,' 'self' and 'system.'
> (1995: 28)

Despite this 'gap' most therapies assume a coherent 'ego' self when they consider the self at all.

Ego theories

The psychodynamic self

Although family therapy has rejected many of psychodynamic therapy's ideas there have remained curious examples of the psychodynamic conception of the self being reflected in family therapy. The self is often discussed in terms of the difference of it being felt from the 'inside' (e.g. 'embodied') and experienced within the context of relationship (e.g. 'embedded'). Nichols (1987) indeed utilised the 'self psychology' of another psychoanalytical thinker, Kohut, which itself functions as a link between a systemic sense of self and a Freudian one. Clearly the history of psychodynamic thought has produced a number of theories of self. Some of these originated in Freud's ideas of the 'conflicted' self, which contained the ego, id and super ego. But others such as those prevalent in the object relations school followed by attachment theorists have variously proposed that the internal self contains 'objects' such as significant carers.

Within this assumption, the 'self' is said to 'split' itself into perceptions of 'good' and 'bad' objects. Later variations of this school have proposed ideas about 'false' and 'true' selves (Winnicott, 1960) – an idea that was important in Laing's work (1965).

We have referred to another variation within psychodynamic therapy already: this is the 'self psychologists' of whom Kohut is one. Kohut's (1977) view is that at the core of human nature is not a raging Freudian id but a more or less insecure self, striving for fulfilment and longing for acceptance and admiration. Kohut also disagrees with the basic Freudian vision that psychological maturation proceeds to independence via a separation from the family. He rejects the view that a mature adult is one who stands alone. He argues that we never outgrow our need for self-affirmation and thus a network of loving and supportive relationships is crucial throughout life. Hence to retain psychological 'health' we cannot escape from being a member of a system that is larger than ourselves. Kohut's model can be considered either an object relations theory or an intrapsychic one as the 'self-object' is not real (Nichols, 1987).

Erwin (1997) has argued that the various psychodynamic formulations of 'self' compound metaphysical distinctions with contradictory definitions. Here our focus is on how frequently these conceptions have been imported into family therapy. Schwartz (1995), for example, works in therapy with the various 'parts' of his clients. In a sense he helps clients understand which parts of their 'selves' come from a family of origin experiences and then he applies systems theory to the relationships between these parts. His method of working has been acclaimed as an 'integrative' one as it combines individual and systems therapy (Nichols & Schwartz, 1998). Equally involved in integrating ideas from individual and family systems is Byng-Hall (1995a; 1995b). His work proposes that 'attachments lie at the heart of family life' (1995b: 45) and that therapy needs to ensure that these secure bonds are fostered within and outside therapy. Clearly, 'attachments' happen for individuals who have a 'self' that can attach.

In more recent years family therapy has undergone a much vaunted *rapprochement* with psychoanalysis (Luepnitz, 1997; McFadyen, 1997) which, amongst other developments, has led to family therapists returning to 'useful' ideas such as transference and fragmented selves (Flaskas, 1997; Woodcock, 2001). Paterson (1996) indeed argues that family therapists need to acknowledge that they work with the 'relational self' rather than the 'autonomous self', which is what psychodynamic therapists work with. Before we return to conceptions of 'relational self' and before we move onto humanistic ideas of self, it is relevant to point out the two elements that the psychodynamic description of self introduces to the psychotherapeutic world. Firstly, it establishes the requirement of the therapist to relate to the self of the other (e.g. the client) and secondly it emphasises the self of the therapist as relevant to the therapeutic endeavour (e.g. note the concepts of transference and counter-transference).

The humanistic self

In this section we will take Rogers' work as an example of a humanistic approach to self in therapy. Rogers has been generally neglected by family therapists (Anderson, 2001; Bott, 2001). Now is not the time for a discussion of the relevance of this model to family therapy practice. However, Rogers added both a new element to self in therapy and created a premium on *relatedness* by his emphasis on empathy. Firstly, Rogers saw therapy as a means to enable the client to reach a *human potential*. In a paper originally written in 1961, Rogers (1990) outlines his view that therapy should enable individuals to be more open to experience, increasingly aware of existential living, to have greater trust in their own abilities and a greater creativity. The whole context of Rogers' work was to contribute to human freedom and individuality. The 'self', in other words, could develop by becoming more accessible to emotions and more aware of its needs. Erwin (1997) summarises this:

> one other idea that Rogers makes important use of is that of 'self-actualisation', ... in most if not all individuals there are growth forces, tendencies toward self-actualisation, that may act as the sole motivation for therapy. (1997: 44)

Secondly, Rogers emphasised empathy as essential in the therapeutic encounter. This basic foundational skill is the skill *par excellence* of client-centred therapy and has received scant attention in the family therapy literature (Street, 1994). We highlight it here as the skill of empathically following an individual in a family session is a very complex process that requires four activity processes by the 'self' of the therapist:

1 The therapist requires emotional openness and receptivity – it involves an emotional suspension of self-awareness ('this is me') in order to be to awareness of the other ('this is what it is like for the other person').

2 It requires an oscillation between thinking and feeling. This involves a shift from experiencing to observing; moving between feeling *with* the individual to thinking *about* the individual.

3 It requires an oscillation between 'awareness of the other' and an 'awareness of the family'. Each family member's internal frame of reference will interconnect with all the others to form a composite reality.

4 It requires an oscillation between the family's composite 'reality' and the observable (to the therapist) interactive patterns that are present both in and outside of the room.

Interestingly these humanistic ideas about self in therapy have been rarely addressed by family therapists who have rather lamely suggested that family therapists can be 'empathic' with systems rather than with individuals (Wilkinson, 1992).

'Bundle' theories of self

An interpersonal self: a temporary 'self'

Implicit in a number of variations of family therapy and other therapies is that there is indeed a 'relational' self (Paterson, 1996). This is summarised by the assertion that 'my perception of you is affected by your perception of me, which is affected by my perception of you'. But at its core this perspective follows the original path of Sullivan (1954) who held a view of 'self' which also assumes there is a stable entity that constitutes the self. The only difference is that here the self is reflected in the appraisals of others. The self becomes a repository of reflections derived from our interpersonal matrix. Selves must also multiply in that the other's self is also a reflected appraisal, and that our selves are reflections of reflections.

Although these ideas were made popular in some of Laing's writing (1972) they pose a number of conceptual problems. In interactional terms the 'self' becomes lost in a maze of mirrors as does the 'other'. Moreover, the reflections imply a 'thing' that can be reflected *even if this thing is behaviour or interpretations of behaviour.* Hence, the interpersonal frame which might look like a 'bundle' theory of self, in fact remains an 'ego'. The way out of this dilemma is to acknowledge that it is a fiction to see an object as existing independent of its context. As postmodernist and feminist writers have argued (e.g. Jordan, Miller, Stiver & Surrey, 1991) in a lived world, objects exist only in relationship. Here, however, the conception of self goes beyond this description of the interpersonal self.

A systemic self

As we have mentioned, Bateson (1972) is perhaps the most erudite proponent of a view that the self is systemic. In his famous description of mind in the 'tree–eye–brain–muscles–axe–stroke–tree' system (1972: 317), Bateson argues that the mind is immanent in the whole system. We might assume that for Bateson 'mind' is a close approximation to what might otherwise be called the 'active self' (or agent). This view has been frequently assumed to be the sort of 'self' to which family therapists have referred. There is a marked difference in this idea of self from previous ones. Here the self is not just 'in relationship' but constituted 'by relationship'. Willi (1987) develops this view by arguing that rather than relationships hampering self-development, self-development can only occur *in relationship*. He presents an ecological model in which self-realisation relies on relations with others in order to make it real. Rosenbaum and Dyckman (1995) point out that once we realise that objects exist only in the context of relationship, we implicitly are saying that there is no such 'thing' as self and no such 'thing' as other and that 'identity' is always fluid, lacking any core essence. 'Self' and 'other' have no independent, permanent existence other than their appearance in relationships that are 'constantly arising in immediate experience in the present moment' (1995: 29). The notion of a 'full' self promotes an illusion that we are somehow separate from what we do. However, asserting that this is so cannot escape the fact that individuals feel and think, which are experienced as activities residing in an individual mind. Varela, Thompson and Rosch (1991) attempted to avoid this difficulty in the theory of the systemic self by stating that cognition or self-awareness is embodied enaction. Thus returning to a 'bundle' theory they state that the self does not exist apart from these enactions. When self and experience are united in embodied action, the difficulty is resolved, since there is then no separation between self and experience, and therefore no need to 're-present' experience 'out there' to a self 'in here.' When the self is immersed in the immediacy of the moment, the separateness of 'self' and 'other' drops away: there is neither 'knower' nor 'known,' but only knowing. As contexts change, 'self' changes or, more precisely, self-in-context is a constantly changing process. Bohart (1993) has made this existential experience, this total immersion in the actions of being alive, an essential prerequisite of any psychotherapy. Equally, this version of the self is replicated in many post-modern texts (Gergen, 1991; 1999). Thus the systemic view of self is that:

(a) Self is not a thing, but a process.
(b) Self is not unitary, but the product of multiple drafts.
(c) Self is not an accrual of experience but an ongoing, ever-changing manifestation of potentiality.
(d) Self is undivided activity.
(e) Self is self-in-action and as such is always contextual.
(f) Self is embodied action.

Family therapy therefore ascribes to a 'bundle' theory of self. Rosenbaum and Dyckman (1995), for instance, say:

> If we conceive of the self as the entire nexus of potentialities, with certain ones being manifested at this particular time, then changing the self requires no act of subtracting from the self, adding to the self, or 'rewiring of the pathways.' Self-changes require a turning, a rediscovery of potentialities that have always been there but have been temporarily excluded. The self as an accumulation of experience is a prison; the self as empty, as shimmering potentiality, is a prism that, depending on its positioning, gives forth many different colours. (1995: 36)

Clearly such a conception of self is both radical and fits a therapy that works with meanings and relationships (including narrative postmodern techniques).

Unfortunately, there are certain difficulties with this version of the bundle theory of self. Firstly, it simply does not accord with most people's everyday reality. For most of us the 'self' is a relatively stable thing which abides within our bodies and which is made up of memories, intentions *and* relationships. Just as systems theory can be seen as taking away free will (Morton, 1987), this systemic description of self can be seen as taking away all that is unique about who we are. This poses a difficulty for therapists who might wish to free individuals from a view about *who they are* which is experienced as restricting whilst at the same time denying there is a self to liberate (Dell, 1986) Secondly, although this bundle theory is intellectually exciting, it does not resolve some of the old philosophical problems about definitions of self (Erwin, 1997). For instance, it is a common error to locate self/other dichotomies solely in language. But experience is a non-verbal process. The self therefore is both linguistic and non-linguistic: a dichotomy that is hard to reconcile within this systemic theory of self. Lastly, in practice, most family therapists rarely maintain such a view about self. We have already referred to those who have reasserted a traditional idea of self and we will go on to outline the two areas in which such formulations have become significant. It is therefore likely that the systemic version of a bundle theory of self is most appealing to family therapists who have an interest in applying Eastern descriptions of self to therapy, rather than those within the mainstream of practice.

Family therapy's return to an 'ego' self

Having explored the origins of family therapy's view about the self, the various psychotherapeutic versions of self and the complexities of a systemic version of self, we wish to note two areas in which family therapy appears to have reverted to an 'ego' version of self. These are in the areas of individual work with clients and in the self-development of the therapist.

Family therapy with individuals

In recent years systemic therapists have become increasingly willing to work with individuals and there is even a discussion of the need to 're-discover the individual' (Steinglass, 1991). Indeed in Chapter 6 we noted research which showed how common working with individuals is in family therapy practice. Moreover, the professionalisation of family therapy has increased the pressure for family therapy to present itself as being equal to other psychotherapies. Thus it needs to be able to do what they do, which is of course predominantly to work with individuals.

Jones (1993) has speculated that because the systemic approach is now sufficiently mature to relax it is able to open itself up to a wide range of influences and be confident about those clients who do not seem to respond positively to their methods. Thus she suggests that individual therapy might be seen as a new and appropriate response rather than simply a return to the past. However, she retains a systemic scepticism when she states that in individual therapy, the systemic therapist will have to take into account those relationship phenomena 'more thoroughly explored by psychoanalytically-orientated therapists' (Jones, 1993: 136). Her view is that the greater intimacy of the one-to-one relationship, the absence of 'significant' others from the session and the greater frequency and duration of meetings, the client's feelings for and expectations of the therapist may well require more attention than they usually receive in the systemic family therapy. She states:

> systemic therapists may at times decide to work with individual clients, for reasons of that seem persuasive. They should bear in mind, though, that systemic therapy, developed while working with families, does not have a well articulated theory of individual functioning, nor

has much thinking been done about technique in individual systemic work. A simple extrapolation of theories and skills developed in family settings is unlikely to be good enough; it would imply that systems family therapy possesses a universal theory and technique, while disregarding the theories and skills of therapists much more familiar with the individual work than systems therapists tend to be. (1993: 137)

This does not mean that Jones does not see some value to individual work undertaken by systemic therapists. She considers that systemic thinking and circular interviewing, introduce certain possibilities. The therapist's questions, comments, focus of discussion, chosen in preference to others have the effect of suggesting to the client a particular world-view. This view naturally includes assumptions about interdependence, the relevance of contexts and the effect of multiple views.

This is also the view promulgated by Jenkins and Asen (1992) about *systemic work with individuals:*

Therapists conduct the first session ... in the sense that significant others could join at any time. Sessions are conducted as if other people were present. It is mainly through the process of interactionally framed questions that therapists define their position. ... Other people are brought into the room as 'ghosts', encouraging the client to consider another's views about his behaviour. (1992: 4)

A rather more developed theory about individual work for family therapists came from Boscolo and Bertrando (1996). These authors see family therapy as being based on the relational world, in which the communicative actions of everyone are linked and recursively connected with a context that lends significance. Hence there is an intimate connection between the relational world and the meanings of actions within individuals. In individual work family therapists should seek to create connections between both the inner and the outer world of an individual. At the same time, the therapist (à la Jenkins and Asen) maintains an interest in the interactive patterns that provide a link between actions, relations, emotions and meanings. In individual systemic therapy, this is expressed through the introduction of 'voices', of 'viewpoints', of 'words' of the third parties that are relevant to the life of the client. The skill of the technique is in psychologically evoking the significant third parties in the life of the patient, mainly through circular questions, and in this way summoning their 'presence' to the context of therapy. Boscolo and Bertrando have given this procedure the name of 'personification of the third party':

> Even in a dyadic relationship, such as exists in individual therapy, one can use circular questions very profitably, particularly when employing 'the personification of the third party' technique. In family therapy, circular questions in general, and triadic ones in particular, have among other things the effect of placing each member of the family in the position of observer of the thoughts, behaviour and emotions of others, creating thus a community of observers. This may be reproduced even in individual therapy as well; significant third parties belonging to either the external or internal ('voices') world are presented, thus creating a 'community' which contributes to the development of different points of view. One of the effects of this method is to challenge the egocentricity: the client is placed in a position of reflective condition and makes hypotheses that take into account the thoughts and emotions of others and not just his own. (1996: 110)

Boscolo and Bertrando (1996) therefore provide a number of reasons for and methods to use in, individual work. What is significant is that their approach assumes that the self is embedded in relationship (a variation of an ego theory) not constituted by relationship (a systemic 'bundle' theory). In this case the aim of therapy is to assist the client in dealing with the potentialities and limitations of their interactive world. It aims to create a different self. The aim is not to move the client towards an experience of selflessness.

One of the criticisms of this approach is that it does not constitute 'family therapy' at all. This view is central to one of Minuchin's (1998) comments about the direction of contemporary family therapy. After observing Karl Tomm conduct an 'internalised other' interview with a mother whose daughter had mental health difficulties, he commented that although this was a valuable technique: 'why [does] this therapy ... not deal directly with family interactions' (1998: 401). Minuchin's view is that this form of systemic therapy misses important opportunities for family members and therapists alike, to observe the interaction of others and to listen to the reflections of others. Many would view these as the *sine qua non* of any family therapy. Essentially, it has proved impossible for family therapists to develop individual work within the theoretical frame of self that they have inherited from their tradition. Yet the individual work they do is clearly informed by a different concept of self than that which most other psychotherapies hold. This new conception often contains ideas about self in relation as well as ideas about relationships constraining the self. Such elements, which may or may not constitute an ego theory of self, also exist when we turn to the person of the therapist and the idea of self-development.

Development and the use of self

In the opening sections of this chapter, we noted that family therapy had ideologically avoided the concept that family therapists needed to undergo therapy to train in their field (Hildebrand, 1998). Yet it has also been true that there has been an undercurrent that has always bordered on this assumption. Thus, for instance, Simon (1989) noted that dissonance and confluence between therapist's life cycle and client life cycle might cause difficulties for the 'treatment system'. Moreover, there has been a currency for the concept of 'trigger families' within the field for some time. This concept was crucial in Bowen's description of how he 'differentiated himself from his family of origin' in a paper which was so radical within the family therapy world that it had to be published anonymously (Bowen, 1972). Indeed, British and American authors have variously developed the term 'use of self' (Baldwin & Satir, 1987; Lieberman, 1980) which includes attention to the self of the therapist within the therapeutic encounter. It would therefore be more accurate to say that within family therapy there has always been a strong, though less widely recognised, tradition that has assumed that the therapist's self needs attention and that it is a fairly static entity that can be observed (by supervisors) and changed (by supervisees). A concise but comprehensive definition of the term 'use of self' proves elusive. This is because the therapist's 'use of self' is a multifaceted and individualised phenomenon. Some therapists (influenced by person-centred counselling) would see it is a process of accepting one's self as a fellow human being who offers something that is more than mere technical professional expertise. For others, being aware of and acknowledging personal vulnerabilities and capabilities provides a personal clarity that informs the therapist about which parts of the self to share and which to withhold in order to retain health and integrity. For others, use of self refers to the straightforward process of reflecting and sharing one's own thoughts about what is happening in the therapy room. However, implicit in the idea of the use of self is that awareness of 'who you are' can help a therapist decide which clients he or she will be able to serve best. More crucially, it might alert a therapist to which families, because of personal issues, should be avoided. To understand and consequently use one's self, therefore, a therapist must consider various factors. Some of these influential factors are one's temperament, personal and professional experiences and realities, theoretical orientation, and, of course, each interpersonal context. Self disclosure has also often demonstrated how therapists use their 'selves'.

Disclosure and the use of self

A study of the variety of the use of self-styles used by family therapists (Shadley, 1987) presents a very interesting continuum of self-disclosure styles that allows for a fuller discussion of this issue.

1 **Intimate interaction.** Here the self is shared through both verbal and non-verbal expressions of therapeutic reactions. References to present or past personal issues are likely.
2 **Reactive response.** In this category there is a typical expression of both non-verbal and verbal feelings of emotional connectedness within the therapeutic relationship. Generally, however, there is no verbalisation of personal life details or parallels.
3 **Controlled response.** Here the therapist is inclined to maintain a slight distance by limiting self-disclosures to past experiences, non-verbalised feelings, anecdotes or literary parallels.
4 **Reflective feedback.** Here the exposure of self is through questioning or challenging families and by giving impressions. The therapist seldom shares personal information or strong emotional reactions.

These four descriptions indicate distinctions among styles and they seem to form a continuum from most to least personal self-disclosure. Use of such a continuum implies that, depending on the context, therapists may actually use a combination or variety of styles. It is clear, however, that each therapist had a preferred position on the continuum. Shadley's (1987) research also indicated that there were self-disclosure differences with different groups of therapists. For instance, therapists with less than seven years' experience were more likely to adopt a controlled or reflective feedback style. Gender also correlated with these differences. Interestingly personal transitions and life events were the most likely to induce therapeutic style change. Of these circumstances, having children and experiencing the death of a parent were particularly significant. These changes of style did not move in uniform ways: for some these experiences led to more distancing strategies whilst others became more emotionally open with clients. Shadley (1987) concluded that theoretical orientation was only one of several critical factors contributing to a therapist's use of self. Gender, the amount of clinical experience and significant life events also played important roles.

This study, which can very easily be criticised methodologically, nevertheless does allow us to place all the discussion of 'use of self' in some framework. It does question whether some of the discussion about 'use of self' is more about therapeutic technique rather than considering self-disclosure as a process. A curious outcome of accepting this continuum is that each person is entitled to only one version of his or her 'therapist self.' Yet we would assume from the systemic version of self that in different contexts, different therapists' 'selves' will be called upon – namely, those that best fit the experience and frame of the clients being served. Haber (1990) has pointed out that different selves are likely to emerge from, and be maintained by, certain patterns of client/therapist interaction over time. However, what this discussion by Haber highlights is that increasingly family therapy is assuming that the therapist's self needs to be considered in training.

Personal growth and training

Nichols (1987) has indicated that in family therapy's early days, when there was a focus on interactions and homeostasis, there was not so much resistance as *disinterest* to the consideration of personal growth within the field. Apart from the notable exceptions of Whitaker (1967) and Bowen (1976) personal growth has tended to be an issue that has been paid scant regard, particularly when we compare family therapy with the individual therapies. Bowen argues:

> I believe and teach that the family therapist usually has the very same problems in his own family that are present in families he sees professionally and that he has the responsibility to define himself in his own family if he is to function adequately in his professional work. (1976: 467)

This 'wounded healer' view (Miller & Baldwin, 1987) of the family therapist has not often been delineated in family therapy. Nor have the implications of this for training been routinely explored. Indeed when this issue has been raised, the tendency has been to argue that training is not therapy. This argument lead Aponte (1994) to suggest that although this dichotomy is true, training cannot be effective if it does not address 'personal issues primarily to improve their [trainees'] performance as therapists' (1994: 5).

There has therefore been an increasing attentiveness to the fact that personal awareness is necessary for therapeutic practice. Therapists work in a context that is gendered, discriminatory, rhetorical, political and obviously unavoidable. The effects of this operate at micro and macro levels. At the micro level therapists have individual and familial influences; at the macro level they are influenced by politics and by the influence of ongoing societal forces that include factors of racism and sexism as discussed in Chapter 6. These, then, are some of the parameters of personal growth within therapeutic practice; attention to the development of self also raises another facet. Within the need for personal awareness, there is also a need for a professional and a personal support system. The consequences of not providing this are cynicism, burn out, illness, retreat from practice, disempowerment and poor personal relationships (Street & Rivett, 1996).

Within a framework of therapist development, personal growth should be planned and based on intentional questioning of the self. It requires an acceptance of doubt. It indicates a rigorous curiosity which leads to an ability to be reflective about one's 'self'; an ability which is integrative with the individual's general functioning. It is assumed that these processes will occur allowing for the development of capacities that result in the person adopting good practice as a therapist. A systemic version of this practice would imply that this process is further characterised by a watchfulness of one's self in interaction and therefore essentially seen as being developed within relationships. The current literature on how to develop these qualities (Aponte, 1992; 1994; Hildebrand, 1998) suggests a number of methods:

1 **By engaging in activities with the self**. These may involve writings, maintaining diaries, keeping observations of one's 'self'. These would be at the recorded level. At the unrecorded level there are the activities related to spiritual practice and autobiographical study (Rivett & Street, 2001; Street, 1989).
2 **Within close relationships**. Activities in and around our intimate and friendship relationships – how they are formed and maintained. This may be through consultations with systemic practitioners or in separate settings.
3 **Family**. This will involve activity connected to our families of origin and the families which we inhabit now (Bowen, 1972). Again the furtherance of this reflection on self might be achieved through systemic consultations.
4 **Colleagues**. Here in the work setting the therapist would be inviting feedback from co-workers. In teams family trees might be collectively drawn. Once more this aspect of 'self in relation' could be explored in peer support groups, consultations or in less formal settings.
5 **Clients**. Clients clearly allow us to learn about ourselves as they struggle with their own processes. Here the therapist can reflect

upon their own 'self' in supervision, live consultation, or by relying on feedback from the client family.

6 **Therapy.** This is a formal approach to undertaking personal growth in which we receive those services that we also attempt to provide.

In regard to the later method of self-development, one of the essential issues is the nature of therapy that family therapists should seek. In an American study, Deacon, Kirkpatrick, Wetchler and Neidner (1999) found in a sample of 178 family therapists that 89 per cent had received some form of personal therapy since entering the profession of which some 34 per cent reported that their first experience was during their post-graduate training. The most frequently indicated theoretical orientation of the therapy received was psychodynamic (45.4%), cognitive (29.6%) and emotion-focused (21.7%). These family therapists rarely included their children or families of origin in their therapy and only included their spouses or partners 24 per cent of the time. This contrasts with a British survey (Street & Rivett, 1996) in which 54 per cent had undergone therapy of some kind but only 9 per cent had received family therapy. This rather paradoxical finding might merely be replicating the theme of this chapter: family therapists remain uncertain about addressing the self when they practise a therapy that also rarely addresses the 'self'.

Conclusion

This chapter has explored family therapy's approach to the self and to individual work from a systemic perspective. We have been unable to expand in depth on theories of self in therapy, but we have shown that despite a potential 'articulated theory of individual functioning' (Rosenbaum & Dyckman, 1995) within a bundle theory of self, most family therapy is predicated on a more traditional idea of self. We have also shown that in the evolution of family therapy there has been a tendency to emphasise its similarity to such theories rather than its difference. Thus in both individual work and in training settings, ideas about self-development and the stability of the self have been increasing. Similar to our conclusions in other chapters, we suggest that family therapy has a *fractured nature*; by this we mean that there are continual conflicts between theory and practice, history and present, promulgators and practitioners. It is also paradoxical because the individual practitioner may need to hold onto different positions at the same time (which is merely a reflection of family therapy's belief in 'double description'). A further source of *fracturing* is that of the empirical basis for family therapy practice, which is the subject of the next chapter.

Chapter 8
Does it work?

With all your science can you tell how it is, and whence it is that light comes into the soul?

Thoreau

Research and family therapy

One of the distinguishing features of the early pioneers of family therapy was their belief that they were establishing empirical evidence for their methods. This was shown in the way they described their work. In particular they were keen to ensure that family therapy recognised the need to prove its validity in contrast to psychoanalysis. For example, in a satirical piece Jay Haley stated:

There has been surprisingly little scientific investigation of what actually occurs during psychoanalytic treatment. (1986: 7)

Although this attitude that 'we are different from' was exaggerated in order to make a point, it does highlight the view of all the early protagonists, that family therapy was claimed to be based on a form of empirical enquiry.

In his essay 'Development of a theory: a history of a research project' (1981b), Jay Haley described how this particular team evolved. The research team began when Bateson, then a respected anthropologist who had settled in America, requested some funding to study human communication. He collected under him a disparate number of researchers who were also concerned with human communication and who later became established family therapy writers. These included Haley himself, Weakland and later Jackson. This team eventually observed a number of families who had a schizophrenic member and formulated the theory of the 'double bind' (Haley, 1981b; Bateson, 1972). Although subsequent studies have severely criticised this concept, it undoubtedly influenced the communication school of family therapy and led as a development to many MRI techniques. It also clearly influenced the Milan school, whose work *Paradox and counter-paradox* (Palazzoli et al., 1978) verifies the connection. The early work of Lyman Wynne, Theodore Lidz, Salvador Minuchin, Carl Whitaker, Virginia Satir etc. were all associated with research projects. From these authors distinctive schools of family therapy developed. The early workers therefore at that time considered themselves to be, if not empirically based, then very closely associated with the research process.

In retrospect there was much to critique from a methodological perspective in this early work. The research experience was largely theory driven and therefore was biased towards proving theory, rather than constructing theory from data. Indeed Haley's own description of the emergence of the 'double bind' theory acknowledges that it was based upon previous investigations of the behaviour of otters, popular cinema, the training of dogs for the blind and 'the utterance of a schizophrenic patient' (1981b: 4). Nevertheless, what was unique about research at this time was that it established a tradition of studying communication where verbatim transcripts were often reported. They therefore could make some claim to being empirical. Whether or not this tradition has continued is very much a matter of debate.

The process of research and the development of therapy

At this juncture it is worthwhile considering the process by which research aids the construction of therapeutic theory and clinical practice. At the core of this there is a need for a view of how one should move from clinical innovation to research and back to clinical practice. The starting point has to begin in the therapist wanting to provide a helpful and satisfactory outcome for clients and we should acknowledge immediately that in the last analysis the client will be the sole arbiter of that. From reflecting on and observing clinical practice, the therapist, sometimes aware of theoretical development, can go on to perfect a technique or place together a set of techniques that can be described as an innovation. This can result in new approaches to traditional clinical problems, or the application of therapy to new areas. The full empirical investigation of a new therapeutic approach should be preceded by a phase of case studies and small-scale research aimed at developing a theory and practice of the technique. Salkovskis (1995) describes the process of clinical development as an 'hourglass' model in which the initial ideas about techniques are tested through single case studies. At this stage it is possible to investigate the matter only with less stringent methodological criteria that reflect the exploratory nature of the work and usually the clinician/researcher's constraints of time and resources. However, once the initial development is complete there is a requirement for research that conforms to the more rigorous standards of inquiry – the narrowing of the hourglass. Salkovskis notes that at this point considerations of internal validity take priority, recognising the fact that this then will raise questions about generalisability to other client groups and the relationship of the approaches to other therapeutic activities. These are questions that can then be answered in a subsequent phrase of research where methodological criteria are again not so stringent – a widening out of the hourglass. This cycle of testing of an approach can be taken further in a process involving several well-recognised and distinct phases. For example, evaluation frequently starts by comparing the new approach with a no-treatment control group and then later with an established treatment procedure. Only at the later stage does it involve more refined analysis such as varying the components of the treatment to establish which are necessary and sufficient and which variations enhance outcome. Later in the research cycle comes the question of comparing two reasonably well-optimised approaches and later still come questions about patient or therapist characteristics that significantly influence the effectiveness of one approach. Clearly a body of research of this nature takes a considerable time to accumulate and few of the psychotherapies have programmatically taken on this full cycle. In this respect family therapy is no different to most schools of psychotherapy. However, family therapy only seems to be at the beginning of the process. Although the reviewers and organisers of the field have described the field well, the general impression is of a field whose research activity is at an early chaotic phase. Naturally in the process of therapeutic theory development, it is unlikely that this pathway will be followed exactly; however, considering matters in this way does offer a plan of the process. This then offers any technique, approach or model a framework for evaluating where it stands in its own development. Unfortunately this type of theoretical reflection would appear to be missing from some parts of the family therapy endeavour.

The philosophy of research in family therapy

Despite the importance of research there continue to be large divisions within the field about the value of considering research at all. In their review Gurman, Kniskern and Pinsof (1986) summarised this issue as one of *epistemology*, by which they meant that the philosophical basis upon which the research question is based. Gurman *et al.* noted that since family therapy relies upon systems theory (and at that time particularly second-order cybernetics) it therefore posits the idea of multiple realities. This view stands in contrast to a positivistic assumption that the researcher can take a position on reality and study it from an outside (and hence 'truer') perspective. Gurman *et al.* (1986) therefore argued that research if done well lends itself to the dominant philosophy of family therapy. However, there are those who argue that research into the systemic properties of phenomena is not possible; Cecchin, Lane & Ray (1994) for example make the point that standard experimental designs assume the ability to control for different variables. However, a systemic perspective is built upon the belief that A influences B, which influences C, and therefore the researcher cannot control for all these variables and hence the research process is inherently flawed. Over the years a number of writers have maintained this position and Cecchin, Lane & Ray (1994) have argued quite clearly against the possibility of researching their therapy at all. This 'anti-research' attitude is clearly present in a part of the family therapy community and it highlights an uncertainty in the field about this issue.

Gurman *et al.* (1986) nevertheless believe that the many critics of positivism misunderstand the differences between the approaches to science and research. They note that researchers acknowledge the bias of their techniques but seek to minimize these:

> Despite the fervour of the arguments raised recently about the 'old' and 'new' epistemologies, the chasm between the two may not be as great as has been perceived. (1986: 569)

Indeed the authors recognise the value of this debate:

> Perhaps the major implication of all this recent philosophic ferment in the family therapy field is that there lurks a genuine danger for a field that has always creatively and productively challenged established tradition and that uncritical and unreflecting yielding up to traditional thinking and practice in the research domain may stifle the emergence of alternative methods of systemically coming to 'know' the mechanisms of change in family therapy. (1986: 569)

One of the consequences of this ferment, as in many other social sciences, has been a shift to the development of qualitative research methods within practitioner groups. The historical antagonism between proponents of qualitative methods and quantitative methods has prevented recognition of the benefits to be gained by employing both methods. Increasingly, however, family therapy researchers have begun to recognise the value of a multi-method approach in bridging the current gaps in theory, research and practice, Sells, Smith & Moon (1996) show the relative merits of integrating both quantitative and qualitative methods in family therapy research by illustrating how the two methods can iteratively build upon each other to offer information that neither can provide alone. By using such data it may then be possible to construct 'low-level' theories on process research that can set the stage for outcome research. This approach to research and qualitative methodology has its greatest potential at the first wide part of the 'hourglass' in Salkovskis' (1995) schema. The use of qualitative methods in family therapy research has only just begun (Burck, Frosh, Strickland-Clark & Morgan, 1998; Kogan, 1998; Kogan & Gale, 1997) and most of the work to date focuses on client perceptions (Strickland-Clark, Campbell & Dallos, 2000; Sells et al., 1996; Dallos & Hamilton-Brown, 2000). The debate about research and research strategies further demonstrates the separation of the family therapy field with regard to research. There are those who adopt a traditional therapy research perspective; there are those who eschew research and there are those who are willing to be creative and innovative in how they answer the question as to whether they are helpful to their clients.

Clinical judgement in research and clinical practice

Within these arguments about the value of research some issues need to be borne in mind by the clinician. Certainly the role and function of research in clinical practice needs to be recognised but the correspondence between the aims of researchers and practitioners is more apparent than real. Their activities in achieving the aim of shedding light on questions about best practice are not the same. They adopt methods that best address their particular lines of inquiry and although the fields are interested in the same phenomena each is constructed and equipped to answer different questions: one through the application of psychotherapy in its clinical context, the other through the strategy, protocols and methods aimed at obtaining data and testing hypotheses. In this, however, it must be recognised that in the last analysis the requirements of the therapists should predominate.

The priority of researchers in clinical trials is to demonstrate an underlying causal relationship between the intervention and, hopefully, improvement. The researcher requires tight controls on the way the treatment is structured, administered, the way the sample is selected, and how outcomes are assessed. By contrast, the therapist's priority is more pragmatic, being less concerned with the demonstration of the value of specific components and more interested in the process towards the final outcome. Clearly this difference of priorities means that therapy being undertaken in research trials is very different from the therapy that is conducted in the clinical setting.

The skill of the 'good' therapist lies in his or her ability to detect obstacles that would make it difficult to implement a therapy and to make the adaptation necessary to aid the clients. In other words, a therapist should have the capacity to monitor and maintain the therapeutic alliance in the face of all the problems of everyday practice. These are obstacles that the researcher attempts to eliminate. There is a risk that the sophistication of research trials which demand clear causal influence can over-regulate therapy content and under-emphasized the freedom of action available to individual therapists (Roth & Fonagy, 1996). The task of applying research findings to daily clinical practice calls for the capacity on the part of the therapist to see the pertinence of specific discoveries to the individual case. It is in the application of the general to the individual that marks out the skilful clinician.

Clinical effectiveness: outcomes

There are two frameworks for considering the research outcomes of any therapeutic practice. The first is the traditional approach that attempts to prove the value of particular strategies to particular problems. This follows the notion stated most clearly by Bergin in 1971 that the foremost question in the field of psychotherapy research is the specificity question: 'What are the specific effects of specific interventions by specified therapists upon specific symptoms of patient types?' (Bergin, 1971: 245). This is the formulation that underlies the 'clinical effectiveness' model in which the effort is focused on demonstrating the helpfulness or otherwise of particular therapy techniques for particular specified conditions. This approach rests on the assumption that the condition can indeed be specified and that clients 'with' the condition can be treated in similar ways.

The second approach takes a different tack and argues that if research demonstrates anything it is that there are core features of any and every therapeutic practice and these factors are those that should be enhanced and demonstrated by therapists. This position leads to the view that it is the similarities in therapeutic techniques that are important, not the differences in theoretical orientation. We will consider the first position in this chapter and the second in the following chapter.

There have been a number of excellent reviews of the research literature in recent years (Carr, 2000b; 2000c; Friedlander, 1998; Friedlander, Wildman, Heatherington & Skowron, 1994; Gurman et al., 1986; Pinsof & Wynne, 1995). There has also been a substantial growth in literature looking at which forms of family therapy work with what problem. It must be noted that all outcome research automatically advantages those methods of therapy that can be easily quantified and which can be applied to problems that can also be easily identified and described. This may indeed be the reason that cognitive behavioural therapy has been so well researched and psychoanalysis has not. In the 1995 special edition of *Journal of Marital and Family Therapy,* evidence was provided to justify a number of substantive conclusions (see Pinsof & Wynne, 1995):

1   Marital and family therapy works.
2   Marital and family therapy is not harmful.
3   Marital and family therapy is more efficacious than standard and/or individual treatment for specific conditions (including adult schizophrenia; depressed outpatient women in distressed marriages; marital distress; adult alcoholism and drug abuse; adolescent drug abuse; adolescent conduct disorders; anorexia in young adolescent females; and various chronic physical illnesses in adults and children).
4   There is no scientific data at this time to support the superiority of any particular form of marital or family therapy over any other.
5   Marital and family therapy is not sufficient in itself to treat effectively a variety of severe disorders and problems.

Underlying these conclusions, however, are a number of implications and interpretations concerning how we should define family therapy itself; it is to some of these that we now turn.

The case of 'treating' 'schizophrenia'

One of the important beginnings of family therapy was undoubtedly in the treatment of schizophrenia. Subsequent decades appear to have consolidated the early work. However, on a number of parameters the later studies established the efficacy of a totally different form of family therapy from that considered by the pioneers. All the research reviews available (Burbach, 1996; Fadden, 1998; Goldstein & Miklowitz, 1995) suggest that psychoeducational approaches based upon the *expressed emotion* research (Leff & Vaughn, 1985) are effective in reducing the relapse rates of the patient with schizophrenia. Many of these studies are remarkable for their experimental designs and long-term follow-ups. Goldstein and Miklowitz state:

> There is now convincing evidence that family interventions are more effective than routine care. ... There is also evidence from ... studies that family interventions are more effective over 2-year periods in delaying relapses and improving social functioning than are individual therapies. (1995: 373)

However, in the early period of family interventions into schizophrenia there were differences between the proponents of 'family management' and those of 'family therapy'. Each was critical of the other because of the negative implications that they perceived to be inherent in one another's approach. In some senses family management approaches were a reaction to earlier family therapy models that appeared to imply that there was an identifiable type of family uniquely associated with schizophrenia (Fallon, Pederson & Al-Khayyal, 1986; Terkelsen, 1983). Furthermore, many criticised these family therapy approaches for suggesting implicitly or explicitly that the family has caused schizophrenia, thereby causing a family to feel pain, guilt and anxiety. The family management approach differentiated itself by adopting a non-blaming stance.

Given these two orientations, research then proceeded initially in two directions. The family management school became more interested in the relapse of the condition whilst others attempted to relate family characteristics to the precipitation of schizophrenia. Clear evidence emerged in the relapse work but this soon became clearly related to the development of the expressed emotion concept:

> Families in which significant others, usually parents, expressed strongly critical and/or emotional overinvolved (intrusive) attitudes are at a higher risk for onset of and relapse for schizophrenia. (Goldstein, 1983: 17)

Clearly as Johnstone (1993) has argued, the implications of the family management research also provided some support for the family therapy models. This led to the realisation that the models were not mutually exclusive and they could become integrated. As family therapy models had an impact on the family management process, the anti-psychiatry attitude inherent in some family therapy thinking diminished and the scepticism of the term 'schizophrenia' was placed to one side. The empirical basis of family management and the theoretical basis of family therapy have begun to achieve a degree of complementariness, and as Burbach (1996) has noted there has been a move towards integration.

Fadden (1998) has outlined the current practice in this field: programmes have as their aim the prevention of relapse and improvement in functioning rather than direct amelioration or 'cure' of the condition. All assume that it is useful to regard schizophrenia as an illness that can be more likely to recur when major stress is present. Importantly none regard the family as the cause of schizophrenia but take as their focus the family burden imposed in attempting to care for the ill member. Two factors appear to be protective and additive in their effect: firstly, regular maintenance therapy with a neuroleptic medication, hence the programme is always associated with ongoing medical treatment; secondly, the establishment of a beneficial emotional atmosphere between the patient and relatives. There are several components to intervention programmes:

1 The patient and family members are seen together.
2 The therapist has a non-blaming stance.
3 There is a didactic element regarding the illness and family functioning.
4 A therapeutic orientation broadly behaviourally based and focused on day-to-day family functioning and an emphasis on acquiring practical skills to overcome these difficulties.
5 Issues of communication within the family are addressed.

Fadden (1998) notes how in this area there are a multitude of terms describing programmes that utilise the notion of 'family' but she indicates that it is only the presence of the above components that constitute a psychoeducational intervention. Burbach (1996) has further considered the nature of family management interventions and their relation to systemic family practice in this field. He points out how it has been clearly demonstrated that the family education input does not lead to a reduction of relapse rates directly but it is the existence of all the above (systemic) components that are crucial to success. However, interventions aimed at enhancing family structure and encouraging positive social interaction lead to a decreased relapse rate. Continued contact with the therapy team would appear to enhance effectiveness leading to a more prolonged reduction in relapse rates. The efficacy of intervention in everyday clinical practice remains to be demonstrated, particularly since a substantial proportion of patients no longer live with their families. There is evidence that family intervention programmes may reduce the cost of services largely as a result of reducing in-patient admissions. Such findings have clear implications for the operation of services that Fadden (1998) has considered. The primary one is the ensuring of the adoption of a family focus in routine clinical practice and how this can pose a challenge for mental health services which typically have developed from medical models and institutional systems.

However, even though authors discuss a process of integration between family management and family therapy, it is not as straightforward an integration as might be assumed. Both Fadden (1998) and Burbach and Stanbridge (1998) comment on the need for appropriate training and supervision in the use of these techniques and they identified the centrality of family therapy conceptions to that. However, it is implicit that the training is not of family therapists *per se* or of individuals who are to become family therapists, but of professionals who already work in adult mental health. They argue for *context-specific training*, which may not be as extensive or focused as family therapy training. In certain parts of the country such training has been devised by mental health services for community psychiatric nurses but such training is not integral to the formal training of family therapists. Therefore, employers of family therapists would be correct in assuming that a graduate of a family therapy course has had no specific training or even experience in this critical area. It will only be by prior professional experience that a family therapist is likely to have had even a clinical introduction to this work. Given the likelihood that psychoeducational family interventions will remain within a state-provided mental health provision and that family therapy training will consider its priorities to be different, it is likely that this situation will continue. In fact the current practice pattern is one in which psychoeducational approaches are led by clinical psychologists and nurses rather than by family therapists. This therefore confirms one of the themes in Chapter 5, namely that there are many professionals who implement family therapy techniques but who do not claim to be family therapists. This also introduces another paradox: a form of intervention that is routinely praised as giving evidence for family therapy's effectiveness is rarely part of family therapy training and is rarely practised by family therapists themselves.

Specific effectiveness: behaviour, drugs and other things

Carr (2000b; 2000c) has provided the most thorough review of the clinical effectiveness of family therapy both with adults and with children and adolescents. He notes the conclusion from meta-analyses for child- and adult-focused problems that family therapy is effective in that the average treated case fares better than 70 per cent of untreated controls (Shadish, Montgomery, Wilson, Wilson, Bright & Okwumabua, 1993). This underlines the value of family therapy as a viable intervention strategy. Correctly, Carr goes on to note that such broad conclusions are of limited value for, in addition to such statements, there is a clear need for specific evidence-based statements about which precise types of family-based interventions are most effective with particular types of problems. Carr goes on to outline those researched techniques that are effective in:

- child abuse and neglect;
- conduct problems;
- emotional problems;
- psychosomatic problems.

An example of one of these areas can be provided in the area of childhood behaviour disorders. Within this field of childhood behaviour the Oregon Social Learning Centre has consistently studied family therapy with conduct disorders for the last twenty years (Patterson, 1982). Chamberlain and Rosicky (1995) describe the three major methods that family therapists have used with this group: social learning family therapy; structural family therapy and multi-target ecological treatment. After comparing all studies published between 1988 and 1994 they concluded that these studies provided evidence of the efficacy of such treatments. However, the kind of treatment offered by all these therapies includes a high level of what has been called 'parent training'. This line of treatment has become widely approved, so much so that recent legislation in Britain allows one of the sanctions for delinquency to be the imposition of a 'Parent Training Order' on the youngsters' parents. Once more in this area we return to the definition of what constitutes family therapy. In practice, 'parent training' may have more in common with schools of behavioural treatments than with models of family therapy. Moreover, until research is able to quantify what it is about the therapy that improves the young person's aggression, it is unlikely that family therapists can be confident that they represent the best intervention. Linked to this it is also interesting to note that reviews of the use of family therapy in cases of ADHD state that it

> Increases confidence, reduces stress and improves family relationships ... but much of this research demonstrates reductions in children's non-compliance and aggression rather than in primary or core symptoms of ADHD ... we conclude that the research definitely supports the use of psychostimulant medication. (Estrada & Pinsof, 1995: 421)

The features of this particular area fall in well with Carr's general conclusions and he notes two important features of the 'political' nature of research that have implications for family therapists. Firstly, that managers of healthcare and social facilities are increasingly the motivating force behind the establishment of clinical effective techniques and the decision of which technique to apply is increasingly becoming a non-clinical one. Secondly, in the research the problems are invariably couched in individualistic terms (e.g. 'does the child's behaviour improve?'). Certainly even if the systemic conception has penetrated the therapy world it still has not made any notable impact on the professional and political arena in which family therapists operate.

The principal conclusions from Carr's review are that:

1 Well-articulated family-based interventions have been shown to be effective for a wide range of problems.
2 The interventions are brief and may be offered by a wide range of professionals on an out-patient basis.
3 For many of the interventions treatment manuals have been developed which clinicians in treating individual cases may flexibly use.
4 The bulk of interventions for which there is evidence of effectiveness have been developed within the cognitive, structural and strategic models.

To Carr's list we can add a fifth and important point.

5 That a significant proportion of interventions are provided in combination with other treatment types.

Clearly in the 'real' world of work effective treatment for a whole range of problems involves major elements of a behavioural frame and are provided within a treatment context where other varieties of activities are also ongoing. What is therefore emerging from the research about the efficacy of family therapy is a confirmation of the paradoxes discussed in Chapter 5. From an 'evidence-based' practice perspective, family therapy needs to be part of a larger treatment package and the form of family therapy that might be indicated is one which draws as much from a behavioural and cognitive model as from a systemic one.

Clearly within this sits the recurring problem of how we should define family therapy. Different definitions result in different conclusions in the research. Roy & Frankel (1995), for example, arrive at some different conclusions from those discussed above when they apply a stricter definition – one that does not allow for non-systemic elements. As regards using family therapy with psychosis the authors comment:

> Family therapy appears to be an adjunct to drugs. ... This gives rise to a major methodological problem, namely, how to separate the treatment effects of all the other modalities from those of family therapy. (1995: 79)

Similarly when these authors considered 'delinquent youth' they comment:

> These studies have not provided consistent evidence to support the assumption that there is a relationship between changes in family functioning and behavioural changes in the delinquent youth. (1995: 58)

Roy and Frankel conclude their book with these words:

> Family therapy still operates, to a very large extent, on belief and indirect evidence. The relationship between aetiology and treatment must be demonstrated. Time is upon us to shake loose from antipathy to research. We must move family therapy from an act of faith to a valid scientifically proven therapeutic intervention. (1995: 183)

This confirms the view that controversy remains alive in the question of what is evidence-based family therapy practice. In this chapter we have provided one perspective on this issue. We are neither sceptical nor 'convinced believers'. What we hope we have demonstrated is that in this arena some of the same paradoxes and fractures exist within family therapy theory and practice that have haunted our analysis so far. One particular theme has been that of training and we return to this before leaving the arena of evidence-based practice.

Finally – training

In discussing the relationship between family therapy and research we have focused on two of the better-validated interventions as these well illustrate definitional and boundary issues. Many family therapists would see these approaches as outside of the mainstream of thinking and yet they are or should be very much in the mainstream of service provision for substantially large client groups. Clearly family therapy is developing in many areas as a part of various multimodal treatment activities, some of which may be led by family therapists and some not. However, one significant point about the training of family therapists emerges from this clinical reality. Family therapists do not seem to be following the model of other professions who have developed 'generic' bases for their training. Clinical psychologists, for example, are required as part of their training to work in contexts with children, the elderly, learning disabilities etc. Psychiatric nurses are similarly required to have a variety of experiences in differing clinical areas. Family therapy training does not replicate this tradition, and by not creating specialist skills continues to leave other professions to lead in the field of psychoeducational family interventions. In this sense training has not adopted the evidence from research.

This chapter has explored the research basis for family therapy practice (does it work?), but it is to another research issue, 'how does it work?', that we turn to in Chapter 9. This question will lead us back to the opening theme of our book: that family therapy is part of the family of psychotherapies and therefore issues of integration rather than distinction may be relevant to a tradition that has reached 'maturity'.

Chapter 9
How does it all go together?

Get up and do something useful, the work is a part of the *koan*.

Hakuin

I'm astounded by people who want to 'know' the universe when it is hard enough to find your way around Chinatown.

Woody Allen

Introduction

In this chapter we shall continue with our investigation of what we can learn about family therapy from an empirical framework but our focus here is not on outcome but on understanding what the core ingredients may be. We will not so much discuss research studies but rather models of therapy and therapeutic activity that have been informed by the empirical tradition. This perspective will essentially build upon previous chapters in that emphasis will be given to the commonalities between family therapy and other therapies. We noted in Chapters 2 and 3 that family therapy's theoretical base poses a number of dilemmas. We noted in Chapters 4 and 5 that, sociologically, family therapists are very like other therapists. In Chapter 7 we noted that family therapists probably retain an individualist concept of 'self' despite their systemic theory. And finally in Chapter 8 we explored the growing research evidence for family therapy which seems to imply that family therapy 'works' when it combines with other interventions. This discussion is therefore moving towards an argument that family therapy needs to integrate itself with other therapies. This theme therefore is taken up in the second part of this chapter after we have considered the idea of common 'active ingredients' of therapy.

Conceptualising the active ingredients of therapy

The notion that the active ingredients of the therapies have more in common than they have differences is not a new one. The idea was first broached in the 1930s by Rosenzweig (1936) who suggested that the effectiveness of different therapeutic approaches had more to do with common elements than with the particular theoretical canons on which they were based. However, this idea was not fully taken up until Frank discussed it in his work entitled *Persuasion and healing* (Frank, 1961). He placed psychotherapy within a number of human activities, which were focused on healing and saw it as a social process. He identified four features shared by all effective therapies:

(i) 'an emotionally charged, confiding relationship with a helping person';
(ii) 'a healing setting';
(iii) 'a rationale, conceptual scheme, or myth that provides a plausible explanation for the patient's symptoms and prescribes a ritual or procedure for resolving them';
(iv) 'a ritual or procedure that requires the active participation of both patient and therapist and that is believed by both to be the means of restoring the patient's health'. (Frank, 1961: 40)

Within individual therapy in the 1980s, there was a discernible increase in writing and research on what could be identified as the common factors of psychotherapy (Wineberger, 1995). However, not until Sprenkle et al.'s paper in 1999 has the field of family therapy attended to these. These authors consider this to be in large part due to family therapy's interest in itself as different from other psychotherapeutic activities. In Chapter 1 we have alluded to this. In our discussion of the common factors here we will focus on models that derive from the empirical psychological tradition. As such we will be describing family therapy without relying upon its own jargon and models. Firstly, we will delineate three ways of describing the common features of all the psychotherapies.

Models for describing the 'common features'

Thinking, feeling and behaviour

It has long been recognised that human experience and activity can be categorised into one of three areas: the behavioural, the emotional and the cognitive. The psychotherapies are orientated to this threefold division and most models have attempted change through at least one of these areas. For example, the behavioural school has focused on behaviour; psychodynamic psychotherapy has focused on the emotional; and the cognitive aspect has been attended to by rational emotive therapy. Although different models have attempted to concentrate on one of these elements to facilitate the change process, change eventually must occur in the other two modalities. In practice, therefore, each school of psychotherapy has tended to emphasise one of these elements as a way of changing all three. This way of considering the process has been developed by Karasu (1986) within an individual therapy framework. It is also possible to categorise family therapy models in this way (Sprenkle et al., 1999).

Clearly the behavioural, cognitive and affective categorisation is an arbitrary one, as each element naturally contains aspects of the other. It is indeed difficult to escape intellectually from the integrity of human activity. However, in keeping with other schools of therapy traditional family therapy models have varied in the extent to which they have given each of these three domains priority. From a 'common factors' perspective it might be argued that the 'best' treatment would be one which addressed each domain equally. This itself would be an argument for the development of new integrated methods of therapy rather than separate 'pure' models.

Explanation, rewarding, gently approaching and education

Garfield (1992) provided a technique-orientated way of describing the common features of therapy. His schema primarily applied to individual therapy but again this can be seen as relevant to family therapy.

Re-attribution

Garfield suggests that therapy gives the client an explanation of his or her difficulty that is understandable and applicable and then provides a healing ritual to overcome them. The explanation must be both credible and acceptable. Hoffman (1993) points about family therapy's shift to meanings rather than on behaviour are clearly an indication of the importance of this.

Reinforcement

Garfield noted that reinforcement is one of the most commonly used therapeutic techniques. Not only do therapists set up environmental situations where the client receives behavioural reinforcement but there is also a way in which every client will receive verbal reinforcement from the manner in which the therapist engages in conversation. This point is well made by Bandler and Grinder's (1975) seminal investigation of Virginia Satir and Milton Erickson.

Desensitisation
Garfield indicated that one of the most common techniques across all therapies is the process of allowing a client to slowly approach an anxiety-provoking stimulus in a graded manner both in imagination and in reality. Again this technique is clearly identified in behavioural models of family therapy.

Information and skills training
Garfield suggested that an educational role and the facilitation of specific skills are common techniques across all forms of therapy. As already noted, for instance, many of the family-orientated approaches for child behavioural disorders entail an educational element. Another example is the way family therapists in medical contexts are encouraged to become familiar with up-to-date information about the illnesses of the patients and to share it where appropriate (McDaniel, Hepworth & Doherty, 1992).

Four core factors
The most recent approach to the common features of therapy has been one that has been proposed by Lambert (1992). He suggested that there are four therapeutic factors that account for improvements in clients. Although not derived from a strict statistical analysis he suggested that these four factors could be seen to be embodied in the findings of empirical studies of psychotherapeutic outcome. These factors have been developed and discussed further by Miller, Duncan and Hubble (1997) and Hubble, Duncan and Miller (1999) and we discuss them below. Even though family therapy researchers have not paid a great deal of attention to the four core factors, Sprenkle et al. (1999) have organised research studies in accordance with this schema (also Street, 2003).

Extra-therapeutic factors
What the client brings to therapy and how the client connected to a social network are seen as being the most common and powerful factors in therapy. It is recognised that the part of the client and the client's particular life circumstances are most important in recovery or the overcoming of any problem. These factors consist of the client characteristics, the immediate and hopefully supportive elements of the client's immediate social environment and even serendipitous events. These factors are in essence the enduring features of clients that are brought into the therapeutic space and influences their lives outside of that space. Lambert (1992) estimates that these factors

account for approximately 40 per cent of outcome variance. Sprenkle et al. (1999) discuss these in terms of the 'static and non-static' characteristics of individuals, couples and families, motivational characteristics, fortuitous events and social support.

Relationship factors

These represent a wide range of variables focusing on the relationship between the therapist and client. This therapeutic relationship is separate from a therapist's particular theoretical orientation. Genuineness, empathy, warmth, acceptance, affirmation, encouragement and general caring are the characteristics that are central to this group of factors. Lambert (1992) estimates that 30 per cent of the successful outcome variance can be largely attributed to these factors. In their early review of the field, Gurman and Kniskern (1978) concluded that the ability of the therapist to establish a positive relationship with his or her clients was the factor that received the most 'consistent' support as an outcome-related factor in marital and family therapy. Certainly research has provided consistent evidence that if clients do not feel listened to, understood and given respect, then the likelihood of them dropping out of treatment is high as is the poor outcome (Howe, 1993; Reimers & Treacher, 1995). There is also some evidence that this bond grows as sessions go on, with a deeper respect for each other emerging as treatment progresses. Friedlander (1998) summarizes this research for family therapy by suggesting that it implies that families prefer a 'nurturant, authoritative parent'. The question that is often asked by practitioners is whether or not relationship skills are sufficient in themselves for effective therapy. Gurman and Kniskern (1978) explicitly state that they are not. This statement, however, comes from a time when the main thrust of family and marital therapy was more involved in active methods. Now that family therapy has moved in the direction of narrative, conversational and collaborative approaches it may well be that the relationship element is coming more to the fore.

Placebo, hope and expectancy

These are therapeutic factors linked to those features of the client's pre-knowledge, estimation and expectancy of therapy. They also refer to the client's ongoing assessment of the treatment, its rationale and the therapist's techniques. The client and indeed the therapist need to believe that the therapy *will work*. The therapist and the client need to have some expectancy of gain at the end. Lambert (1992) estimates that these account for some 15 per cent of the successful outcome variance. There is no significant family therapy research in this area.

Model or technique factors

These factors refer to the beliefs and procedures unique to specific therapeutic approaches and treatments. They are the factors of specific theories and they refer to the differences between therapeutic approaches and theories. Lambert (1992) suggests that these specific model factors account for 15 per cent of improvement in therapy. When one considers the research effort in this area for family therapy some clear conclusions emerge. As noted in the previous chapter the evidence clearly indicates that no orientation has been demonstrably shown to be superior to any other. The meta-analysis by Shadish, Ragsdale, Glaser and Montgomery (1995) has clearly demonstrated that in keeping with the other psychotherapy literature family therapy has been shown to have no one school which is superior to another. They note, however, that it is difficult to compare marital therapy and family therapy because of their increasing methodological divergence.

Lambert has reviewed psychotherapy research and his set of conclusions (Asay & Lambert, 1999) are:

(a) The effects of therapy are positive at treatment termination. Generally we know that therapy can work.
(b) The beneficial effects of therapy can be achieved in short periods (5–10 sessions) with at least 50 per cent of clients seen in routine clinical practice. For most clients, therefore, therapy will be brief.
(c) A sizeable minority of clients (20 to 30%) require treatment lasting more than 25 sessions. This group may need alternative interventions with more intensive multifaceted treatment approaches. Even when intensive efforts are required clients will improve.
(d) The effects of treatment are lasting for most clients, with follow-up studies suggesting little decline one to two years after termination. Encouraging and reinforcing the clients' belief in their ability to cope with the inevitable temporary setbacks likely to be experienced after therapy can reduce relapse.
(e) Client outcome is principally determined by clients' variables and extra therapeutic factors rather than by the therapist or therapy.
(f) Outside of client and extra-therapeutic variables, the best predictor of success is therapist–client relationship factors. Therapist

relationship skills, such as acceptance, warmth and empathy, are absolutely fundamental in establishing a good relationship. These are all related to positive outcomes.

(g) Therapists can contribute to the therapeutic process by enhancing the effects of client expectations and placebo factors in their approach. Positive expectations about treatment include the belief that there is a hope for overcoming problems and feeling better.

(h) Some specific techniques look to be especially helpful with certain symptoms and disorders.

Given that many of these factors are relational and contextual, it is surprising that family therapists have not paid them more attention. Certainly family therapy shares more with other psychological treatment modalities than it has acknowledged. Indeed many of the concepts in common therapeutic currency about how therapy may work have been underplayed by family therapy theory and focus little in its practice and training. This may represent another of the family therapy 'fracture' points.

Unique features of marital and family therapy?

Clearly all family therapists will be asking themselves the question as to whether the nature of their practice contains some features that are separate from individual psychotherapy and unique to itself. After all, family therapy was originally conceived to be somehow different from the manner of practice of those therapists who saw only individuals. Certainly what family therapy claims to do more than any other type of therapy is to translate problems of the human condition into interactive and relational terms. In their discussion of the common factors, Sprenkle et al. (1999) have suggested that some factors are unique to family therapy. In essence what these authors do is to suggest a model of basic theoretical underpinnings and discuss the 'uniqueness' of family therapy factors from this framework. What is of interest is how the discussion of core features leads to the elucidation of 'base-level' models. They suggest that the theoretical basis of family therapy involves a *relational conceptualisation* which leads the therapist to undertake work with an *expanded direct treatment system;* this work naturally involves an *expanded therapeutic alliance.* It is these elements that Sprenkle and his colleagues see as being a separate and distinguishing feature of marital and family therapy but of such a nature that they form a communality within the field itself.

We include the above discussion as it provides an indication to family therapists of other frames that can be placed on their activities – frames that implicitly critique family therapy's theoretical formulations. A central difficulty with the domination of theory-based training and practice is that it limits the practitioner in appreciating the nature of the therapeutic activity. The perspectives of others on our activity may allow us to come to a fuller awareness of the important components of that activity. Undoubtedly in an era of 'managed care' and 'evidence-based practice' there is still much uncertainty about family therapy efficacy; this can only be overcome by a comprehensive approach to developing research programmes. However, as Carr (2000b) notes, the political climate may be against the funding of family therapy research and so the impetus and motivation must rest with practitioners themselves. Thus it is clear that small-scale research and audit should become a common element of practitioner practice.

All this argument presupposes that in many ways there are some relatively stable aspects of family therapy practice. However, as we have seen in early chapters the field continues to be easily influenced by new and exciting ideas that would appear to prevent a foundational base for empirically understanding family therapy. In contrast to this constant theoretical innovation, the perspective of core features implies that family therapists should be seeking to integrate their theory and practice not only with each other but also with the wider therapeutic community. It is therefore to this theme that we now turn.

Why integration?

We have argued in earlier chapters that the principal critiques of family therapy have focused on the philosophical, sociological and psychological dimensions. However, other developments (such as the empirical findings discussed above), seem to move us towards an integrative model and these also inherently involve a critique. The theme of integration has not received the attention it deserves. Indeed individual practitioners who seek to integrate their work often do so because of frustration with the limits of any one approach or perspective (Liddle, 1982). Clearly the orderly application of theory and technique from differing but compatible schools of thought cannot be taken as a simple task: integration is a multifaceted, complex process that has different foci and outcomes. Indeed the process of integration can be different in different circumstances. In the final analysis the end product for each and every therapist is how he or she puts into practice their theoretical understanding. However, within the context of this critical review of family therapy, integration has a wider significance. Our review of empirical models, we can note, suggests that there is a confluence within the psychotherapies in terms of their understanding of the 'active ingredients' of therapy. We have also noted how the practice of family therapists might differ less than presumed from the practice of their psychotherapeutic colleagues. Here, therefore, we wish to explore the possibilities of integration to see if family therapists can integrate their methods with those of the other psychotherapies and to reflect upon what might be lost if that were to happen.

What is integration?

Integration can be described as a *theoretical* process or a *clinical* one. *Theoretical* attempts at integration join elements of different schools of psychotherapy into one theory. This might be the melding of disparate pieces of theory into a 'meta' theory. Within family therapy, examples of this include combining structural and strategic methods. Alternatively it may involve the blending of a variety of theories where the foundation comes from one model. In this respect Lebow (1997) has argued that as systems theory is essential to family therapy, an integrative therapy should include more than the combination of systems theory and one other approach. For example, approaches that combine psychodynamic principles and systems theory are more appropriately labelled as 'psychoanalytic family therapy' rather than as 'integrative.'

Clinical integration describes the process by which a therapist uniquely assimilates his/her own personal practice which itself reflects the variety of influences that are encountered in a typical professional life. It is in the latter process that the therapist primarily articulates the pragmatics of his/her own context whilst all the other influences are a part of the intellectual and ideological system that surrounds her/him. The risk of clinical integration is that the therapist becomes purely pragmatic and eclectic, which would imply that the therapist is a 'technocrat'. This would contradict the concept of 'reflective practice', which implies that the therapist learns from the use of theory in practice. It would seem, therefore, that there is more value in developing integrative models which can be publicly discussed than in therapists developing their own personal paradigm in a private non-verbalised manner.

Advantages and disadvantages of integration

The advantages of an integrative approach are many. Firstly, such approaches draw from a broad theoretical base and are more able to account for the range of human behaviour. Therefore, they allow for greater flexibility in the treatment of any individual and family. Hence they offer the opportunity for increased acceptability and efficacy of care. Secondly, they are more readily adapted to diverse client populations and to diverse therapeutic style. Indeed, it could be said that integrated models offer a wide range of powerful interventions specifically designed for specific problems. Thirdly, they permit greater objectivity in the selection of strategies for change and because of this can easily be adapted to new developments in research and practice. Lastly, as noted above, these advantages are particularly pertinent to family therapists adapting and adjusting their practice to the needs of the workplace.

However, integrative models do have disadvantages (Lebow, 1997). For instance, they may lack a theoretical focus. They may be inconsistent. They may give rise to utopian goal setting that results in interminable treatment. The complexity of the approach may have adverse effects on the therapeutic relationship. They can be difficult to teach and also difficult to monitor in empirical terms. For these reasons, Grunebaum (1997) argues that despite its attractiveness integration in its purest form is a misguided, probably impossible, and an unnecessary goal. He claims that there is an inherent incompatibility of the central theoretical constructs necessary for such integration; and that many human endeavours such as medicine do well without striving for or achieving integration. Grunebaum also points out the importance of understanding commonalities between approaches and drawing a distinction between this and the integration of treatment models.

Having said this, the current reality is that therapists put their ideas together in a personal framework, largely without discussion on training courses or in practice. Because of this we will now outline a number of ways of integrating family therapy with the findings from research.

Models of integration

From its outset family therapy knew that it was integrating ideas from different therapeutic traditions. The pioneers of family therapy freely assimilated concepts and interventions from diverse sources in their clinical practice and model building (e.g. Ackerman, 1958;

Bowen, 1976; Whitaker & Keith, 1981). However, the methods they taught and emphasised in their writing were more narrowly focused and, with the passage of time, as their treatments became reified as schools, the original integrative nature of these efforts became obscured.

More recently, a literature concerned with integration has emerged (Grunebaum, 1988; Lebow, 1984; 1987; Liddle, 1984; Moultrop, 1981; 1986), and numerous integrative models been developed (Feldman, 1985; 1990; Gurman, 1981; L'Abate, 1986; Pinsof, 1995). These can largely be divided into those that combine a number of models of therapy; those that provide integrated methods for specific client groups; those that try to provide a universal integration for all therapies; and those that provide a value base which is claimed as integrative.

Combining models

Methods often cross the boundaries of what earlier were distinct schools of couple and family therapy. Methods of 'behavioural' therapists now often include strains of strategic (Barton & Alexander, 1981) and even experiential treatments (Jacobson, 1992). 'Structural' therapists draw on multigenerational explorations of family of origin (Breunlin, Schwartz & MacKune-Karrer, 1992; Melito, 1988). Work with 'object relations' frequently involves the teaching of communication skills and pragmatic help in solving problems. Integration is continually a part of the ongoing theoretical process of family therapy theory development. We can see, therefore, that within the theoretical and practical environment of family therapy the pressure is towards a pragmatic approach. The processes of integration clearly influence one another: changes at the clinical level can affect the theoretical and vice versa. For the therapist at his/her reflective best, the levels of theory, strategy and clinical necessity should remain recursively linked and consistent with one another. The most common integrative efforts combine behavioural notions of learning with a systemic understanding of family process and the individual psychodynamics that are brought to bear in these patterns. Examples are Feldman's multidimensional family therapy (Feldman, 1985; 1990) and Gurman's integrative marital therapy which involves an innovative combination of object relations, behavioural and systemic procedures for working with couples (Gurman, 1981). Others combine these in different patterns (Kirschner & Kirschner, 1986; Nichols, 1987; Wachtel & Wachtel, 1986). Other authors have taken other directions. Seaburn, Landau-Stanton and Horwitz

(1995) mix what they term here and now (primarily structural, strategic and behavioural tasks), transgenerational (primarily Bowen and experiential work) and ecosystemic approaches. Again, others combine narrative and strategic approaches (Eron & Lund, 1993), strategic and behavioural (Duncan & Parks, 1988), and experiential and systemic (Greenberg & Johnson, 1988). Some integrative approaches focus on the therapist developing a personal method (Moultrop, 1981; 1986; Lebow, 1987; Carpenter & Treacher, 1993).

Models for specific client groups

Much of the recent, creative edge in integration has been concerned with the development of specific treatments for specific populations. It is in this area that there has been development in treatment protocols and manuals. Some (Liddle, Dakof & Diamond, 1991; Piercy & Frankel, 1989) have brought structural, systems and behavioural principles together in the treatment of adolescent chemical dependency. Similarly, integrative approaches have been described for the treatment of sexual problems (Kaplan, 1974), physical illness (Rolland, 1994; Wood, 1993; Wright & Leahey, 1994) and alcoholism (Vetere & Henley, 2001). The much-quoted approach by Goldner et al. (1990) to domestic violence merges feminist, narrative, systemic and psychodynamic concepts. Probably the most widely practised integrative models are the psychoeducational approaches used in the treatment of severe mental illness discussed earlier.

In the development of such approaches there may well be some dangers. For example, we may be left with numerous distinct yet overlapping treatments for different problems. This may ultimately block our understanding of the factors that transcend disorders and of common pathways towards change. This of course rests on the hope that some 'grand' understanding may be possible. Grunebaum (1997) argues from the opposite perspective that most progress is made by finding integrated ways of working with particular kinds of situations, with families when there is mental illness, or with couples when there is sexual dysfunction. His argument is for 'local' knowledge and the integration that this entails.

Models that describe a universal framework

Carr (2000a) provides a pragmatic approach to the issue of integration termed the 'formulation model'. Theoretically this is based on the domains of behaviour that parallel the tripartite division of human experience into 'behaviour', 'cognition' and 'affect' discussed earlier. Carr's model therefore suggests that the family therapist use whatever method is most likely to alter the 'problem maintaining behaviour patterns, belief systems or contextual factors'. By categorising which family therapy methods are designed to change these three areas, he is able to describe how to intervene.

Pinsof (1994; 1995), however, has described a more thorough model which integrates both family and individual therapy. His model shares an emphasis upon the 'problem' with Carr, but he provides a 'hierarchy' of intervention levels. Thus 'direct' interventions such as behavioural task assignment and structural enactment precede those that emphasise affective experience, which, in turn, precede investigation of the individual psychodynamic level. In problem-centred therapy, parsimony is emphasised: additional levels of intervention are included only when treatment is blocked from achieving its goals through the use of simpler, more directive measures. For Pinsof, therefore, individual, couple and family therapy do not necessarily differ in their basic understanding of the client system; they only differ in the point at which they draw the boundary between who is actively involved in problem maintenance. The therapeutic process moves in a sequence from the interpersonal 'here and now' behavioural focus through the interactive 'meaning' levels to the individual historically focused approaches. The therapist moves through the levels when systems' 'resistance' prevents the implementation of an adaptive solution. As the therapist moves through the levels, the focus and quality of therapeutic behaviour changes. The therapist typically becomes less active, less directive, more exploratory and more reflective. This shift requires different therapeutic skills at different levels. It requires therapists with extensive skills in working in different orientations in different contexts. From this perspective, family, couple and individual therapy are simply three different interventions into the same terrain. Pinsof's model implicitly suggests that therapists need a range of knowledge and skills that transcend the separate therapeutic traditions. It implies that the qualification of 'therapist' should have some universal definitions. Interestingly, the research quoted in Chapter 5 does suggest that American therapists see themselves as qualified to intervene at these different levels of treatment. Such genericism does not preclude a degree of specialism, but it is a long way from the training and attitudes of British therapists. Perhaps only in the training of counsellors does such genericism apply.

Pinsof's model shows that it is possible to integrate schools of family therapy and also to integrate family therapy and individual therapy. This emphasises the point that the process of integration within the psychotherapy field is not a question of either/or, but of both/and.

An integrative value base: the personal perspective

Lebow (1987) has argued that individual therapists need to develop their own personal paradigm which respects client views but provides an understanding of personal growth and professional change. Such models of personal integration assume that there are both general principles of psychotherapy and that there is a consistent need to relate these principles to the specific therapeutic relationship. In many senses it outlines an ethical position of how therapists should conduct their thinking about their practice. There are, however, few such models to draw on. The closest has been that described by the term '*user-friendly practice*' as outlined by Carpenter and Treacher (1993) and Reimers and Treacher (1995). These authors consider that the family therapy movement has been dominated by the views of the 'benefactors not the beneficiaries'. Their aim is to

> contribute to a perspective in the family therapy movement that has largely been ignored because of the impact and fashionableness of models which too readily absorbed the alienating and dehumanising facets of systems theorising. ... This alternative perspective insists that therapy needs to be viewed as a cooperative project between user and therapist which takes seriously users' experience of family therapy.
> (Reimers & Treacher, 1995: 3)

Reimers and Treacher (1995) identify the humanness of the therapeutic endeavour. They point out that it is a mistake to think that the primary nature of what we do is to 'do therapy'. Therapy in all its constructions and convulsions is merely another form of helping. The humanity and the humanness of helping are what are central, and they note that within this activity there can be problems because of the inherent power differentials. Thus this is an approach based on the assumption that the building of a therapeutic alliance between users and therapist(s) is crucial to the success of therapy. They highlight the ethical nature of the encounter and also point out that the therapist is a person also in this. They suggest that therapists should consider the experience of 'becoming a client' and connect to this experience for their service users. It is under this heading that Treacher (1995) offers his criticism of the way family therapy technology such as the screen, teams and video have been used. These authors further state that the family should be seen as unique in relation to other families. They emphasise cultural differences as well as those of 'class, gender, sexual orientation, power, age, disability, ethnic origin, religion and a socio-cultural background', pointing out that it is the therapist's job to understand these in the context of the wider culture. As part of understanding what it is like to be a client of family therapy, Reimers and Treacher argue that therapists should be willing to attend therapy themselves. We have indicated in Chapter 7 that family therapists appear to be reluctant to use family therapy as consumers but these authors clearly suggest that family therapists should *experience* family therapy. Undoubtedly there is a world of the difference between sitting in a therapist's room and discussing one's feelings concerning your relationship with your mother and father and sitting in the same room with your mother and father and telling them how you feel. Similarly, hearing one's own adolescent children complain about your own behaviour as a parent is very different to seeking support and encouragement from the privacy of a one-to-one therapy session. These experiences might produce mindful and humble family therapists: they perhaps should be part of training. Implicit in this proposal is that therapy should 'fit' the problem: so a marital problem would suggest marital therapy; a problem with children would suggest some family sessions; personal doubt and loss of direction would suggest individual work.

The user-friendly authors go on to suggest that sometimes therapists do not need to act as therapists but more as supporters and advocates in general ways and that due consideration should to be given to the way in which therapists assist clients in developing resources for themselves. This clearly links to the Miller et al. (1997) argument that extra-therapeutic activities are an important ingredient of therapeutic effectiveness. It also echoes the suggestion (in Chapter 5) that sometimes family therapists need to adopt other skills in order to help families.

In summary, therefore, the user-friendly approach (Carpenter & Treacher, 1993; Reimers & Treacher, 1995; Treacher, 1995) states that family and marital therapy is a human activity that has at its core an ethics. It occurs in a relationship in which there is an inherent power differential. Therapy occurs in a context in which the therapist attempts to facilitate change through the process of the relationship (the therapeutic alliance). Therapists should be aware of themselves and their limitations and attempt to be focused on what the client requires. In the construction of this ethical practice the therapist should:

1 Appreciate what it is like being a client both practically and experientially.
2 Acknowledge difference and uniqueness.
3 Base a practice on evidence from a research foundation.
4 Create and utilise integrated models.
5 Attend to personal issues away from therapy with clients.
6 Support trainee-friendly training.
7 Be available to assist clients in whatever ways are needed.

In some ways, the central guidelines of the user-friendly approach are a restatement of well-established principles of psychotherapeutic endeavour. It is a reaffirmation of an understanding that has served the psychotherapeutic community well over many years. These guidelines may be seen as echoing Rogers' (1957) 'necessary and sufficient conditions' for therapeutic change. Indeed, their argument can be applied to any form of the psychological therapy. There is nothing in this approach that marks it out as a uniquely systemic approach. We have therefore presented this perspective as an example of a personal integrative approach centred upon values which effectively states the commonalities between family and other therapies. Ultimately, integration has brought family therapy around full circle in establishing not difference but sameness to other therapies.

Conclusions

Within this chapter we have provided an overview of an empirical model that deconstructs the ingredients of therapeutic change. This has enabled us to explore what form an integrated family therapy might take. We have noted that it is not helpful to consider that the boundaries of core ingredients and integration can be limited to the marital and family therapy field alone. Rather than developing family therapy's own integrated theories we should be looking towards the development of integrated theories of psychotherapy generally. We have used Pinsof as an exemplar of this approach and demonstrated that the integrated practice approach of the user-friendly therapists is merely a restatement of the values and ethics of the psychotherapeutic community at large. Within this context it must be recognised that individual practitioners may rarely consider the core ingredients and integration. Moreover, training courses still emphasise difference not similarities. We have suggested that within family therapy the ethical source of psychotherapy (with its roots in individual suffering) is rarely addressed. But equally if family therapy lost its uniqueness the diversity of thought, practice and wisdom that family therapy has brought into the realm of therapy would also be lost! Yet one of the themes of this book, running through each specific chapter, is that family therapy has become more and more like other therapies as it has matured. So once more as we end a chapter, we return to paradoxes. Integrative models bring with them important lessons. But they might lack creativity and might miss the 'radical edge' of family therapy. Once more, we must recommend a 'both/and' mind which not only allows contradictions but welcomes them!

Chapter 10
Beginning at an ending: beyond 'both/and'

For the time being mind arrives, but words do not.
For the time being words arrive, but mind does not.
For the time being both mind and words arrive.
For the time being neither mind nor words arrive.

Shexian Guixing

Beginning

At the outset of this book we identified a number of features that characterised family therapy at its inception. Its origins lay in developments of psychotherapeutic practice; it was a clinical (not a research) creation, with a method and theory that proclaimed a unity of purpose. It was unique in its radical stance towards the methods and theories of other psychotherapies. In this book we have extended this critical stance towards family therapy itself: we have attempted to perturb its very own self-conception. We have found that its psychotherapeutic nature has sometimes been relegated in importance to theoretical and philosophical discussions. We have suggested that some of the theoretical justifications of marital and family therapy do not actually make a lot of sense. In particular systems theory and post-modernism, though useful as 'maps', are not sufficient to describe the 'territory' of family therapy. We have also found that although family therapy claimed to have a unity of purpose at its origins, this has been far from the reality of its practice. Far from there being a unity, there are and always will be different types of family therapy and different types of therapists. Those who deal with families in psychoeducational ways are different from those who offer behavioural approaches to struggling parents. These are different from those who conduct their professional practice in the financial isolation of private practice or those in educational institutions in which clients are ultimately seen as training examples. Moreover, professional requirements add another layer of complexity to the definition of 'family therapy'. Indeed, this conclusion highlights a limitation of our endeavour: marital therapy and family therapy, for instance, occupy significantly different places in the British professional context. Thus, our use of the term 'family therapy' throughout this book might have privileged the very idea of unity that we doubt.

Equally our critical review might have obscured the role of family therapy as a psychotherapy that seeks to heal psychological distress. Certainly we have acknowledged the controversy about the role of psychotherapy in contemporary society. Thus some would argue that psychotherapy is becoming a mythological (and dubious) structure which fuels 'pop psychology' (Dawes, 1994). Others would argue that the healing conversation is only compromised once it is turned into a professional activity (House, 2001). This points to the fact that our review is itself not 'outside the flux'. This book too is both context-bound and time-bound. It has also crafted reality into some shape.

Indeed, family therapy in common with other similar activities is at best *time-bound*. Each generation of family therapists will engage in activities in terms of their own time, place and context. Every generation of psychotherapists will be faced with certain abstract questions of morality, fairness and justice that will only find answers within the concreteness of the actual practice of therapy. The construction of past concrete arrangements – 'solutions' – will always create burdens, injustice and new questions for those who operate in the present. Rappaport and Stewart (1997) note in their discussion on the development of a critical psychology that

> liberation in the context of relationships can never be perfectly known or obtained, but for an instant. It is only the moment of 'change' itself, when a new comprehension, respect and pattern of behaviour emerges, that liberates, albeit for an instant, before the dust of a new status quo settles on the product of reform or revolution, requiring yet another long battle against the forces of privilege. It is in the battle itself, when people cross boundaries to commune with one another in mutual respect, that one glimpses liberation. (1997: 304)

This is to propose a view of psychotherapeutic practice as being a continual process in which no ideas could or should remain dominant because dominant ideas result in certainties that do not exist. Within this conception the question of the institution of the profession will for us always be problematic. Not, that is to say, that there should not be professional activity: that is the way the world works. But that the profession itself has to be creative in finding ways to encourage individual members to be 'disrespectful' of its thinking so that thinking can always develop.

We have also presented a picture of family therapy being indelibly *context-bound*. The sociology of its theory and practice emphasises that it has a role in society and that its practitioners cannot escape that role. This role does not prevent radical practice (in the spirit of its inception), but it marks out the differences between different sorts of family and systemic therapists. We have also noted that as family therapy has matured, research evidence has grown and specialist posts have been created. There has been a move away from a pure and 'standalone' practice towards an inclusive, integrative model. But we have also found 'fractures', contradictions and 'paradoxes' that continue to shake the field: within any family therapy text these fractures function as land mines that threaten and weaken the certainty aspired to.

Beyond 'both/and'

How can we deal with these paradoxes? We might begin by providing a list of some of the things that appear to stand in opposition to each other:

wholly new – part of a tradition
process – content
evidence–based practice – an art
professional expertise – simple commonsense friendship
assisting the state – assisting resistance
professional organisation – flexible rules
experience – naivety
theorists – practitioners
individuals – families
self – other
self – no self
family therapists – systemic practitioners
map – territory
both/and
either/or

These numerous dilemmas of family therapy are an integral part of its practice: it is, as we have said, a paradoxical pursuit. To be a family therapist necessarily involves having to confront all these issues. Here, as we commented earlier, family therapists need to 'Go back to one'. 'One' is the expectation that family therapists have of multiple or 'double description'. Some have called this the 'both/ and' scenario. In this sense the paradoxes are not ones that need answers, but need to be *lived*. The ambiguity and ambivalence of practice in which multiple ideas are all valued at the same time, points towards a moment where these contradictions, paradoxes and fractures are known to be 'true' but also to be subsumed in the experience of therapy. We therefore can also say that there is

list – no list

In some way this transcends the 'both/and' idea. It is 'Not two and not one', as the Zen masters say, and this may be Bateson's 'naked skeleton of Truth'. There is the 'and' and the 'both'. There is 'both' together with 'and'. Then there is neither 'both/and'. Such a suggestion rests heavily upon Eastern philosophical spiritual ideas as they apply to psychotherapy (e.g. Claxton, 1986; Crook & Fontanna, 1990; Kopp, 1979; Rosenbaum, 1998; Welwood, 1983). We cannot explore these here as they are explored in depth elsewhere (Rivett & Street, 2000; 2001). All we wish to do is to highlight an essential, if not 'the' essential aspect of psychotherapy: namely its experiential nature. In a sense our text therefore has become a *koan*: an unsolvable riddle which points towards experience not theory! Family therapy and its psychotherapeutic roots can and do contribute to the confusing beauty of this human process.

There can be no 'final solution' to evaluating family therapy either for individual clients or as an abstract intellectual endeavour. But there are criteria by which we can judge all outcomes. For us these criteria are that outcomes should be seen as being fair, just and respectful. They should also carry the hopefulness of human beings in their quest for satisfying lives. To achieve this the lessons are clear: instead of becoming self-satisfied with our conceptions and presuppositions, we should stop to consider and continually reflect on the inherent fractures, tensions, ambiguities, dilemmas, paradoxes and contradictions in our practice. Not only do we need to be explicit about our values but also about our own subjectivity. A continual process of focusing on the dilemmas and tensions will truly take us beyond them.

Endings

In the spirit of self-reflexivity, we now wonder where this text and family therapy in general fit in the model of a life cycle that so predominated discussions at the turn of the century. There are many ways to describe the history of a field. Kaslow (1990a; 1990b) in her formulation of the history of the family psychology offered a generational categorisation that has clear echoes for family therapy. She stated that in her field:

1 The first generation were pioneers and renegades.
2 The second generation were innovators and expanders.
3 The third generation were challengers, refiners and researchers.
4 The fourth generation were integrators and seekers of new horizons.

We can see from this categorisation that different developmental phases and different contexts present different dilemmas and issues. Equally, 'hindsight' may be helpful (or biased) but being in the middle of a process is not a very good place for describing and defining it. So where are we in terms of our review of family therapy? If we were at the end of the period of pioneering and renegade activity, we would be enthusiastic and even proselytising (although we might secretly dislike its delinquency). If we were at the end of a period in which expansion and innovation has occurred we might come to the conclusion that the field has stabilised itself and become clearer in its focus. We might applaud developments and congratulate family therapists on forming an identity for themselves. If we were in a period characterised by refinement and research we might say that the field had come of age and was attending to issues in a mature manner. If we were in a period of integration we might applaud the way issues and themes that were once separate are brought together. We might be pleased to report that the once rigid boundary of the field is becoming blurred and outside influences were making impacts for the good.

  Clearly this form of speculation is appropriate when we consider the activity of an intellectual pursuit solely within terms of itself. When that pursuit is linked to people's jobs, to activities in the public arena and to professional organisations, other processes are at work. The need to maintain and enhance a professional activity and to support a professional organisation can limit the cycle of intellectual development. Certainly the theorist, the researcher, the professionaliser and the practitioner will all have different views of the phase we are in. Each family therapist will need to answer the question for herself or himself. Is it possible to be in one phase and all four at the same time? Many questions remain unanswered. Will integration continue to expand? Will psychoanalysis and family therapy continue their *rapprochement*? Will evidence-based practice dominate?

Will professional 'family therapy' debilitate 'systemic practice'? Will a new form of generic therapist emerge? Readers will reach their own conclusions about these questions. Our analysis is itself context- bound and perhaps quite 'traditional'. However, as we quite liked the label of 'renegades' when we were younger, we hope that some part of our early radicalism has seeped into this presentation of family therapy.

References

Ackerman, N.P. (1958). *The psychodynamics of family life*. New York: Basic Books.

Ackerman, N.P. (1962). Family psychotherapy and psychoanalysis: the implications of difference. *Family Process, 1*, 30–43.

Adams, D. (1988). Treatment models of men who batter: a pro-feminist analysis. In K. Yllo & M. Bograd (Eds.), *Feminist perspectives on wife abuse*. Newbury Park, CA: Sage.

Akister, J. (1998) Attachment theory and systemic practice: research update. *Journal of Family Therapy, 20*, 353–366.

Allen, W. & Olson, D. (2001). Five types of African-American marriages. *Journal of Marital and Family Therapy, 27*, 301–314.

Almeida, R. (1998). The dislocation of women's experience in family therapy. In R. Almeida (Ed.), *Transformations of gender and race: family and developmental perspectives*. New York: Haworth Press.

Almeida, R. & Bograd, M. (1991) Sponsorship: men holding men accountable for domestic violence. In M. Bograd (Ed.), *Feminist approaches for men in family therapy*. Binghamton, NY: Harrington Park Press.

American Psychiatric Association. (1994). *Diagnostic and statistical manual of mental disorders*. Washington, DC: APA.

Andersen, T. (1987). The reflecting team: dialogue and meta-dialogue in clinical work. *Family Process, 26*, 415–428.

Andersen, T. (1991). *The reflecting team: dialogues and dialogues about the dialogues*. New York: Norton.

Andersen, T. (1997). Researching client–therapist relationships. *Journal of Systemic Therapies, 16*, 125–133.

Anderson, H. (2001). Post-modern collaborative and person centred therapies: what would Carl Rogers say? *Journal of Family Therapy, 23*, 339–360.

Anderson, H. & Goolishian, H. (1986). Problem determined systems: towards transformation in family therapy. *Journal of Strategic and Systemic Therapies, 5*, 1–13.

Anderson, H. & Goolishian, H. (1988). Human systems as linguistic systems: preliminary and evolving ideas about the implications for clinical practice. *Family Process, 27*, 371–393.

Anderson, H. & Goolishian, H. (1992). The client is the expert: a not-knowing approach to therapy. In S. McNamee & K. Gergen (Eds.), *Therapy as social construction*. London: Sage.

Anderson, S. & Schlossberg, M. (1999). Systems perspectives on battering: the importance of context and pattern. In M. Harway & J. O'Neil (Eds.), *What causes men's violence against women?* Thousand Oaks, CA: Sage.

Aponte, H. (1992). Training the person of the therapist in structural family therapy. *Journal of Marital and Family Therapy, 18*, 269–281.

Aponte, H. (1994). How personal can training get? *Journal of Marital and Family Therapy, 20*, 3–15.

168 References

Asay, T.P., & Lambert, M.J. (1999). The empirical case for the common factors in therapy: quantitative findings. In M.A. Hubble, B.L. Duncan & S.D. Miller (Eds.), *The heart and soul of change: what works in therapy*. Washington, DC: American Psychological Association.

Association for Family Therapy [AFT]. (1996). Personal communication.

Association for Family Therapy [AFT]. (1999). *Blue Book: requirements for training courses in family and systemic psychotherapy and systemic practice*. London: AFT.

Atkinson, B. & Heath, A. (1990). Further thoughts on second order family therapy – this time it's personal. *Family Process, 29*, 145–155.

Atkinson, D.R. & Lowe, S.M. (1995). The role of an ethnicity, cultural knowledge and conventional techniques in counselling and psychotherapy. In J.G. Ponterotto, J.M. Casas, L.M. Suzuki & C.M. Alexander (Eds.) *Handbook of multi-cultural counseling*. Thousand Oaks, CA: Sage.

Attneave, C. (1969). Therapy in a tribal setting and urban network intervention. *Family Process, 8*, 192–210

Audit Commission. (1994). *Seen but not heard*. London: HMSO.

Audit Commission. (1999). *Children in mind*. London: Audit Commission.

Avis, J. (1992). Where are all the family therapists? Abuse and violence within families and family therapy's response. *Journal of Marital and Family Therapy, 18*, 225–232.

Baldwin, D. (1987). Some philosophical and psychological contributions to the use of self in therapy. In M. Baldwin & V. Satir (Eds.), *The use of self in therapy*. New York: Haworth Press.

Baldwin, M. & Satir, V. (Eds.). (1987). *The use of self in therapy*. New York: Haworth Press.

Bandler, R., & Grinder, J. (1975). *The structure of magic I*. Palo Alto, CA: Science and Behavior Books.

Barnes, M. & Maple, N. (1992). *Women and mental health: challenging the stereotypes*. Birmingham: Venture Press.

Barrett, M. & McIntosh, M. (1982). *The anti-social family*. London: Verso.

Barratt, S., Burck, C., Dwivedi, K., Stedman, M. & Raval, H. (1999) Theoretical bases in relation to race, ethnicitry and culture in family therapy training. *Context, 44*, 4–12.

Barrett-Lennard, G.T. (1998). *Carl Rogers' helping system: journey and substance*. London: Sage.

Barton, C. & Alexander, J.F. (1981). Functional family therapy. In A.S. Gurman & D.P. Kniskern (Eds.), *Handbook of family therapy*. New York: Brunner/Mazel.

Baruch, G. & Treacher, A. (1978). *Psychiatry observed*. London: Routledge & Kegan Paul.

Bates, Y. (2000). Still whinging: the professionalisation of counselling. *Changes, 18*, 91–99.

Bateson, G. (1972). *Steps to an ecology of mind*. New York: Ballantine.

Bateson, G. (1979). *Mind and Nature*. New York: Dutton.

Bateson, G. & Bateson, M.C. (1987). *Angels fear: towards an epistemology of the sacred*. New York: Bantam Books.

Berger, P & Luckman, T. (1966). *The social construction of reality*. New York: Anchor.

Bergin, A.E. (1971). The evaluation of therapeutic outcomes. In A.E. Bergin & S.L. Garfield (Eds.), *Handbook of psychotherapy and behaviour change*. (2nd Ed.). New York: John Wiley.

Bertalanffy, L. von. (1968). *General systems theory*. New York: George Braziller.

Bogdan, J. (1984). Family organisation as an ecology of ideas: an alternative to the reification of family systems. *Family Process*, *23*, 375–388.

Bograd, M. (1984). Family systems approaches to wife battering: a feminist critique. *American Journal of Orthopsychiatry*, *54*, 558–569.

Bograd, M. & Mederos, F. (1999). Battering and couples therapy: universal screening and selection of treatment modality. *Journal of Marital and Family Therapy*, *25*, 291–312.

Bohart, A. (1993). Experiencing: the basis of psychotherapy. *Journal of Psychotherapy Integration, 3*, 51–68.

Bor, R., Mallandain, I. & Vetere, A. (1998). What we say we do: results of the 1997 UK Association of Family Therapy members survey. *Journal of Family Therapy*, *20*, 333–351.

Boscolo, L. & Bertrando, P. (1996). *Systemic therapy with individuals*. London: Karnac.

Bott, D. (2001). Client centred therapy and family therapy: a review and commentary. *Journal of Family Therapy*, *23*, 361–377.

Bott, D. & Hodes, M. (1989). Structural therapy for a West African family. *Journal of Family Therapy, 11*, 169–179.

Bowen, M. (1972). Towards the differentiation of a self in one's own family. In J. Framo (Ed.), *Family interaction: a dialogue between family researchers and family therapists*. New York: Springer.

Bowen, M. (1976). *Family therapy in clinical practice*. New York: Aronson.

Box, S., Copley, B., Magagna, J. & Moustaki E. (Eds.). (1981) *Psychotherapy with families: An analytic approach*. London Routledge & Kegan Paul.

Boyd-Franklin, N. (1989). *Black families in therapy*. New York: Guilford.

Boyd-Franklin, N. & Bry, B. (2000). *Reaching out in family therapy*. New York: Guilford.

Braham, P., Rattansi, A. & Skellington, R. (1992). *Racism and antiracism: inequalities, opportunities and policies*. London: Sage.

Brazier, D. (1995). *Zen therapy*. London: Constable.

Breunlin, D., Schwartz, R. & MacKune-Karrer, B. (1992). *Metaframeworks: transcending the models of family therapy*. San Francisco: Jossey-Bass.

Broderick, C.B., & Schrader, S.S. (1981). The history of professional marriage and family therapy. In A.S. Gurman & D.P. Kniskern (Eds.), *Handbook of family therapy*. New York: Brunner/Mazel.

Brown, G. & Harris, T. (1978). *The social origins of depression*. London: Tavistock.

Brown, J.A.C. (1961). *Freud and the post Freudians*. Harmondsworth. Penguin.

Brown, P. & O'Leary, K.D. (1997). Wife abuse in intact couples: a review of couples treatment programs. In G.K. Kantor & J. Jasinski (Eds.), *Out of Darkness: contemporary perspectives on family violence*. Thousand Oaks, CA: Sage.

Burbach, F.R. (1996). Family based interventions in psychosis – an overview of, and comparison between, family therapy and family management approaches. *Journal of Mental Health, 5*, 111–134.

Burbach, F.R. & Stanbridge, R.I. (1998). A family intervention in psychosis service integrating the systemic and family management approaches. *Journal of Family Therapy, 20*, 311–326.

Burck, C. (1978). A study of families' expectations and experiences of a child guidance clinic. *British Journal of Social Work, 8*, 145–158.

Burck, C. & Daniel, G. (1995). *Gender and family therapy*. London: Karnac.

Burck, C., Frosh, S., Strickland-Clark, L. & Morgan, K. (1998). The process of enabling change: a study of therapist interventions in family therapy. *Journal of Family Therapy, 20,* 253–268.

Burnham, J. (1986). *Family therapy: first steps towards a systemic approach.* London: Routledge.

Burrell, G. & Morgan, G. (1979). *Sociological paradigms and organisational analysis.* London: Gower.

Busfield, J. (1996). *Men, women and madness: understanding gender and mental disorder.* Basingstoke: Macmillan.

Byng-Hall, J. (1995a). *Rewriting family scripts.* New York: Guilford.

Byng-Hall, J. (1995b). Creating a secure family base: some implications of attachment theory for family therapy. *Family Process, 34,* 45–58.

Byrne, N. & McCarthy, I. (1999). Feminism, politics and power in therapeutic discourse: fragments from the Fifth Province. In I. Parker (Ed.), *Deconstructing psychotherapy.* London: Sage.

Carpenter, J. (1987). Some reflections on the state of family therapy in the UK. *Journal of Family Therapy, 9,* 217–229.

Carpenter, J. (1992). Naivety and family therapy. *Context, 13,* 20–22.

Carpenter, J. & Treacher, A. (1993). User-friendly family therapy. In J. Carpenter & A. Treacher (Eds.), *Using family therapy in the 90s.* Oxford: Blackwell.

Carr, A. (1990). Failure in family therapy: a catalogue of engagement mistakes. *Journal of Family Therapy, 12,* 371–386.

Carr, A. (2000a). Evidence-based practice in family therapy and systemic consultation. I. *Journal of Family Therapy, 22,* 29–60.

Carr, A. (2000b). Evidence-based practice in family therapy and systemic consultation. II. *Journal of Family Therapy, 22,* 273–95.

Carr, A. (2000c). *Family therapy: concepts, process and practice.* Chichester: John Wiley.

Carter, B. & McGoldrick, M. (Eds.). (1989). *The changing family life cycle.* Boston, MA: Allyn & Bacon.

Cecchin, G., Lane, G. & Ray, W. (1993). From strategising to non-intervention: toward irreverence in systemic practice. *Journal of Marital and Family Therapy, 19,* 125–136.

Cecchin, G., Lane, G. & Ray, W. (1994). *Irreverence: cybernetics of prejudice in the pratice of psychotherapy.* London: Karnac.

Chamberlain, P. & Rosicky, J.G., (1995). The effectiveness of family therapy in the treatment of adolescents with conduct disorders and delinquency. *Journal of Marital and Family Therapy, 21,* 441–459.

Child Guidance Special Interest Group. (1975). *The child guidance service.* Cardiff: BASW.

Chimera, C., Cooklin, A & Miller, A. (1999). Organisations for training and service delivery in relation to race, ethnicity and culture. *Context, 44,* 25–31.

Claxton, G. (Ed.), (1986) *Beyond therapy: The Impact of Eastern Religions on Psychological Theory and Practice.* London: Wisdom Publications.

Cochrane, R. (1983). *The social creation of mental illness.* Harlow: Longman.

Coleman, H.L.K., Wampold, B.E. & Casali, S.L. (1995). Ethnic minorities' ratings of ethnically similar and European American counsellors: A meta analysis. *Journal of Counseling Psychology, 42,* 55–64.

Conference Collective. (1999). *Narrative therapy and community work.* Adelaide: Dulnich.

Conran, T. & Love, J. (1993). Client voices: unspeakable theories and unknowable experiences. *Journal of Systemic Therapies, 12*, 1–19.

Cooklin, A. (1996). Happy orgy of reminiscences. *Context, 29*, 9–12.

Cred Subcommittee of AFT. (1993). The case for the registration of family therapists. *Context, 14*, 4–5.

Crook, J & Fontanna, D. (Eds.). (1990). *Space in Mind: East–West Psychology and Contemporary Buddhism*. Shaftesbury, Dorset: Element.

Cupitt, D. (1991). *What is a story?* London: SCM.

Cupitt, D. (1994). *After all*. London: SCM.

Dallos, R. & Draper, R. (2000). *An introduction to family therapy*. Buckingham: Open University Press.

Dallos, R., & Hamilton-Brown, L. (2000). Pathways to problems – an exploratory study of how problems evolve vs dissolve in families. *Journal of Family Therapy. 22*, 375–393.

Dallos, R. & Urry, A. (1999). Abandoning our parents and grandparents: does social constructionism mean the end of systemic family therapy? *Journal of Family Therapy, 21*, 161–186.

Dankoski, M., Penn, M., Carlson, T. & Hecker, L. (1998). What's in a name? A study of family therapists' use and acceptance of the feminism perspective. *American Journal of Family Therapy, 26*, 95–104.

Dawes, R.M. (1994). *House of cards: psychology and psychotherapy built on myth*. New York: Free Press.

de Shazer, S. (1982). *Patterns of brief family therapy*. New York: Guilford.

de Shazer, S. (1985). *Keys to solution in brief therapy*. New York: Guilford.

de Shazer, S. (1991). *Putting difference to work*. New York: Guilford.

Deacon, S., Kirkpatrick, D., Wetchler, J. & Neidner, D. (1999). Marriage and family therapists' problems and utilization of personal therapy. *American Journal of Family Therapy, 27*, 73–93.

Dell, P. (1982). Beyond homeostasis: toward a concept of coherence. *Family Process, 21*, 21–41.

Dell, P. (1989). Violence and the systemic view: the problem of power. *Family Process, 28*, 1–14.

Dell, P.F. (1986). In defence of 'lineal causality'. *Family Process, 25*, 513–521.

Dienhart, A. (2001). Engaging men in family therapy: does the gender of the therapist make a difference? *Journal of Family Therapy, 23*, 21–45.

Dienhart, A. & Avis, J. (1994). Engaging men in family therapy: an exploratory Delphi Study. *Journal of Marital and Family Therapy, 20*, 397–417.

Doherty, W. & Beaton, J. (2000). Family therapists, community and civil renewal. *Family Process, 39*, 149–159.

Doherty, W. & Simmons, D. (1996). Clinical practice patterns of marriage and family therapists: a national survey of therapists and their clients. *Journal of Marital and Family Therapy, 22*, 9–25.

Doherty, W.J. & Baird, M.A. (1987). *Family-centered medical care: A clinical casebook*. New York: Guilford.

Duncan, B.L. & Parks, M.B. (1988). Integrating individual and systems approaches: Strategic-behavioral therapy. *Journal of Marital and Family Therapy, 14*, 151–161.

Dwivedi, K. (Ed.). (1999). Sowing the seeds of cultural competence. *Context, 44*, 2–4.

Epstein, E. (1993). From irreverent to irrelevance: the growing disjuncture of family therapy theories from social realities. *Journal of Systemic Therapies, 12*, 15–27.

Erickson, B. (1992). Feminist fundamentalism. *Journal of Marital and Family Therapy, 18*, 263–267.

Eron, J.B. & Lund, T.W. (1993). How problems evolve and dissolve: Integrating narrative and strategic concepts. *Family Process, 32*, 291–309.

Erwin, E. (1997). *Philosophy and psychotherapy*. London: Sage.

Estrada, A.U. & Pinsof, W.M. (1995). The effectiveness of family therapies for elected behavioural disorders of childhood. *Journal of Marital and Family Therapy, 21*, 403–440.

Fadden, G. (1998). Research update: psychoeducational family interventions. *Journal of Family Therapy, 20*, 293–311.

Fallon, I.R.H., Pederson, J. & Al-Khayyal, M. (1986). Enhancing of health giving family support versus treatment of family pathology. *Journal of Family Therapy. 8*, 339–350.

Feldman, L.B. (1985). Integrative multi-level therapy: a comprehensive interpersonal and intrapsychic approach. *Journal of Marital and Family Therapy, 11*, 357–372.

Feldman, L.B. (1990). *Multi-dimensional family therapy*. New York: Guilford.

Fernando, S. (1989). *Race and culture in psychiatry*. London: Routledge.

Fernando, S. (1991). *Mental health, race and culture*. Basingstoke: Macmillan.

Flaskas, C. (1997). Engagement and the therapeutic relationship in systemic therapy. *Journal of Family Therapy, 19*, 263–282.

Font, R., Vecchio, K.D.-D. & Almeida, R. (1998) .Finding the words: instruments of liberation. In R. Almeida, (Ed.), *Transformations of gender and race*. Binghamton, NY: Haworth Press.

Foucault, M. (1965). *Madness and civilisation: a history of insanity in the age of reason*. New York: Random House.

Foucault, M. (1976). *The birth of the clinic*. London: Tavistock.

Foucault, M. (1986). *The Foucault reader* (P. Rabinow, Ed.). Harmondsworth: Penguin.

Frank, J.D. (1961). *Persuasion and healing: a comparative study of psychotherapy*. Baltimore, MD: Johns Hopkins University Press.

Frankland, A. (1996). Accreditation and registration. In R. Bayne, I. Horton & J. Bimrose (Eds.), *New directions in counselling*. London: Routledge.

Friedlander, M. (1998). Family therapy research. In M. Nichols & R. Schwartz *Family therapy: concepts and methods*. New York: Allyn & Bacon.

Friedlander, M., Wildman, J., Heatherington, L. & Skowron, E. (1994). What we do and don't know about the process of family therapy. *Journal of Family Psychology, 8*, 390–416.

Friedman, S. (1993). *The new language of change*. New York: Guilford.

Garfield, S.L. (1992). Eclectic psychotherapy: a common factors approach. In J.C. Norcross & M.R. Goldfried (Eds.), *Handbook of psychotherapy integration*. New York: Basic Books.

Gergen, K. (1991). *The saturated self*. New York: Basic Books.

Gergen, K. (1999). *An invitation to social construction*. London: Sage.

Golann, S. (1988). On second order family therapy. *Family Process, 27*, 51–65.

Goldenberg, I. & Goldenberg, H. (2000). *Family therapy: an overview*. Pacific Grove, CA: Brooks/Cole.

Goldner, V. (1985). Feminism and family therapy. *Family Process, 24*, 31–47.

Goldner, V. (1991). Generation and gender: normative and covert hierarchies. In M. McGoldrick, C. Anderson, & F. Walsh (Eds.), *Women in families: a framework for family therapy*. New York: Norton.

Goldner, V. (1998). The treatment of violence and victimization in intimate relationships. *Family Process*, *37*, 263–286.

Goldner, V. (1999). Morality and multiplicity: perspectives on the treatment of violence in intimate life. *Journal of Marital and Family Therapy*, *25*, 325–336.

Goldner, V., Penn, P., Sheinberg, M. & Walker, G. (1990). Love and violence: gender paradoxes in volatile attachments. *Family Process*, *29*, 343–364.

Goldstein, M.J. (1983). Family interaction: patterns predictive of the onset and course of schizophrenia. In H. Stierlin, L.C. Wynne & M. Wirching (Eds.), *Psychosocial intervention in schizophrenia. An international View*. Berlin: Springer-Verlag

Goldstein, M.J. & Miklowitz, D.J. (1995). The effectiveness of psychoeducational family therapy in the treatment of schizophrenic disorders. *Journal of Marital and Family Therapy*, *21*, 361–376.

Goodrich, T. (Ed.). (1991). *Women and power: perspectives for family therapy*. New York: Norton.

Goolishian, H. & Anderson, H. (1992). Strategy and intervention versus non-intervention: a matter of theory? *Journal of Marital and Family Therapy*, *18*, 5–15.

Gorell Barnes, G. (1998). *Family therapy in changing times*. London: Macmillan.

Greenberg, L.S. & Johnson, S.M. (1988). *Emotionally focused therapy for couples*. New York: Guilford.

Grunebaum, H. (1988). The relationship of family theory to family therapy. *Journal of Marital and Family Therapy*, *14*, 1–14.

Grunebaum, H. (1997). Commentary: why integration may be a misguided goal for family therapy. *Family Process*. *36*, 19–21.

Gurman, A.S. (1981). Integrative marital therapy: toward the development of an interpersonal approach. In S. Budman (Ed.), *Forms of brief therapy*. New York: Guilford.

Gurman, A.S. & Kniskern, D.P. (1978). Research on marital and family therapy: progress, perspective and prospect. In A.E. Bergin & S.L. Garfield (Eds.), *Handbook of psychotherapy and behaviour change* (2nd Ed.). New York: John Wiley.

Gurman, A.S., Kniskern, D.P. & Pinsof, W.M. (1986). Research on marital and family therapies. In S.L. Garfield & A.E. Bergen (Eds.), *Handbook of psychotherapy and behavior change* (3rd ed.). New York: John Wiley.

Haber, R, (1990). From handicap to handy capable: training systemic therapists in use of self. *Family Process*, *29*, 375–384.

Haley, J. (1962). Whither family therapy? *Family Process, 1*, 68–100.

Haley, J. (1963). *Strategies of psychotherapy*. New York: Grune & Stratton.

Haley, J. (1976). *Problem solving therapy*. San Francisco: Jossey Bass.

Haley, J. (1980). *Leaving home: the therapy of disturbed young people*. New York: McGraw-Hill.

Haley, J. (1981a). Why a mental health clinic should aviod family therapy. In J. Haley, *Reflections on therapy and other essays*. Washington DC: Family Therapy Institute.

Haley, J. (1981b). Development of a theory: a history of a research project. In J Haley, *Reflections on therapy and other essays*. Washington DC: Family Therapy Institute.

Haley, J. (1986). *The power tactics of jesus Chirst and other esays*. Rockville, MD: Triangle press.

Hardy, K. & Laszloffy, T. (1995). The cultural genogram: key to training culturally competent family therapists. *Journal of Marital and Family Therapy*, *21*, 227–237.

Hardy, K. & Laszloffy, T. (1998). The dynamics of a pro-racist ideology: implications for family therapists. In M. McGoldrick (Ed.), *Re-visioning family therapy*. New York: Guilford.

Hardy, K. & Laszloffy, T. (2000). Uncommon strategies for a common problem: addressing racism in family therapy. *Family Process*, *39*, 35–50.

Hare-Mustin, R. (1978). A feminist approach to family therapy. *Family Process*, *17*, 181–194.

Hare-Mustin, R.T. & Marecek, J. (1997). Abnormal and clinical psychology: the politics of madness. In D. Fox & I. Prilleltensky (Eds.), *Critical psychology: an introduction*. London: Sage.

Harre, R. (1972). *The philosophies of science*. Oxford: Oxford University Press.

Harway, M., Hansen, M. & Cervantes, N. (1997). Therapist awareness of appropriate intervention in treatment of domestic violence: a review. *Journal of Aggression, Maltreatment and Trauma*, *1*, 27–40.

Hawley, D.R. & DeHaan, L. (1996). Toward a definition of family resilience: integrating life-span and family perspectives. *Family Process*, *35*, 283–298.

Hawley, D.R. & Olson, D.H. (1995). Enriching newlyweds: an evaluation of three enrichment programs. *The American Journal of Family Therapy*, *23*(2), 129–147.

Health Advisory Service [HAS]. (1995). *Together we stand*. London: HMSO.

Held, B. (1995). *Back to reality: a critique of post-modern theory in psychotherapy*. New York: Norton.

Held, B. (1996). Solution-focused therapy and the post-modern. In S. Miller, M. Hubble & B. Duncan (Eds.), *Handbook of solution-focused brief therapy*. San Francisco: Jossey-Bass.

Held, B. (2000). To be or not to be theoretical: that is the question. *Journal of Systemic Therapies*, *19*, 35–49.

Hildebrand, J. (1998). *Building bridges*. London: Karnac.

Hill, J. (1994). Ethnicity, culture, race and family therapy. *Context*, *20*, 2–3

Hoffman, L. (1988). A constructivist position for family therapy. *Irish Journal of Psychology*, *9*, 110–129.

Hoffman, L. (1990). Constructing realities: an art of lenses. *Family Process*, *29*, 1–12.

Hoffman, L. (1993). *Exchanging voices: a collaborative approach to family therapy*. London: Karnac.

Hoffman, L. (1998). Setting aside the model in family therapy. *Journal of Marital and Family Therapy*, *24*, 145–156.

House, R. (2001). The statutory regulation of psychotherapy. *The Psychotherapist*, *17*, 12–17.

Howe, D. (1989). *The consumers' view of family therapy*. Aldershot: Gower.

Howe, D. (1991). The family and the therapist. In M. Davies (Ed.), *The sociology of social work*. London: Routledge.

Howe, D. (1992). *An introduction to social work theory*. Aldershot: Arena.

Howe, D. (1993). *On being a client: understanding the process of counselling and psychotherapy*. London: Sage.

Hubble M.A., Duncan, B.L. & Miller, S.D. (Eds.). (1999). *The heart and soul of change: what works in therapy*. Washington, DC: American Psychological Association.

Ivey, A.E., Ivey, M.B. & Simek-Morgan, L. (1993). *Counselling and Psychotherapy: a multi-cultural perspective* (3rd Ed.). Needham Heights, MA: Allyn & Bacon.

Jackson, D. (1965). The study of the family. *Family Process*, *4*, 1–20

Jacobson, N.S. (1992). Behavioral couple therapy: a new beginning. *Behavior Therapy*, *23*, 493–506.

Jacobson, N.S. & Gottman, J. (1998). *When men batter women: new insights*. New York: Simon & Schuster.

Jenkins, H. & Asen, K. (1992). Family therapy without the family: a framework for systemic practice. *Journal of Family Therapy, 14*, 1–14.

Johnstone. L. (1993). Family management in schizophrenia: its assumptions and contradictions. *Journal of Mental Health, 2*, 255–269.

Jones, E. (1990). Feminism and family therapy: can mixed marriages work? In R. Perelberg & A. Miller (Eds.), *Gender and power in families*. London: Routledge.

Jones, E. (1993). *Family systems therapy*. Chicester: John Wiley.

Jordan, J., Miller, J., Stiver, I. & Surrey, J. (Eds.). (1991). *Women's growth in connection: writings from the Stone Center*. New York: Guilford.

Kaplan, H.S. (1974). *The new sex therapy*. New York: Brunner/Mazel.

Karasu, T.B. (1986). Specificity versus and non-specificity. *American Journal of Psychiatry, 143*, 687–695.

Karl, Cynthia, Andrew & Vanessa. (1992). Therapeutic distinctions in an on-going therapy. In S. McNamee & K. Gergen (Eds.), *Therapy as social construction*. London: Sage.

Kaslow. F.W. (1990a). *Voices in family psychology. Vol.1*. Newbury Park, CA: Sage.

Kaslow. F.W. (1990b). *Voices in family psychology. Vol.2*. Newbury Park, CA: Sage.

Kaufman, G. (1992). The mysterious disappearance of battered women in family therapists' offices: male privilege colluding with male violence. *Journal of Marital and Family Therapy, 18*, 233–243.

Keeney, B. (1983). *Aesthetics of change*. New York: Guilford.

Kirschner, D.A. & Kirschner, S. (1986). *Comprehensive family therapy: an integration of systemic and psychodynamic treatment models*. New York: Brunner/Mazel.

Klein, D.M. & White, J.M. (1996). *Family theories*. Thousand Oaks, CA: Sage.

Kogan, S.M. (1998). The politics of making meaning: discourse analysis of a 'postmodern' interview. *Journal of Family Therapy, 20*, 229–252.

Kogan, S.M. & Gale, J.E. (1997). Decentering therapy: textual analysis of a narrative therapy session. *Family Process, 36*, 101–126.

Kohut, H. (1977). *The restoration of the self*. New York: International Universities Press.

Kopp, S. (1979). *If you meet the Buddha on the road, kill him!* Palo Alto, CA: Science and Behavior Books.

Kuehl, B., Newfield, N. & Joanning, H. (1990). A client based description of family therapy. *Journal of Family Psychology, 3*, 310–321.

L'Abate, L., (1986). *Systemic family therapy*. New York: Brunner/Mazel.

Laing, R. (1965). *The divided self*. Harmondsworth: Penguin.

Laing, R. (1972). *Knots*. Harmondsworth: Penguin.

Lambert, M.J. (1992). Implications of outcome research for psychotherapy. In J.C. Norcross & M.R. Goldfried (Eds.), *Handbook of psychotherapy integration*. New York: Basic Books.

Larner, G. (1994). Para-modern family therapy: deconstructing post-modernism. *Australian and New Zealand Journal of Family Therapy, 15*, 11–16.

Larner, G. (1995). The real as illusion: deconstructing power in family therapy. *Journal of Family Therapy, 17*, 191–217.

Larner, G. (2000). Towards a common ground in psychoanalysis and family therapy: on knowing not to know. *Journal of Family Therapy, 22*, 61–82.

Lask, B. (1987). Cybernetico-epistobabble, the emperor's new clothes and other sacred cows. *Journal of Family Therapy*, 9, 207–215.

Lebow, J.L. (1984). On the value of integrating approaches to family therapy. *Journal of Marital and Family Therapy*, 10, 127–138.

Lebow, J.L. (1987). Developing a personal integration in a family therapy: principles for model construction and the practice. *Journal of Marital and Family Therapy*. 13, 1–14.

Lebow, J.L. (1997). The integrative revolution in couple and family therapy. *Family Process, 36*, 1–17.

Leff, J. & Vaughn, C.E. (1985). *Expressed emotion in families*. New York: Guilford.

Leitch, L. & Thomas, V. (1999). The AAMFT–Head Start training partnership project: enhancing MFT capacities beyond the family system. *Journal of Marital and Family Therapy*, 25, 141–154.

Liddle, H.A. (1982). On the problems of eclecticism: a call for epistemologic clarification and human-scale theories. *Family Process, 21*, 243–250.

Liddle, H.A. (1984). Toward a dialectrical–contextual–coevolutionary translation of structural–strategic family therapy. *Journal of Strategic and Systemic Therapies* 3, 66–79.

Liddle, H.A., Dakof, G.A. & Diamond, G. (1991). Adolescent substance abuse: Multidimensional family therapy in action. In E. Kaufman & P. Kaufmann (Eds.), *Family therapy with drug and alcohol abuse* (2nd Ed.). Boston, MA: Allyn & Bacon.

Lieberman, S. (1980). *Transgenerational family therapy*. London: Croom Helm.

Littlewood, R. & Lipsedge, M. (1982). *Aliens and alienists: ethnic minorities and psychiatry*. Harmondsworth: Penguin.

Luepnitz, D. (1988). *The family interpreted: feminist theory in clinical practice*. New York: Basic Books.

Luepnitz, D. (1997). Feminism, psychoanalysis and family therapy: reflections of telos. *Journal of Family Therapy*, 19, 303–317.

Lyon, D. (1994). *Postmodernity*. Buckingham: Open University Press.

Lyotard, J.-F. (1986). *The postmodern condition: a report on knowledge*. Manchester: Manchester University Press.

Macionis, J. & Plummer, K. (1997). *Sociology*. Harlow: Pearson Education.

Markowitz, L. (1993). Walking the walk. *Family Therapy Networker*, July/August, pp. 19–31.

Marsh, P. & Crow, G. (1997). *Family group conferences in child welfare*. Oxford: Blackwell.

Marx, K. (1975). *Early writings*. Harmondsworth: Penguin.

Masson, J. (1988). *Against therapy*. New York; Atheneum.

Masson, J. (1992). The tyranny of psychotherapy. In W. Dryden & C. Feltham (Eds.), *Psychotherapy and its discontents*. Buckingham: Open University Press.

May, T. (1993). *Social research*. Buckingham: Open University Press.

McCarthy, I. (1998). Power, abuse discourses and women in poverty. *Human Systems, 8*, 239–249.

McCarthy, I. (2001). Fifth Province re-versings: the social construction of women lone parents' inequality and poverty. *Journal of Family Therapy*, 23, 253–277.

McCubbin, H.I., Thompson, E.A., Thompson, A.I. & Frommer, J.E. (1998). *Stress, coping, and health in families: sense of coherence and resiliency*. London: Sage.

McDaniel, S.H., Hepworth,J. & Doherty, W.J. (1992). *Medical family therapy: a biopsychosocial approach to families with health problems*. New York: Basic Books.

McFadyen, A. (1997). Rapprochement in sight? postmodern family therapy and psychoanalysis. *Journal of Family Therapy, 19*, 241–262.

McGoldrick, M. (1998). A framework for re-visioning family therapy. In M. McGoldrick (Ed.), *Re-visioning family therapy*. New York: Guilford.

McGoldrick, M., Almeida, R., Preto, N., Bibb, A., Sutton, C., Hudak, J. & Hines, P. (1999). Efforts to incorporate social justice perspectives into a family training program. *Journal of Marital and Family Therapy, 25*, 191–209.

McGoldrick, M., Anderson, C. & Walsh, F. (1989). Women in families and in family herapy. In M. McGoldrick, C. Anderson & F. Walsh (Eds.), *Women in families: a framework for family therapy*. New York: Norton.

McLeod, J. (1997). *Narrative and psychotherapy*. London: Sage.

McNamee, S. & Gergen, K. (Eds.). (1992). *Therapy as social construction*. London: Sage.

Mederos, F. (1999). Batterer intervention programs. In M. Shepard & E. Pence (Eds.), *Coordinating community responses to domestic violence: lessons from Duluth and beyond*. Thousand Oaks, CA: Sage.

Melito, R. (1988). Combining individual psychodynamics with structural family therapy. *Journal of Marital and Family Therapy, 14*, 29–43.

Meltzer, H., Gatward, R., Goodman, R. & Ford, T. (2000). *Mental health of children and adolescents in Great Britain*. London: The Stationery Office.

Mental Health Foundation. (2000). *Bright futures: promoting children and young people's mental health*. London: Mental Health Foundation.

Messent, P. (1992). Working with Bangladeshi familes in the East of London. *Journal of Family Therapy, 14*, 287–304.

Messent, P. (2000). Social workers in child mental health: securing a future. *Child Psychology and Psychiatry, 5*, 102–107.

Miles, A. (1987). *The mentally ill in contemporary society*. Oxford: Blackwell.

Miller, D. (1984). Commentary: a family is a family is a family. *Family Process, 23*, 389–395.

Miller, G. & Baldwin, D. (1987). Implications of the wounded healer paradigm for the use of self in therapy. In M. Baldwin & V. Satir (Eds.), *The use of self in therapy*. New York: Haworth Press.

Miller, G. & de Shazer, S. (1998). Have you heard the latest rumor about...? Solution-focused therapy as a rumor. *Family Process, 37*, 363–377.

Miller, S.D., Duncan, B.L. & Hubble, M.A. (1997). *Escape from Babel: towards a unifying language for psychotherapy practice*. New York: Norton.

Ministerial Group on the Family (1998). *Supporting families*. London: The Stationery Office.

Minuchin, P., Colapinto, J. & Minuchin, S. (1998). *Working with families of the poor*. New York: Guilford.

Minuchin, S. (1974). *Families and family therapy*. Cambridge Mass: Harvard University Press.

Minuchin, S. (1998). Where is the family in narrative family therapy? *Journal of Marital and Family Therapy, 24*, 397–403.

Minuchin, S., Montalvo, B., Guerney, B., Rosman, B. & Schumer, F. (1967). *Families of the slums*. New York: Basic Books.

Morton, A. (1987). Who started it? Remarks about causation. In S. Walrond-Skinner & D. Watson (Eds.), *Ethical issues in family therapy*. London: Routledge & Kegan Paul.

Moultrop, D.J., (1981) Towards an integrated model of family therapy. *Clinical Social Work Journal, 9*, 111–125.

Moultrop, D.J. (1986). Integration: a coming of age. *Contemporary Family Therapy, 8*, 157–167.

Mowbray, R. (1995). *The case against psychotherapy registration: a conservation issue for the human potential movement.* London: Trans Marginal.

Muncie, J., Wetherall, M., Langan, M., Dallos, R. & Cochrane, A. (1997). *Understanding the family.* London: Sage.

Natoli, J. & Hutcheon, L. (1993). *A post-modern reader.* New York: State University of New York Press.

Nichols, M. & Schwartz, R. (Eds.). (1995) *Family therapy: concepts and methods* (3rd Ed.). Boston, MA: Allyn & Bacon.

Nichols, M. & Schwartz, R. (Eds.). (1998). *Family therapy: concepts and methods* (4th Ed.). Needham Heights, MA: Allyn & Bacon.

Nichols, M.P. (1987). *The self in the system: expanding the limits of family therapy.* New York: Brunner/Mazel.

Nock, S. (2000). The divorce of marriage from parenthood. *Journal of Family Therapy, 22*, 245–263.

O'Hagan, K. (2001). *Cultural competence in the caring professions.* London: Jessica Kingsley.

Olson, D.H. & Olson, A.K. (1999) PREPARE/ENRICH program: Version 2000. *Journal of Family Ministry, 11*, 4, 28–53.

Osborne, K. (1983). Women in families: feminist therapy and family systems. *Journal of Family Therapy, 5*, 1–10.

Padilla, A.M. & De Snyder, S.N. (1987). Counselling hispanics: strategies for effective intervention. In P. Pederson (Ed.), *Handbook of cross cultural counselling and therapy.* Westport, CT: Greenwood.

Pakman, M. (1995). Therapy in contexts of poverty and ethnic dissonance: contructivism and social constructionism as methodologies for action. *Journal of Systemic Therapies, 14*, 64–71.

Palazzoli, M.S., Boscolo, L., Cecchin, G. & Prata, G. (1978). *Paradox and counterparadox: a new model in the therapy of the family in schizophrenic transaction.* Northvale, NJ: Aronson.

Parfit, D. (1987). Divided minds and the nature of persons. In C. Blakemore & S. Greenfield (Eds.), *Mindwaves.* Oxford: Blackwell.

Parker, I., Georgaca, E., Harper, D., McLaughlin, T. & Stowell-Smith, M. (1995). *Deconstructing psychopathology.* London: Sage.

Parry, A. (1991). A universe of stories. *Family Process, 30*, 37–54.

Paterson, T. (1996). Leaving well alone: a systemic perspective on the therapeutic relationship. In C. Flaskas & A. Perlesz. (Eds.), *The therapeutic relationship in systemic therapy.* London: Karnac.

Patterson, C.H. (1996). Multi-cultural counselling: from diversity to universality. *Journal of Counselling and Development, 74*, 227–231.

Patterson, G.R. (1982). *A social learning approach to family intervention.* Eugene, OR: Castalia.

Pearson, G. (1974). Prisons of love: the reification of the family in family therapy. In N. Armistead (Ed.), *Reconstructing social psychology.* Harmondsworth: Penguin.

Pence, E. & Paymar, M. (1993). *Education groups for men who batter.* New York: Springer.

Perlesz, A., Young, J., Paterson, R. & Bridge, S. (1994). The reflecting team as a reflection of second order therapeutic ideals. *Australian and New Zealand Journal of Family Therapy, 15*, 117–127.

Piazza, J. & del Valle, C. (1992). Community based family therapy training: an example of work with poor and minority families. *Journal of Strategic and Systemic Therapies, 11*, 53–69.

Piercy, F.P. & Frankel, B.R. (1989). The evolution of an integrative family therapy for substance-abusing adolescents: toward the mutual enhancement of research and practice. *Journal of Family Psychology, 3*, 5–25.

Pilgrim, D. (1983). Politics, psychology and psychiatry. In D. Pilgrim (Ed.), *Psychology and psychotherapy*. London: Routledge & Kegan Paul.

Pilgrim, D. (1992). Psychotherapy and political evasions. In W. Dryden & C. Feltham (Eds.), *Psychotherapy and its discontents*. Buckingham: Open University Press.

Pilgrim, D. (1997). *Psychotherapy and society*. London: Sage.

Pilgrim, D. & Rogers, A. (1993). *A sociology of mental health and mental illness*. Buckingham: Open University Press.

Pinsof, W.M. (1994). An overview of integrative problem-centered therapy: a synthesis of family, and individual psychotherapies. *Journal of Family Therapy, 16*, 103–121.

Pinsof, W.M. (1995). *Integrative problem centered therapy*. New York: Basic Books.

Pinsof, W.M. & Wynne, L.C. (1995). The efficacy of marital and family therapy: an empirical overview, conclusions and recommendations. *Journal of Marital and Family Therapy, 21*, 585–613

Pocock, D. (1995). Searching for a better story: harnessing modern and postmodern positions in family therapy. *Journal of Family Therapy, 17*, 149–173.

Pocock, D. (1999). Loose ends. *Journal of Family Therapy, 21*, 187–194.

Poster, M. (1978). *The critical theory of the family*. London: Pluto Press.

Rabinow, P. (1984). *The Foucault reader*. New York: Pantheon Books.

Rack, P. (1982). *Race, culture and mental disorder*. London: Tavistock.

Ranade, W. (1994). *A future for the NHS?* London: Longman.

Rappaport, J. & Stewart, E. (1997) A critical look at critical psychology: elaborating the questions. In D. Fox & I. Prilleltensky. (Eds.), *Critical psychology: an Introduction*. London: Sage.

Rayner, P. (1986). On asking the right questions. *Family Process, 25*, 123–131.

Reimers S. & Treacher, A. (1995). *Introducing user-friendly family therapy*. London: Routledge.

Richeport-Haley, M. (1998). Ethnicity in family therapy: a comparison of brief strategic therapy and culture focused therapy. *American Journal of Family Therapy, 26*, 77–90.

Rieff, P. (1966). *The triumph of the therapeutic*. Chicago: Chicago University Press.

Rivett, M. (1997). Myths, legends and redescriptions. *Context, 34*, 3–4.

Rivett, M. (1999). A thematic review of the family therapy journals of 1998. *Journal of Family Therapy, 21*, 377–389.

Rivett, M. (2001). Comments–working systemically with family violence: controversy, context and accountability. *Journal of Family Therapy, 23*, 397–404.

Rivett, M. & Smith, G. (1997). Celebrating British family therapy. *Context, 34*, 2–16.

Rivett, M. & Street, E. (2000). The snowy heron in the bright moon hides. *Context, 48*, 27–28.

Rivett, M. & Street, E. (2001) Connections and themes of spirituality in family therapy. *Family Process, 40*, 457–465.

Rivett, M., Tomsett, J., Lumsdon, P. & Holmes, P. (1997). Strangers in a familiar place: the evolution of a family therapy clinic within an in-patient adolescent unit. *Journal of Family Therapy, 19*, 43–57.

Rogers, A. & Pilgrim, D. (1996). *Mental health policy in Britain.* Basingstoke: Macmillan.

Rogers, C. (1957). The necessary and sufficient conditions of personality change. *Journal of Consulting Psychology, 21,* 95–103.

Rogers, C. (1990). A therapist's view of the good life: the fully functioning person. In H. Kirschenbaum & V. Henderson (Eds.), *The Carl Rogers reader.* London: Constable.

Rolland, J.S. (1994). *Families, illness, and disability: an integrative treatment model.* New York: Basic Books.

Rose, N. (1999). *Governing the soul.* London: Free Association Books.

Rosenbaum, R. (1998). *Zen and the art of psychotherapy.* New York: Brunner/Mazel.

Rosenbaum, R. & Dyckman, J. (1995). Integrating self and system: an empty intersection? *Family Process, 34,* 21–44

Rosenzweig, S. (1936). Some implicit common factors in diverse methods in psychotherapy. *Journal of Orthopsychiatry, 6,* 412–415.

Roth, A. & Fonagy, P. (1996). *What works for whom? A critical view of psychotherapy research.* London. Guilford.

Routledge, D. (1996). Personal communication.

Roy, R. & Frankel, H. (1995). *How good is family therapy?* Toronto. University of Toronto Press.

Russell, G.F., Szmukler, G.I., Dare, C. & Eisler, I. (1987). An evaluation of family therapy in anorexia nervosa and bulimia nervosa. *Archives of General Psychiatry, 44,* 1047–1056.

Rutter, M. (1999). Resilience concepts and findings: implications for family therapy. *Journal of Family Therapy, 21,* 119–144.

Salkovskis, P.M. (1995). Demonstrating specific effects in cognitive and behavioural therapy. In M. Aveline & D.J. Shapiro (Eds.), *Research foundations for psychotherapy practice.* Chichester: John Wiley.

Samuels, A. (1999). Therapy in/and/of/by the world. *Australian and New Zealand Journal of Family Therapy, 20,* 121–127.

Sanders, B. (1998). Why post-modern theory may be a problematic basis for a therapeutic practice: a feminist perspective. *Australian and New Zealand Journal of Family Therapy, 19,* 111–119.

Sarup, M. (1993). *An introductory guide to post-structuralism and postmodernism.* Hemel Hempstead: Harvester Wheatsheaf.

Satir, V. (1978). *Conjoint family therapy.* London: Souvenir Press.

Schneider, C. (1990). The struggle towards a feminist practice in family therapy: practice. In R. Perelberg & A. Miller (Eds.), *Gender and power in families.* London: Routledge.

Schwartz, R. (1995). *Internal family systems therapy.* New York: Guilford.

Seaburn, D.B., Landau-Stanton, J. & Horwitz, S. (1995). Core techniques in family therapy. In R.H. Mikesell, D.D. Lusterman & S.H. McDaniel (Eds.), *Integrating family therapy: handbook of family psychology and systems therapy.* Washington, DC: American Psychological Association.

Sedgwick, P. (1982). *Psycho politics.* London: Pluto Press.

Sells, S., Smith, T. & Moon, S. (1996). An ethnographic study of clients' and therapists' perceptions of therapeutic effectiveness in a university based clinic. *Journal of Marital and Family Therapy, 22,* 325–342.

Shadish, W., Montgomery, L., Wilson, P., Wilson, M., Bright, I., & Okwumabua, T. (1993). The effects of family and marital psychotherapies: a meta-analysis. *Journal of Consulting and Clinical Psychology. 61,* 992–1002.

Shadish, W.R., Ragsdale, K., Glaser, R.R. & Montgomery, L.M. (1995). The efficacy and effectiveness of marital and family therapy: a perspective of meta-analysis. *Journal of Marital and Family Therapy, 21*, 345–360.

Shadley, M.L. (1987). Are all therapists alike? Use of self in family therapy: a multidimensional perspective. In M. Baldwin & V. Satir (Eds.), *The use of self in therapy*. New York: Haworth Press.

Shaw, E., Bouris, A. & Pye, S. (1996). The family safety model: a comprehensive strategy for working with domestic violence. *Australian and New Zealand Journal of Family Therapy, 17*, 126–136.

Shek, D. & Lai, K. (2001). The Chinese version of the self-report family inventory: reliability and validity. *American Journal of Family Therapy, 29*, 207–220.

Shields, G.C., Wynne, L.C., McDaniel, H. & Gawinski, B.A. (1994). The marginalisation of family therapy: a historical and continuing problem. *Journal of Marital and Family Therapy, 20*, 117–138.

Showalter, E. (1987). *The female malady: women, madness and English culture 1830–1980*. London: Virago.

Simon, D. (1991). Developing a profession: opportunities to emerge. *Context, 9*, 22–23.

Simon, G. (1995). A revisionist rendering of structural family therapy. *Journal of Marital and Family Therapy, 21*, 17–26.

Simon, R. (1989). Family life cycle issues in the therapy system. In B. Carter & M. McGoldrick (Eds.), *The changing family life cycle*. (2nd Ed.). Boston, MA: Allyn & Bacon.

Simon, R. (1997). Fearless foursome. *Family Therapy Networker*, November–December, pp. 57–68.

Skellington, R. & Morris, P. (1992). *'Race' in Britain today*. London: Sage.

Smart, B. (1993). *Postmodernity*. London: Routledge.

Speck, R. & Attneave, C. (1974). *Family networks*. New York: Vintage Books.

Speed, B. (1984). Family therapy: an update. *ACPP Newsletter, 6*, 2–14.

Speed, B. (1987). Over the top in the theory and practice of family therapy. *Journal of Family Therapy, 9*, 231–240.

Speed, B. (1991). Reality exists OK? An argument against constructivism and social constructionism. *Journal of Family Therapy, 13*, 395–409.

Speed, B. & Carpenter, J. (1998). Editorial: looking back and looking forward. *Journal of family therapy, 20*, 111–112.

Sprenkle, D.H., Blow, A.J. & Dickey, M.H. (1999). Common factors and other nontechnique variables in marriage and family therapy. In M.A. Hubble B.L. Duncan, & S.D. Miller. (Eds.), *The heart and soul of change: what works in therapy*. Washington, DC: American Psychological Association.

Stahmann, R.F. (2000). Premarital counselling: a focus for family therapy. *Journal of Family Therapy. 22*, 104–116.

Steinglass, P. (1991). An editorial: finding a place for the individual in family therapy. *Family Process, 30*, 267–269.

Stewart, K. & Amundson, J. (1995). The ethical postmodernist: or not everything is relative all at once. *Journal of Systemic Therapies, 14*, 2: 70–78.

Street, E. (1989). Challenging the White Knight. In: L. Spurling & W. Dryden (Eds.), *On becoming a psychotherapist*. London: Routledge.

Street, E. (1994). *Counselling for Family Problems*. London: Sage.

Street, E. (2003). Counselling psychology and naturally occurring systems. In R. Woolfe, W. Dryden & S. Strawbridge (Eds.), *Handbook of Counselling Psychology*. (2nd Ed.). London: Sage.

Street, E. & Reimers, S. (1993). Using family therapy in child and adolescent services. In J. Carpenter & A. Treacher (Eds.), *Using family therapy in the 90s*. Oxford: Blackwell.

Street, E. & Rivett, M. (1996). Stress and coping in the practice of family therapy. *Journal of Family Therapy, 18*, 303–319.

Strickland-Clark, L., Campbell, D. & Dallos, R. (2000) Children's and adolescents' views on family therapy. *Journal of Family Therapy, 22*, 324–341.

Sue, D.W. & Sue, D. (1990). *Counselling and the culturally different: theory and practice*. New York: John Wiley.

Sue, S., Zane, N. & Young, K. (1994). Research on psychotherapy with culturally diverse populations in A.E. Bergin and S.L. Garfield op cit. (Eds.), *Handbook of psychotherapy and behavior change*. (4th Ed.). New York. Wiley.

Sullivan, H.S. (1954). *The psychiatric interview*. New York: Norton.

Tamasese, K. & Waldegrave, C. (1993). Cultural and gender accountability in the 'Just Therapy' approach. *Journal of Feminist Family Therapy, 5*, 29–45.

Terkelsen, K.G. (1983). Schizophrenia and the family: II. Adverse effects of family therapy. *Family Process. 22*,191–200.

Totton, N. (2000). *Psychotherapy and politics*. London: Sage.

Treacher, A. (1987). 'Family therapists are potentially damaging to families and their wider networks.' Discuss. In S. Walrond-Skinner & D. Watson (Eds.), *Ethical issues in family therapy*. London: Routledge & Kegan Paul.

Treacher, A. (1993). The case against the registration of family therapists. *Context, 14*, 7.

Treacher, A. (1995). Steps towards a user-friendly approach. In S. Reimers & A Treacher. *Introducing user-friendly family therapy*. London Routledge.

UKCP. (2001). *National register of psychotherapists*. London: Routledge.

Varela, F.J., Thompson, E. & Rosch, E. (1991). *The embodied mind*. Cambridge, MA: MIT Press.

Vetere, A. & Gale, A. (1987). *Ecological studies of family life*. Chichester: John Wiley.

Vetere, A. & Henley, M. (2001). Integrating couples and family therapy into a community alcohol service: a pantheoretical approach. *Journal of Family Therapy, 23*, 85–101.

Wachtel, P.L. & Wachtel, E.F. (1986). *Family dynamics in individual psychotherapy: a guide to clinical strategies*. New York: Guilford.

Waldegrave, C. (1990). Just Therapy. *Dulwich Centre Newsletter, 1*, 5–48.

Waldegrave, C. & Tamasese, K. (1993). Some central ideas in the 'Just Therapy' approach. *Australian and New Zealand Journal of Family Therapy, 14*, 1–8.

Walrond-Skinner, S (1976). *Family therapy. The treatment of natural systems*. London: Routledge & Kegan Paul.

Walrond-Skinner, S. (1987). Feminist therapy and family therapy: the limits to the association. In S. Walrond-Skinner, & D. Watson (Eds.), *Ethical issues in family therapy*. London: Routledge & Kegan Paul.

Walrond-Skinner, S. & Watson, D. (Eds.). (1987). *Ethical issues in family therapy*. London: Routledge & Kegan Paul.

Walsh, F. (1996). The concept of family resilience: crisis and challenge. *Family Process, 35*, 261–281.

Walsh, F. & Scheinkman, M. (1989). (Fe)male: the hidden gender dimension in models of family therapy. In M. McGoldrick, C. Anderson & F. Walsh (Eds.), *Women in families: a framework for family therapy*. New York: Norton.

Walters, M. (1990). A feminist perspective in family therapy. In R. Perelberg, & A. Miller (Eds.), *Gender and power in families*. London: Routledge.

Walters, M., Carter, B., Papp, P. & Silverstein, O. (1989). *The invisible web: gender patterns in family relationships*. New York: Guilford.

Watzlawick, P. Weakland, J. & Fisch, R. (1974). *Change: principles of problem formation and problem resolution*. New York: Norton.

Waugh, P. (1992). *Postmodernism: a reader*. London: Edward Arnold.

Webster, J. (2002). Family therapy and workforce planning. *Journal of Family Therapy, 24,* 134–149.

Weldon, F. (1997). *The Guardian*, 11 January, p. 21.

Welwood, J. (1983). *Awakening the heart: East/West approaches to psychotherapy and the healing relationship*. Boston, MA: Shambala.

Werner-Wilson, R. (1997). Is therapeutic alliance influenced by gender in marriage and family therapy? *Journal of Feminist Family Therapy, 9,* 3–16.

Whitaker, C. (1967). The growing edge. In J. Haley & L. Hoffman (Eds.), *Techniques of family therapy*. New York: Basic Books.

Whitaker, C. & Keith, D.V. (1981). Symbolic–experiential family therapy. In A.S. Gurman & D.P. Kniskern (Eds.), *Handbook of family therapy*. New York: Brunner/Mazel.

White, C. (Ed.). (2000). Living positive lives. *Dulwich Centre Journal, 4,* 3–37.

White, M. (1984). Pseudo-encopresis: from avalanche to victory, from vicious to virtuous cycle. *Family Systems Medicine, 2,* 150–160.

White, M. (1993) Deconstruction and therapy. In S. Gilligan & R. Price (Eds.), *Therapeutic conversations*. New York: Norton.

White, M. (1995). *Re-authoring lives*. Adelaide: Dulwich Centre Publications.

White, M. & Epston, D. (1990). *Narrative means to therapeutic ends*. New York: Norton.

Wieselberg, H. (1992). Family therapy and ultra-orthodox Jewish families: a structural approach. *Journal of Family Therapy, 14,* 305–329.

Wilkinson, M. (1992). How do we understand empathy systemically? *Journal of Family Therapy, 14,* 193–205.

Willi, J. (1987). Some principles of an ecological model of the person as a consequence of the therapeutic experience with systems. *Family Process, 26,* 429–436.

Williams, F. (1992). Somewhere over the rainbow: universality and diversity in social policy. *Social Policy Review, 4,* 200–219.

Wineberger, J. (1995). Common factors aren't so common: the common factors dilemma. *Clinical Psychology: Science and Practice, 2,* 45–69.

Winnicott, D. (1960). The theory of parent–child relationships. *International Journal of Psycho-analysis, 41,* 585–97.

Wohl, J. (1995). Traditional individual psychotherapy and ethnic minorities. In J.F. Aponte, R. Young Rivers & J. Wohl (Eds.), *Psychological interventions and cultural diversity*. Boston, MA: Allyn & Bacon.

Wood, B.L. (1993). Beyond the 'psychosomatic family': a behavioural family model of paediatric illness. *Family Process, 32,* 261–278.

Woodcock, J. (2001). Threads from the labyrinth. *Journal of Family Therapy, 23,* 136–154.

Wright, L.M. & Leahey, M. (1994). Calgary family intervention model: one way to think about change. *Journal of Marital and Family Therapy, 20,* 381–395.

Index